humble

WELBECK
BALANCE

humble

The Quiet Power
of an Ancient Virtue

DARYL VAN TONGEREN, PhD

WELBECK
BALANCE

Published in 2022 by Welbeck Balance
An imprint of Welbeck Non-Fiction Ltd
Part of Welbeck Publishing Group
Based in London and Sydney
www.welbeckpublishing.com

Originally published in the U.S. in 2022 by The Experiment, LLC.
This edition published by arrangement with The Experiment, LLC.

A CIP catalogue record for this book is available from the British Library.

ISBN
Hardback – 978-1-80129-095-1
Paperback – 978-1-80129-099-9

Printed in Great Britain by CPI Group (UK) Ltd, Croydon CRO 4YY

10 9 8 7 6 5 4 3 2 1

Note/Disclaimer

Welbeck Balance encourages diversity and different viewpoints.
However, all views, thoughts, and opinions expressed in this book are the
author's own and are not necessarily representative of Welbeck Publishing Group
as an organization. All material in this book is set out in good faith for general
guidance; Welbeck Publishing Group makes no representations or warranties
of any kind, express or implied, with respect to the accuracy, completeness,
suitability or currency of the contents of this book, and specifically disclaims, to
the extent permitted by law, any implied warranties of merchantability or fitness
for a particular purpose and any injury, illness, damage, death, liability or loss
incurred, directly or indirectly from the use or application of any of the information
contained in this book. This book is not intended to replace expert medical or
psychiatric advice. It is intended for informational purposes only and for your own
personal use and guidance. It is not intended to diagnose, treat or act as a substitute
for professional medical advice. The author and the publisher are not medical
practitioners nor counsellors, and professional advice should be sought
before embarking on any health-related programme.

Every reasonable effort has been made to trace copyright holders of
material produced in this book, but if any have been inadvertently
overlooked the publishers would be glad to hear from them.

For Sara

Contents

PART III

How Humility Can Change Your Life

Introduction

Pride comes before the fall.

This ancient warning has spanned cultures and time, has been described in Greek myths and proclaimed in religious teachings. Consider the story of Narcissus, who was so enamored with his own reflection that he ignored amorous pursuers and eventually longed for death, revealing the dangers of self-absorption. The myth of Arachne cautions the perils of over-confidence and the unwillingness to listen to and learn from others, lest you be like a weaver turned into a spider, spending your days endlessly spinning webs in vain. Religions—from Buddhism to Christianity to Islam—warn their adherents to avoid the hazards of hubris. The arrogant, cocky, and self-assured are destined to be knocked down, put in their place, or downright humiliated. Think too highly of yourself and you're going to be smitten by an angry god or some force of cosmic justice (or turned into an arachnid).

In modern culture, two lines of thought have developed about what humility is. First, we began to equate humility with humiliation. We were taught that those who brag get their eventual comeuppance through public shame or embarrassment. This can give way to self-deprecation and hiding our accomplishments,

leaving us balancing a desire for ambition with the fear of standing out. Although they have the same root word, *humility* and
humiliation are quite different.[1] Humiliation is about embarrassment, shame, or subjugation. Humility comes from within and
cannot be forced by another person or external situation.
Research has found that people respond negatively to humiliation but positively to humility.[2] When humility is equated with
humiliation, it becomes a punishment, like a bar of soap for the
vulgarity of boasting, and its taste starts to sour.

Alternatively, those who have long abandoned any notion of
gods or karmic justice think of humility as an antiquated idea
with no real bearing on modern life. If anything, humility has
been used as a tool of oppression to keep some people down while
others stay in power. Far too many people have been wrongly told
to stay in line or be quiet in the name of "humility." Modern
culture asserts that strength comes from power, aggression, and
dominance. "Nice guys finish last," after all, so those who adhere
to anachronistic notions of modesty aren't going to get anywhere
in life. It's better to be brash, bold, and confident, even if you
"fake it till you make it."

As we can see, humility has often been misunderstood or
exploited.

But true humility is neither humiliation nor oppression. It's
not an attribute of the weak or a penalty for pride. It's not a tool
of the oppressor. In fact, modern science has revealed that true,
authentic humility is a secure openness to the world, where we
can be honest with ourselves and others about our strengths and
limitations, seeking to learn new perspectives and caring deeply
about those around us. It is not shame or guilt, nor is it an excuse
to be a doormat. Humility is a way of approaching ourselves,
other people, and the world around us with a sense of *enoughness*—an unconditional worth and value—that opens us to the
world as it is. And two decades of scientific research agree:

Humility helps strengthen relationships, enhance work, and improve society. It is powerful and transformative and wildly countercultural. And it might be exactly what we all need.

Does Pride Really Come Before the Fall?

I became interested in humility in graduate school. I was part of a positive psychology research group that sought to identify factors that contributed to human flourishing. Most of our work centered on forgiveness, but while I was there, we started branching out into character strengths and their role in relationships. I was studying meaning in life and forgiveness, and my dissertation looked at how we maintain meaningful relationships by offering forgiveness to our romantic partners. My good friend and fellow graduate student colleague Don Davis conducted his dissertation on how humility plays a role in relationships. Slowly, a synergy built around humility. Along with another fellow graduate student, Josh Hook, the three of us sought to advance research in this area that psychology had largely ignored.

At the time, there were two reasons why psychological research hadn't yet explored humility. One stumbling block was that researchers thought measuring humility would be a logistical nightmare. After all, isn't it absurd to ask people how humble they are? Would a truly humble person be honest and report high humility? Or would they think of all the people who are humbler and report more modest levels? And wouldn't a raging narcissist max out on self-reported humility? Researchers feared self-reported humility would be diabolically unreliable. Fortunately, they figured out ways to address these problems, and it didn't turn out to be as difficult as they once imagined. In fact, numerous scholars have joined in the empirical investigation of humility, turning it into a thriving area of scholarly inquiry.

But there was a second and, in my mind, larger stumbling block: Humility is a tough sell. On the surface, many Westernized, individualistic cultures don't reward humility. The "squeaky wheel gets the grease," and often the loudest, brashest, and most selfish people grab the power, resources, and money and appear to reap all the benefits and none of the costs. We elevate vanity and praise peacocking; we see narcissistic displays as the cost of doing business. In fact, we have come to idolize such actions as some misplaced form of confidence.

But any such gains are both superficial and short-lived. A selfish life of narcissistic indulgence is hollow and unfulfilling. This approach leaves a wake of relational carnage and intrapersonal turmoil. Put simply, our psychological and relational motivations for connection and meaning don't align with being a self-centered narcissist. And in the past decade, we finally have the psychological research to support such a claim. We know what the ancient philosophers and poets have proclaimed: Humility is a strength worth cultivating. Despite current cultural myths, arrogant conceit is a trap that will consume our time and attention and leave us disconnected and disillusioned. Humility, on the other hand, is liberating, empowering, and revolutionary.

So, when asking whether or not "pride comes before the fall," consider this: According to the folks at Merriam-Webster, ancient uses of the word *pride* connote an "inordinate self-esteem" and "unreasonable conceit of superiority."[3] It was included in the list of the seven deadly sins. Over time its meaning has shifted to also include self-respect or collective self-worth. The former view of pride is poisonous and more akin to narcissistic arrogance; the latter view is rather healthy. Yet the opposite of humility is not pride; in fact, humility requires a healthy sense of self that springs from security. Rather, humility's foe is arrogance or conceit; a superior view of oneself in which others are viewed as inferior and entitlement reigns supreme. And this creeps into myriad expressions in daily life, is consistently reinforced by culture, is modeled in the highest forms of entertainment and politics—and it is ultimately unfulfilling. Indeed, arrogance comes before the fall. But humility can grant us a life rich with meaning, healthy relationships, and secure wholeness. Culture may tell us to embrace selfishness and conceit as a pathway to make the most of life, but the scientific research tells a different story.

The Fascinating, Fragile Self

I'm a professor of social psychology and I teach at a small liberal arts college near the shore of Lake Michigan. We social psychologists study how our thoughts, feelings, and behavior change in relation to the presence of other people. Essentially, how other people affect us. This research has gathered clues regarding why groups compete, the nature of aggression, and how it feels to be rejected. But of all the various subjects that social psychologists study, one of our favorites—and likely one of yours, too—is the *self*. We can think of the self as a collection of memories, feelings, thoughts, and concepts we hold about ourselves and our identity. We scholars have split the study of the self like a pie with nearly endless slices, examining self-esteem, self-awareness, self-control, self-compassion, and on and on. We're pretty enamored with the self—and so is popular culture.

The past two decades have been a shrine to "the Self." Even though the term *selfie* wasn't in many people's vocabulary a decade ago, just think of how many selfies you've taken in the past six months (or for some people, six days!). Nearly all our phones have cameras on both sides to enable us to take pictures of ourselves. The popular emphasis on the self has been propelled by three converging trends that have left us more miserable and fragile than ever before.

The first trend is an increase in seeking value and worth from external sources. We've put our self-esteem and sense of significance on people outside ourselves, and we work tirelessly to gain their approval. Research has suggested that some people share eight selfies per day,[4] and clever experimental research has found that randomly assigning women to share a selfie on social media increased their anxiety and decreased their feelings of attractiveness, even when they were given the opportunity to touch up the photo.[5] Merely the act of putting ourselves out there for evaluation takes its toll on our mental health. Not only are we worried about how others evaluate us, but we naturally compare ourselves to others. With access to a nearly endless list of exemplars for beauty, wealth, achievement, success, ability, humor, or accomplishment, we usually find that we come up short in comparison. Our evaluations of significance, worth, and value—core factors determining whether we feel as though our life is meaningful— have shifted toward cultural standards and external sources. We've put our meaning and happiness in other people's hands.

Given the influence that others have on our sense of self, you would think that we'd be careful about those with whom we surround ourselves. Not so. Rather, a second trend is the increasingly narrow scope of attitudes, opinions, and beliefs to which we expose ourselves. We selectively choose our friends, news channels, and information sources—all of which confirm our preexisting views—leading to a growing homogeneity of ideas. We've created echo chambers that affirm what we've long believed to be true, and unfollow, unfriend, or unsubscribe to any voice that tells us differently. Entrenched in our way of seeing the world (the *right* way, of course), we are no longer exposed to differing opinions. As a result, we've lost the ability to talk respectfully with people with whom we disagree. It's easy to filter out the uncomfortable voice of dissent in our lives, and our tolerance for difference has diminished. In some cases, this disagreement has turned into contempt, aggression, and violence. We see those who differ from us as ignorant and sometimes inhuman. Our divisions are on full display.

A third force is the strong desire for overly positive self-regard, especially relative to others. We've become accustomed to viewing ourselves as better than average, more often right than wrong, with our capabilities as characteristic and our indiscretions as inadvertent. I teach my students about this tendency, known as the *better-than-average effect*, through an in-class exercise. You can try it as well. I tell them to think about an average person their age and in their stage of life (the average student at our college). I ask them to rank themselves from 1 to 100 percent, with 1 percent indicating that they are the absolute worst on this dimension, and 100 percent indicating that they are the absolute best on this dimension, *compared to the average person*. I ask them, compared to the average student, how

- intelligent are you?
- sociable are you?
- athletic are you?
- attractive are you?

Then I ask them to tally their scores and give an estimated average. They jot down their anonymous answers on index cards, which I collect. I started this exercise when I was teaching in graduate school more than a decade ago, and it plays out nearly the same way every time. When I share the pooled results with the class, no one blinks an eye when I tell them that the average self-rating was somewhere between 65 and 70 percent.

Let that sink in: We're all above average.

You don't have to be gifted at math to realize that we can't all be above average. Half the class should, statistically speaking, be below average. And when I share this insight with them, they nod along, smiling and thinking to themselves: *I can't believe everyone thinks they're above average. Good thing I really* am *above average.*

What score did you get? And what was your response?

Now, not everyone scores above the midpoint of 50 (which would be precisely average), and some people should rank themselves higher on these dimensions (for instance, collegiate athletes should probably rate themselves somewhere around the 90th percentile or higher for athleticism). But we're just so accustomed to thinking we're better than average that we've become unaccustomed to taking feedback, receiving criticism, or accepting failure, which might suggest the opposite. We'd sooner ignore reality or numb the pain of criticism than accept that we have shortcomings and use such information to grow and change.

The result of these three converging forces—external sources of self-worth, ideological isolation, and overly positive self-regard—is a *fragile sense of self*. We relentlessly defend this fragile sense of self, one precariously affirmed by the opinion of carefully selected others yet sheltered from voices that might disrupt our positive view of ourselves. We're left feeling more insecure and defensive than ever, scrambling to protect our sense of self and views rather than being able to interact with people with whom we disagree and to accept criticism from those who see the world differently than we do. We approach the world ready to defend our beliefs rather than learn from the evidence. We can get lost in the anxiety of social comparison and the fear of evaluation, with our attention dedicated to an endless cycle of self-validation-seeking that grants us a momentary dopamine hit for each endorsement from our tribe (that looks like us, believes like us, and talks like us) but ultimately leaves us feeling empty and unfulfilled. In the end, we're externally puffed up and internally hollow; we're sad, lonely, and anxious, because this design does not actually meet any of our core needs as humans. How did we get here?

The Proliferation of Peacocking

In the 1970s and '80s, psychologists (and overwhelmingly, social psychologists) began studying self-esteem. Research took off exponentially, and by the '90s, social policies were being based on a flurry of research findings that purported self-esteem was the great panacea to a host of social ills. The problem is that these interventions didn't work. People were just as lonely, underachieving, aggressive, and miserable as ever. In fact, some have argued that this focus on self-esteem actually made things worse.

Jean Twenge, one of the foremost experts on narcissism, led a meta-analytic review of all results on the Narcissistic Personality Inventory (which gauges one's inflated sense of self; typical respondents are college students in the United States) from 1982 to 2009 and found significant increases over time.[6] That is, American college students reported an increasingly overinflated sense of self, perhaps in part because of the focus on self-esteem during the 1980s and '90s. Because of this analysis, she and Keith Campbell (another narcissism expert) argue that the United States is in the midst of a narcissism epidemic,[7] though other work has found that Westernized, individualistic countries (such as the United Kingdom) around the world also tend to be more narcissistic than Eastern countries. Despite some criticisms of this work, the data remain clear: People report being more self-involved now than in generations before.

What is the result of this uptick in self-aggrandizement? Research suggests parallel drops in empathy and concern for other people and increases in ideological endorsement of tolerance and equality.[8] People are now more focused on themselves and less willing to take the perspective of someone else, even though they ideologically agree with the concept of tolerance and equality. To be sure, decades of focusing on inflating the self appears to have backfired. It didn't solve societal woes or personal insecurities. Instead, the result is that many of us feel disconnected, anxious, and conflicted. Relationships have soured, conflict is persistent, and rifts feel deeper and more unbridgeable than ever. It's time for something different.

Humility as a Possible Solution

Despite the cultural fascination with narcissistic self-aggrandizement, I refuse to accept that this is healthy or beneficial. I can't imagine a society is healthy or flourishing when so many of its citizens are disconnected and unhappy. And we can't be the first generation to try to solve enduring problems of isolation or meaninglessness. These are ancient topics of deep human concern, about which we've amassed a bit of wisdom.

Humility can change our life and society at large for the better. Many great thinkers have bragged about the power of humility. Socrates is credited with saying, "Pride divides the men, humility joins them." Saint Augustine, a Christian theologian in the fourth century, argued, "It was pride that changed angels into devils; it is humility that makes men as angels." Mother Teresa wisely asserted, "If you are humble, nothing will touch you, neither praise nor disgrace, because you know what you are." Albert Einstein remarked, "A true genius admits that he/she knows nothing." Mary Oliver wrote, "Humility is the prize of the leaf-world. Vain-glory is the bane of us, the humans." These represent a fraction of the many people who have glimpsed the value of humility and have exhorted others to practice it.

We are now at a place where modern science has confirmed ancient wisdom: Humility is powerfully transformative. Research in humility has accelerated in the last decade, and the time is ripe for psychological science to speak to the powerful role of humility in private and public life. Scientific interest and effort have increased, and the data are clear and compelling: Humility changes lives. It is a boon for healthy relationships, a necessary component for the workplace, and an important part of any society that seeks to grow and change.

Lest we begin thinking of humility as a cure-all, let's pause and hold our collective excitement (and egos) in check. Just as efforts designed to boost self-esteem indiscriminately didn't work, humility won't solve all of life's problems. Let's take a humble approach to the research on humility, understanding that it's both new and promising while full of nuance and in need of context. Some people are humble in some areas of life (such as with family) but not others (such as at work). And the same people can be humble one day and jerks the next. Some have tried to exploit or subjugate others, inexplicably in the name of humility. People may call something humility that is anything but humble. But true, authentic humility can be liberating. It is transformative and revolutionary—and it's worth cultivating in our own life.

What Is Humility?

Researchers have offered various definitions of humility, but one that has received relative consensus suggests that humility includes three features: an accurate self-assessment, the ability to regulate one's ego, and an orientation toward other people.[9] Put more simply, humility is *knowing yourself, checking yourself, and going beyond yourself*. Let's look at each of these features.

The first part of humility is having an accurate view of yourself, including both strengths and weaknesses—that is, *knowing yourself*. Humble people know what they are good at and what areas could benefit from growth and improvement. Whereas arrogant people know their strengths too well (to the detriment of acknowledging any weaknesses), and those who are self-defeating dwell only on their weaknesses (ignoring their obvious strengths), humble people own their limitations while embracing their strengths.[10] We can think of humility as giving people an accurate view of the world, starting with themselves. Most people fall into the trap of believing that humble people should not think of, let alone speak about, their strengths, but that's simply not true. Humble people can accept the reality of who they are, including the flattering and the unflattering. This also means that humility requires a fair amount of self-awareness. It's hard to take stock of yourself if you're oblivious to your thoughts, feelings, or actions. Moving mindlessly through life can lead to a mild selfishness. However, thinking *too* much about yourself can also lead to an unhealthy preoccupation that might border on narcissistic obsession. Finding the golden mean of being aware of yourself without becoming preoccupied or overly ruminative is a good first step toward humility.

The second part of humility requires that people regulate their ego. It necessitates *checking yourself*. We all tend toward self-ishness—seeking esteem, praise, and glory. Our desire for self-esteem runs deep, and some have argued it may be one of our most fundamental motives.[11] After all, it's natural for us to accept praise and pass the blame; however, humility turns this on its head. A humble person can share the praise and glory with others, acknowledging that many people likely contributed to their successes. They also are willing to accept blame or criticism when it's appropriate to do so. Being humble involves owning decisions that didn't pan out, resisting the desire to shirk responsibility and make excuses, and admitting when you were at fault. Finally, regulating ego means that how you present your ideas or accomplishments matters. Humble people don't think they deserve special attention or are any more important because of their achievements.[12] Remember, humility is being aware of your strengths and what you are good at; however, humble people don't spend their days making sure others are aware of the same. Instead, being honest *and* modest goes a long way.

The third part of humility is being oriented toward other people, or *going beyond yourself*. Humble people think about others and take their needs into consideration. Rather than focusing solely on themselves, those who are humble can *empathize* with those around them. It's a transcendent move that shifts people into a wider perspective, broadening what they consider when they make decisions and reorienting their world such that they are no longer in the center. This profound shift may be the hallmark social feature of humility. It's why we like humble people so much: They are willing to consider us and our needs. And who wouldn't want to be in a relationship with someone like that?

A helpful metaphor for balancing the three features of a humble character is to think of humility as *being the right size*. Humble people match their self-concepts and actions more accurately to reality. They know their strengths and weaknesses and don't need to brag nor shrink in the presence of others. To have this "right size" comes from security in knowing that your value doesn't come from fleeting external standards or elusive approval or adoration. It comes from *enoughness*. The confidence of knowing that you are a person of *inherent* worth and value frees you up from the relentless and futile pursuit of external validation that drives so much arrogant and narcissistic behavior. Humility is not an indication of weakness but rather a marker of strength.

What Does Humility Look Like?

It might be helpful to show what humility looks like in real life. Scholars have argued about how many kinds of humility there are and what are its basic dimensions. (The irony of researchers arguing to defend their view of humility is not lost on me.) In my estimation, the research on humility focuses on four primary areas: people, ideas, ways of life, and life's ultimate questions. The associated types of humility—relational, intellectual, cultural, and existential, respectively—have different personal experiences and behavioral expressions. These are listed in Table 1.

Type of Humility	Focus	Experience	Expression
Relational humility	People	In relationships	Being other-oriented and checking one's ego
Intellectual humility	Ideas	Around ideas	Being open to new insights and seeking learning
Cultural humility	Ways of Life	In cultural interactions	Learning from others and not viewing one's own culture as superior
Existential humility (cosmic/spiritual)	Ultimate Questions	Feeling small relative to nature / the universe / God	Feeling grateful to something larger than oneself

Table 1. Types of humility

Relational humility surfaces in our interactions with other people. Relationally humble people can take in feedback, think of others, and are aware of their strengths and weaknesses. They're kind and caring—the type of friends, coworkers, and partners we all like.

Intellectual humility shows up when discussing our core beliefs and convictions, when we are open to new insights and intent on learning from others. Intellectually humble people can admit when they're wrong and own their limitations. They're also curious, preferring to seek out evidence over ideology and learn from the world around them rather than defend their own views.

Cultural humility has to do with navigating competing cultural perspectives. Culturally humble people realize that each person has a way of seeing the world and they are eager to learn the perspectives of others. These people do not see their own cultural viewpoint as superior. They take the time to listen to others and work hard to make sure everyone has a seat at the table. They are naturally curious and inclusive.

Existential humility addresses how people answer ultimate questions in life, such as: What happens to us after we die? What is the meaning of life? What is my purpose? We often experience existential humility in relation to forces of nature, the universe, the cosmos, or when considering the divine. This type of humility is expressed in feelings of gratitude to something larger than oneself. Existentially humble people want to wrestle with big questions and dig into the deep and pressing concerns of what it means to be human. They accept their finitude and are at peace with their place in the world.

Indeed, other scholars have tried to make their mark studying smaller slices of humility: There might be other "variants of humility." For example, some have suggested that there might be a "religious humility," which would be humility about one's religious beliefs; however, this is likely just a combination of intellectual, cultural, and existential humility. Others have suggested that there is a "political humility," which is a humble approach to political ideology and expression, though this might just be intellectual and cultural humility. When we think about the dimensions—people, ideas, ways of life, and ultimate questions—we can dream up many intersecting domains in which humility is relevant, but these can often be boiled down to the four core elements.

People can vary on the degree to which they are humble across these different dimensions. For example, someone could be existentially humble—feeling small when looking over the Grand Canyon and giving thanks for the existence of such beauty—but display intellectual arrogance when they express their beliefs by being very confident about their ideas about God and their own place in the universe. Alternatively, a relationally humble partner who cares deeply about the needs of their significant other may be stubbornly committed to their own cultural perspective and unwilling to consider the ways of life offered by other cultures.

Or perhaps someone is humble at work and a jerk at home. Thus, humility is not an all-or-nothing characteristic. Not only does it exist in degrees, it also varies in different areas and expressions. Understanding this will help us identify the dimensions that we may need to work to cultivate more strongly. A truly humble person will dedicate time and effort to cultivating humility across all these dimensions.

Putting Humility in Context

Nurturing humility may seem daunting. Who can really know themselves deeply, keep their ego in check, and constantly think of others? And perhaps more concerning, where will it get you in life? You might think, *Sure, that all sounds well and good, but it just doesn't work in the real world.*

I mentioned that this might be a tough sell. Many individualistic cultures, where the tendency is to prioritize the individual over the group, have a strong bent toward self-aggrandizement. Often, the cultural norms are so powerful that it can feel like you're standing on a moving sidewalk toward narcissism and self-obsession. Phrases like "nice guys finish last" assume that power, domination, and self-centeredness are the way to get ahead in life. We implicitly (or explicitly) teach one another that a good life comes from thinking only of yourself: Make sure you get yours first.

The result? Many people are more miserable than ever. Anxiety among people under fifty has increased significantly over the past decade.[13] More than forty million adults in the United States—greater than one in six people—and more than 25 percent of children between thirteen and eighteen, report anxiety.[14] Research consistently documents how Americans are lonely, depressed, disconnected, and mentally unwell.[15] Mental illness is skyrocketing. Suicide is on the rise. The state of mental health in America is deteriorating.[16] Globally, one in four people will report a mental health condition at some point in life, depression contin-ues to rob people of meaningful years of their life, and, tragically, more than one million people commit suicide each year.[17] We're losing the ability to communicate well with those with whom we disagree. Families are fracturing. Relationships are dissolving. People are unhappy. Our preoccupation with ourselves seems to be backfiring.

Here, humility stands out as a stark countercultural statement. It shifts the focus away from solely thinking about yourself and promotes owning your limitations and shortcomings, keeping your ego in check. Of course, humility won't solve all of society's ills. But research confirms that it can make relationships better, improve people's work and productivity, and help groups that typ-ically disagree to get along. It can foster openness, curiosity, and genuine respect for others—including people who might seem so different from us. Humility brings about social change, innova-tion, and discovery. And humility might be exactly what we need to find common ground amid the deep divisions in our world.

Dispelling Myths

In the autumn of 2019, I received an email from a writer at *The New York Times*. He had read a recent review article I published and wanted to craft a piece on the importance of humility. I was flattered and excited—finally, humility—something that I had studied for a decade—was getting the coverage I thought it deserved. It's not that I felt like my work was deserving of such press as much as I thought the topic was timely and powerful. After seeing the benefits of humility in countless empirical stud-ies, I was eager for the world to see it, too.

My immediate (and thankfully inaudible) response was "Why me?"

I began to run through a mental list of people I felt were immensely more qualified to write about humility. There was still so much to learn and so many other people who knew it so well. But then the irony hit me: A humility researcher who has spent a decade of his professional career studying a topic immediately thought of deferring to others rather than stepping into the spotlight. Eventually, I realized that I was indeed qualified: I had worked hard to earn the right to share research I had a hand in creating. And I also realized how humility is a difficult practice; I had spent years studying the topic and still found myself erring on the side of deference.

I wrote this book to help get the truth out about humility. Despite many pervasive cultural (and Greek) myths, humility is not about weakness. In fact, as you'll learn, true humility comes from a place of security. Throughout this book, you'll see how it takes security, confidence, and a realistic view of the world to be humble. Practicing this kind of virtue takes more effort and power than run-of-the-mill selfishness. It also takes courage to be humble, because it requires shifting your standards of worth and value away from external contingencies toward something more stable and lasting.

I've often heard people say that humility is thinking that you're nothing. This, too, is a misguided idea. Humility is about being the right size: not too big, not too small. If the ditch on one side of the humility highway is arrogance, the ditch on the other is timidity. Remember, a truly humble person values themselves the same way they cherish and respect others: as someone who is inherently worthy.

I fear that many of these misconceptions about humility have led people to think that humility is an antiquated idea of no practical value in today's culture. They brush it off and think it doesn't apply in real life. But we need humility now more than ever. We're more anxious, alone, and miserable than we've been in recent memory. We don't get along with others. The relentless pursuit of more has left us feeling empty and unhappy. Our entire system of values is oriented around self-promotion and seemingly rewards narcissism. And it's completely failed us. It's time for something different.

So, let's abandon our misconceptions about humility. It's not a punishment from the gods, nor is it a shameful humiliation or a badge of the weak. It's a powerful way to approach yourself, other people, and the world—and it can transform your life for the better.

PART I

The Benefits of Humility

1

Awareness and Acceptance

HUMILITY HELPS US BECOME self-aware and accept who we are and the world as it is. Scholars have long argued that becoming aware of a reality, and then accepting that reality, are central features of psychological health and well-being.[1] Both awareness and acceptance are often considered to be key components of mindfulness, which is a nonjudgmental awareness of ourselves and the world around us.[2] When we can see ourselves as we are, and the world as it is, we can make wise and informed decisions. We're then in a better position to craft a life of meaning and fulfillment. In short, humility is the honest engagement with reality, and this honest engagement comes with a host of benefits.

Of course, sometimes reality is difficult to accept. In September 2020, actor and podcast host Dax Shepard made a startling confession that he had hoped to never utter: He was no longer sober. For months, he had hidden this fact from his loved ones and audience, until he finally decided to tell the truth. After nearly sixteen years of sobriety, he told his audience that he had become addicted to painkillers and was, as of the recording of that particular episode, seven days sober. Dax had built more than a podcast empire with his honest and engaging Armchair

Expert—he had cultivated a community of listeners who appreciated his vulnerability and authenticity. And it was that desire for authenticity that drove him to share his story of relapse.

Consider the potential risk of such a confession. In 2019, Forbes ranked him as the fourth-highest earning podcaster, earning $9 million that year and amassing twenty million monthly listeners. Part of his identity was being sober, and he was an inspiration for many who thought sobriety was elusive. Some might have seen his relapse as a betrayal, his honesty as a desecration of a sacred bond, or his transgression of succumbing to addiction unforgivable. His professional and financial losses could have been staggering.

Still, Dax had the humility to first become aware that he had a problem and then accept his reality. It wasn't a pleasant situation to embrace. We might imagine that it would have been better for him to keep this relapse hidden. But avoiding and failing to accept this hard reality was taking its toll. As he recounted in the episode, Dax's personal well-being suffered, his relationships were strained, and he couldn't stand the deceit any longer. Humility required him to admit his limitations, own his mistakes, and openly share his struggles. Doing so took courage and vulnerability. It demanded self-awareness and insight, and it was a process that unfolded over time. But he knew that his own well-being required honesty, not only so others could help him work toward continued sobriety but also because his integrity demanded consistency in his values and behaviors. His honesty was as inspiring as it was raw and painful. We ached for him and rooted for him, and were left wondering: If we could all be that honest—and indeed, that humble—to admit our mistakes and own up to own our limitations, would we be better off, both individually and collectively?

The road to humility starts with accurate self-knowledge: seeing ourselves and the world *honestly*. Often, this begins with realizing our biases and admitting our weaknesses, alongside affirming what we're good at. We have to name our privilege and accept our limitations, recognizing where growth is needed. Honesty starts within. Then, it permits us to begin to see the world as it is—not simply as we want it to be. Understanding our cognitive tendencies and areas of vulnerability can be empowering—and can help us work toward being more open, less defensive, and more honest. It can improve our relationship with reality and with other people and contribute to our overall well-being.

Humility for Health

The *well-being hypothesis* argues that humility is good for mental and physical health. People who cultivate humility report better functioning in several areas of their life, including their emotional life and physical bodies. A representative sample of older adults in the United States has shown that humble people report better health.[3] My colleagues and I examined how this works in close relationships between partners dealing with the stress of transitioning to parenthood and experiencing persistent arguments.[4] Examining new parents, we found that when both partners were humble, they reported less stress and less depression during those early months of a baby's life than when one or both partners were arrogant. Similarly, when examining recurring conflicts in the lab by having couples argue over a contentious issue, we found that when both partners were humble, not only did they report being more satisfied with their partner, but their physiological responses (such as blood pressure) were healthier and less reactive than when couples were arrogant. Indeed, researchers have concluded that humility is good for emotional and physical health.[5] But why might humility contribute to a healthier, happier life?

Recall that the first part of humility is having an accurate view of yourself—*knowing yourself*. People who are humble acknowledge their strengths and weaknesses, knowing there's room for growth in both the things they do well and those they don't. They can also admit when they're wrong. This requires two critical ingredients. In order to truly know yourself, you first need to cultivate *self-awareness*. People who are self-aware prioritize learning more about themselves and understanding why they do what they do. They want to develop a realistic picture of who they are and seek to understand their weaknesses and strengths. They investigate their own motives and behaviors in an attempt to identify patterns. They check in with their thoughts and feelings and are attuned to their bodies. In short, they are effectively introspective, motivated by a desire to understand themselves better each day. Similarly, humble people are aware of the world around them. They are motivated to see the world accurately rather than merely in a way that conforms to their preconceived notions about how the world should be. They rely on empirical evidence and data to make decisions because they value reality over fiction, even if that reality is unsettling. They seek the truth, uncomfortable as it is, because they desire to engage with others and the world with integrity.

The second key ingredient for knowing yourself is acceptance. Only once you become aware of who you really are—your strengths and limitations, your patterns and motivations, and your areas for growth—can you accept yourself. True acceptance only comes after a full and honest awareness of what you're accepting. And this acceptance confers a sense of psychological security, improving your well-being.

Most of us rely on external sources to measure self-worth, thinking that only after we make enough money, have enough friends, or earn enough accolades will we be enough. Chasing external sources of self-worth is exhausting and unsatisfying. We can get stuck in a cycle of seeking validation from others that leaves us acting inauthentically and feeling unhappy. How frustrating for our sense of self to be wrapped up in the approval of others or in the ever-changing cultural standards of beauty, wealth, or accomplishment. However, people who have cultivated a sense of humility through developing strong self-awareness can start to avoid this trap by focusing on—and *accepting*—who they are, including our shadow sides. Seeing ourselves for who we really are, including the bad as well as the good, can help us move toward acceptance. We run afoul when we compare *all* of who we are to *parts* of other people. When we measure our athletic abilities against professional athletes who are paid for their prowess and skill, we'll almost always come up short, because we spend our days working a regular job, whereas cultivating athletic skills constitutes their job. Our vacations look less glamorous than social media influencers', our food looks less appetizing, and our lives feel more pedestrian when we're caught in the trap of high-stakes social comparison. But acceptance offers security, which is critical to psychological health.

Humility can help break that cycle of seeking external validation. By helping you know who you are and accept yourself as you are, humility can reduce anxiety, slow patterns of rumination, and stop defensiveness in its tracks. When you feel comfortable with who you are, you have no need to go out of way to prove your worth. You simply know you're a person of worth, deserving of love, and with inherent value. You're enough.

This acceptance does not mean you're ready to stop changing nor that you've got life all figured out. Instead, it requires admitting your limitations and realizing areas for growth. You will be the first to admit when you don't know, that you would like to learn; when you are afraid, that you would like to be brave; when you doubt, that you would like to trust. It's not about unfounded confidence or obsessive certainty. Instead, humility is an acceptance of who you are, and the belief that you are a person of worth and value *as you are*. You don't have to do anything more to be loved or accepted—*you are enough*. This realization is freeing and will change your life.

Why Are Awareness and Acceptance So Elusive?

Few of us engage with reality without bias or view ourselves purely objectively. We're motivated to perceive ourselves—and the world—in ways that uphold our deeply ingrained assumptions. There are two main foes to awareness and acceptance: shame and a desire for unrealistically high self-esteem. Oftentimes, shame keeps us from taking an honest look at ourselves and the world around us. Shame is the feeling when we evaluate ourselves negatively *as a person* for some unwanted or objectionable behavior.[6] Shame focuses on how we think we're inherently bad rather than describing some behavior or action as negative. More simply, shame is when we think we're worthless because we failed to meet some standard. Such a standard can be imagined or impossible to achieve, such as expecting to be incredibly attractive, highly athletic, exorbitantly wealthy, or immensely knowledgeable, or to never make a social, intellectual, or moral mistake. Shame can arise when we don't live up to some ideal that we think we *should* meet or surpass, or shame can come from an internalized perfectionism that creates a performance-based self-worth—we only think others will love us if we meet some metric. The result may be an unwillingness to accept our flaws or receive criticism, because we fear that we are unlovable or unworthy. We might ignore areas in need of growth because we internalize them as flaws that showcase how we don't measure up. We feel shame when we blame ourselves for things that go wrong, so we may not acknowledge anything could ever be wrong. We might adopt a positive bias as a form of protection.

This shame originates from insecurity and creates either distortion or defensiveness. On the one hand, because of shame, we might just distort our view of ourselves or reality to avoid the negative feelings of not living up to some ideal. We might resist seeing ourselves negatively because doing so means also feeling ashamed of ourselves—even though shame is not a necessary emotion when we "don't measure up." Indeed, we could just as easily acknowledge that such standards are unreasonable and that we are enough, just as we are. Shame may lead us to make excuses, justify our behavior, or rationalize our responses out of a place of insecurity. On the other hand, the negative feelings generated when we feel shame might cause us to lash out at others and respond defensively to information that doesn't conform with the way we want to see ourselves or the world. We may fight off any negative feedback because we see it as an indictment of our unlovability and worthlessness. We might take offense at things that we shouldn't and lash out in fear and anger. And we might resist indications that any of our views could be incorrect, preserving our distorted perspective because it temporarily alleviates our feelings of shame. We hope that no one learns the fear we secretly harbor: that if anyone saw the "real me," they wouldn't love me.

The second adversary to awareness is motivation for self-enhancement and high self-esteem.[7] Although some research questions whether this drive is as strong in collectivistic cultures, such as Japan,[8] as it is in individualistic cultures like the United States and United Kingdom, most researchers agree that we want to see ourselves in the best light possible. One of the primary ways that this motivation manifests is through sophisticated cognitive biases. Our minds are designed to preserve the positive views of ourselves that we so deeply cherish. Decades of research have revealed that our default operating mode is biased toward the self, which can make developing humility a formidable challenge.

This drive can distort how we see ourselves. We are motivated to see ourselves positively because high self-esteem serves many ends. For example, a positive view of oneself is a core feature of a meaningful life.[9] When we feel significant and valued, life feels more meaningful. In fact, when we feel like we're making a lasting difference that people will remember, it helps us manage our anxiety about death by granting us a sense of symbolic immortality—the idea that, after our own death, we will live on in the memories of others because of our legacy and achievements.[10] Feeling good about ourselves is an existential resource.

Our motivations also affect how we perceive the world. In fact, self-enhancement has been offered as a default response to cope with adversity and stress: People cling to the belief that life will get better, that they will be better than they were before tragedy struck, and that they will overcome their suffering.[11] Such beliefs, while adaptive when coping with adversity, have been called *positive illusions*. They require interpreting information in a particularly favorable light even when the facts do not justify such a conclusion. This strategy is a trade-off. On the one hand, it enables us to move toward goals that may seem unreachable; we often have to believe that we can make a difference in this world in order to persevere in areas that require a lot of work. On the other hand, we might dismiss warning signs or ignore reality in favor of keeping our positive view of ourselves intact. Those who don't respond this way are called *depressive realists*: Rather than engaging in self-enhancement, they see the world more accurately at the cost of positive emotion.

It feels good to buy into many of these positive illusions and cognitive biases. It helps us maintain a view of ourselves that, despite perhaps lacking sufficient evidence, is elevated and typically positive. Now, not everyone has high self-esteem; some folks indeed suffer from low self-esteem or clinical levels of depression. That, too, is problematic. The experience of depression often feels numbing, like we are in a fog, unmotivated to change, and unconvinced that life is worth the difficulty of trying. In severe cases, depression can lead to self-injurious behaviors. I certainly don't advocate for cripplingly low self-esteem or recommend depression. Rather, remember that humility is the middle road, on which one side is the ditch of arrogant self-aggrandizement, and on the other is the ditch of unwarranted self-abasement.

Humility is the golden mean between pursuing high self-esteem at all costs and the self-loathing of shame. We get into trouble when we favor our positive self-view at the cost of an honest engagement with reality or react out of fear and shame for not meeting or exceeding some unrealistically high standard. Either of these makes us less likely to admit when we're wrong, take feedback from trusted sources, change when it would be to our benefit, or learn from the views and experiences of others, because such feedback is inherently threatening. It can isolate us from others and the world, wreaking havoc on our lives and leaving us miserable, unhappy, and alone.

Only once we become aware of who we are through an honest evaluation can we start on the process toward acceptance. Similarly, we can only accept the reality of the world around us once we see it as it really is. This clarity can transform our shame and uncouple us from the costly chase of external validation. To fully understand how beneficial humility can be, we have to examine some of our mental tendencies; we tend to perceive ourselves and the world with bias, which is problematic. That is, we must understand ourselves and identify some obstacles to achieving that awareness.

Getting to Know Ourselves

If humility brings about awareness and acceptance, it's important to examine some common mental patterns that make the process of objectively viewing and evaluating ourselves and our world so difficult. Here we'll discuss the common barriers that make it hard for us to be unbiased investigators of our own life.

Each of us has these similar cognitive proclivities, and research suggests that being aware of these biases is a good first step to overriding them.[12] We can't change what we don't know.

The first common cognitive tendency that protects our fragile ego is the *self-serving bias*, which is the tendency to take credit for our successes but shift blame to others for our failures. When life goes our way, we naturally think it was our doing; but when things don't go as planned, we quickly discover a new culprit to hold responsible for our misfortune. In this way, we're able to keep a positive view of ourselves, no matter what happens to us. The problem is that if we don't take responsibility for failure (but instead blame others), then we can't learn and grow. If nothing that goes wrong is our fault, how can we avoid a similar situation in the future or develop the necessary skills to achieve a different result? We're hampered by an inability to own our mistakes, but we're also eager to take credit when outside factors played a role in our success. We fail to see the contributions of others and the powerful role of context in shaping our reality.

When we understand this tendency, we're able to counter it by humbly accepting our fair share of the responsibility and blame, while sharing the praise and credit with others—a humble response is to acknowledge the contribution of others in our own successes. By understanding that this self-serving reaction is often automatic, we can choose to override it by pausing and thinking more broadly about what responsibility we should bear for a particular outcome. In the end, we might end up feeling grateful for the ways that others contributed to our well-being.

A second bias is the *better-than-average effect*, which we talked about in the introduction. Thinking that we're above average—even when we know that we can't all be—stops us from accepting that we need to learn, grow, and develop. We already think we're better than most, though we engage in this thinking selectively. I do not think that I'm above average at most athletic endeavors.

In basketball, football, or any activity that requires me to stand and move simultaneously (such as waterskiing), I know for certain that I am decidedly below average. And I've come to terms with that just fine. But I tend to be more biased in areas that I care deeply about or are central to my sense of self. I probably think I'm a better-than-average professor, better-than-average husband, and a (slightly) better-than-average runner—because those are aspects that are central to my self-concept. You, too, might find that the areas you care most about are the ones where you think you are better than most. And perhaps you've developed skill in those areas and truly have become better than average, which has then made those features a central part of your self-concept. But even when we're probably right, we still inflate our comparison and underestimate how much we can still learn and grow.

Humble people leave room for the margin of improvement, even in areas where they excel. They realize that there are areas where they are, indeed, better than average—but certainly not in every area of comparison. Humility begs that we admit our limitations and acknowledge areas for growth and improvement. This allows us to get better in areas where we are not strong or have not yet developed expertise. Humble people can rest in the security of untying their value and worth from their achievements. They know that even though they are not "the best" at something, they still have inherent worth and value. And by knowing where we can grow, we can build in these areas and experience a richer and fuller life.

A third selfish error in our bag of cognitive tricks is the two-sided coin of *false uniqueness* and *false consensus*. On the one hand, we (falsely) believe that we're unique in our abilities and talents; we overestimate how good we are when it comes to positive things about our character, skills, or capabilities. As with the self-serving bias, when things go right, it's easier for us to make sense of why they happened: We're talented, capable individuals who are unique in our ability to navigate life effectively. But when things don't go well, we tend to (falsely) overestimate how many other people would have made the same mistake we made or have the same flaws we have. For example, when we don't stick to our exercise plan, we may tell ourselves that no one regularly makes every workout. We also overestimate consensus with our opinions, reasoning that any intelligent or thoughtful person would believe the same things we believe and see the world the same way we do. We imagine that only the intellectually dormant think differently. Here, the problem lies in that we don't realize that our abilities are pretty common, and we have dark sides just like everyone else, which we could address and improve upon with deliberate personal growth.

Perhaps a humbler response is to embrace our humanity. Humble people realize that, like others, they have flaws. They are not threatened by the achievements or capabilities of other people but instead take joy in celebrating alongside others. They have the security to allow others to shine, and the confidence to know that, like everyone, they, too, are human and make mistakes. They give grace and compassion to themselves and others.

Fourth, nearly all of us suffer from *overconfidence*, which is our tendency to overestimate our ability. When asked how long it would take to solve a common anagram (word puzzle), most people vastly underestimate the time required because they think they are much better at these types of puzzles than they really are. In the same way, I usually think I can mow my lawn or put away laundry much faster than it actually takes me. By placing too much faith in our own ability, we end up failing a lot more because we don't try to learn or seek help when we get stuck. This overconfidence can also lead to the *planning fallacy*: We underestimate how long it takes to do things. College students know this well, when they assume they can write a term paper in mere hours, only to find themselves pulling all-nighters when the task takes much longer than anticipated. And as with students scrambling to complete an assignment, a failure to plan correctly (because we ignore the countless things that can and do go wrong or that take longer than we think) leads to greater stress and contributes to higher chances of failure. Most of us don't work best when we're stressed out, and our shoddy work is evident. Or we get caught up at work trying to do the job right, neglecting our family, friends, or personal health.

Humility helps us take better stock of our own abilities so we're less likely to be overly confident. It's not that humble people lack confidence; rather, it's that they have a more accurate sense of their ability, so they are less likely to plan poorly. Again, their self-knowledge allows them to engage with the world with a greater degree of accuracy and to use that information to make wise and intentional decisions.

Sometimes our biases become clear when we compare our behavior with others. The *actor-observer effect* is our tendency to think that bad things that happen to us are because of external circumstances beyond our control, such as losing a job because the economy is in a recession, but when they happen to other people, it's because of their character flaws—losing their job because they are lazy or irresponsible. Because of this, we may elude responsibility, think poorly of others, and inflate our own relative standing compared to those around us. All of this means that we have to work harder to see other people's perspectives and cultivate genuine empathy for the plight of others. We tend to engage others with a slight penchant for judgmentalism.

The humble response is one of empathy. When we afford others the same benefit of the doubt that we give ourselves, we stop judging them and start asking how we can help them. We cease to see them as a problem and begin to view them as people, like us, who are trying their best. We are motivated by compassion and love, rather than judgment that arises from our own self-doubt and insecurity.

This is a daunting list of cognitive frailties that we humans share. To make matters worse, once we're made aware of these biases, we still tend to think that we're not as biased as everyone else. We're biased about our own bias. Psychologist Emily Pronin calls this the *bias blind spot*, which makes talking about, and addressing, our cognitive biases doubly hard.[13] While reading this list, you might have felt resistant or defensive . . . and then you might have assured yourself that while you're sure you have *some* of these biased characteristics, you surely don't suffer from these biases as badly as others do. You're a bit more enlightened, a bit more fair-minded than others. This tendency reveals just how insidious and deep bias can be. Talking about these biases is not enough. We must take active steps to correct, or account for, these proclivities.

Humble people can receive this feedback less defensively because they realize that we all share a common plight. Once we understand that insight into common psychological barriers is not an indictment, we can begin to use this information to better shape our responses. We can look for how these behaviors manifest in our own lives and start to counteract them. Table 2 shows how these biased tendencies work and why they limit us.

Taken together, this means that we often do not have an accurate or healthy view of ourselves or reality. In many cases, we skew toward the positive. And while that does help our mental health some, its benefits only extend to a point. Letting these biases go unchecked can render us fragile and prone to injury and disappointment. If our mental machinery is designed to maintain a positive view of ourselves, even if that means denying reality, denigrating others, or defending our actions regardless of the situation, then when we meet the unquestionable and harsh reality of

Bias Tendency	How It Works	Why It Limits Us
Self-serving bias	We accept credit for our successes and blame other people or situations for our failures	We can't learn and grow if we never take responsibility
Better-than-average effect	We think that we're better than the average person	We aren't honest about our true standing and areas for improvement
False uniqueness	We think our positive skills and abilities are uniquely ours	We inflate our own egos and don't recognize the skills and abilities of others
False consensus	We think other people believe as we do	We can't imagine how or why other people might hold differing beliefs
Overconfidence	We overestimate our ability and underestimate obstacles	We agree to do more than we can handle (overcommit) and don't give ourselves enough time
Actor-observer effect	We make excuses when we fail but blame others for their shortcomings	We don't grant others the same compassion we give ourselves
Bias blind spot	After identifying biases, we secretly think that we're not as biased as other people	We resist accepting critical information, even when it would make us better human beings

Table 2. Some of our common biases

criticism, opposing views, loss, grief, suffering, relationship stress, or any form of emotional pain, we may be (and often are) ill equipped to handle that reality. We often lack the resilience required to absorb negative feedback or adjust to negative events we encounter in life. In the end, an overly positive view of the world can leave us bitter and broken.

So much emotional pain can be traced back to the combination of lacking self-awareness and having a dysfunctional relationship with reality. Early psychologists catalogued countless defensive mechanisms that people employed to shield themselves from the cold pain of reality. The inability to see the world as it is or understand our place within it makes us unhappy, resentful, and disconnected. Some have argued that acceptance is necessary to find meaning in adversity and suffering.[14] Working to accept ourselves and the world as they are—both good *and* bad— is a step toward good mental health and well-being. And humility eases the way.

How Awareness and Acceptance Enhance Well-Being

Cultivating humility will bring about an awareness and acceptance of the world that is solidly rooted in reality. It takes work, but it's worth it. Without an accurate understanding of ourselves and the world, we're doomed to fall prey to the narcissistic traps of culture and will likely languish under our false delusion: We'll stop growing, keep fighting with others, and direct our energy and effort toward shallow sources of validation and praise. As counterintuitive as it sounds, knowing yourself well, having an accurate sense of the world, and decreasing positive bias is associated with increased well-being. Let's examine how.

Humility grants us autonomy. Developing self-insight is crucial. It's important to know yourself, as well as your relationship to reality, in order to know what works for you (and what doesn't) so that you can get the most out of your life. Knowing, and admitting, that you're not good at something can free you up to spend your time elsewhere. For example, some college students select majors their parents want them to pursue, only to later realize it feels inauthentic and misaligned with their sense of purpose and passion. I went to college as a business major but quickly realized that such a career would be unfulfilling for me. It took courage to break the news to my parents that I was switching my major to psychology, and I know some students who would rather live dutifully and somewhat unfulfilled than admit their mistake or make a decision that could upset others. I can't imagine sticking rigidly to my first (and surely wrong) decision to try my hand at business. I'd be miserable. But humility can free us to live a life more aligned with our values and talents, as well as identify the areas in our own life that we need to develop and grow. Having self-awareness allows us to actively craft our life rather than passively reacting to the world around us.

Humility also allows us to know our limits and set boundaries. Awareness enables you to identify what you don't know—and research has revealed that intellectually humble people are better at identifying what they don't know than arrogant people.[15] Humble people have a better understanding of both the breadth and the limits of their knowledge. Because of this, they know how to spend their efforts to learn and grow, and when to ask for help. And they can do so with a spirit of curiosity and eagerness to learn, rather than shame or embarrassment that they didn't already know the answer. No one knows everything. Many of us have specialized knowledge that we've developed through deliberate training and intentional effort, and some of us are even experts in areas, but it's unrealistic to have an all-encompassing breadth of knowledge and skill. Developing self-awareness helps us realize the scope of our limits, and humility can help us see those as exciting growth "edges" rather than confining boundaries.

In a related vein, humility, via awareness and acceptance, can help us set more realistic goals. When we know our abilities and limitations, we can set goals that we are better able to meet. Then, as we progress, we can also adjust our goals (upward) accordingly. Previous research has revealed that high self-esteem can lead people to set unrealistic goals when they feel threatened. For example, in the absence of threat, people with high self-esteem make fairly accurate predictions and perform mostly well at complex tasks; but when their ego is threatened, they double down and bet on themselves too much, which leads them to fail to achieve the lofty goals they thought they could easily reach.[16] When we think too highly of ourselves, a threat causes us to go out of our way to prove just how great we are. An unchecked—and threatened—ego fails us because we try to do too much, just to reassert to ourselves and others how great we are. When we don't know ourselves well, or when we're arrogantly smitten with ourselves and desperately trying to protect a fragile ego, we miss out on opportunities to grow and improve, and lash out at others when things don't go our way. Remember, humility is about a sense of security that comes from knowing and accepting yourself. But knowing yourself well also helps you set more manageable goals and enables you to monitor your progress along the way, admitting when you're falling behind or might need some help.

Humility also fosters personal growth. How can you learn or grow if you can't take honest feedback and or see the world accurately? If you don't know what you don't know, how can you make new discoveries or acquire knowledge? You'll always be operating out of a positive illusion, protecting your sense of self and the existing way of seeing the world. Humility allows you to achieve authentic personal growth by engaging with the world as it is. You can be more open to feedback and will seek out opportunities to learn. In addition, you'll adopt an incremental mindset— the belief that you can change your characteristics rather than viewing them as fixed and immutable—something that researchers find is critical for happiness[17] and success.[18]

There is yet another upside: Awareness and acceptance lead to self-compassion. Humility is not simply about bracing to face the cold, harsh world as it is; research has found a positive relationship between humility and self-compassion.[19] People who are more honest with themselves (and about the world) tend to also treat themselves with more compassion. The limitations of this research preclude us from determining whether seeing ourselves as we truly are frees us up to be more compassionate toward ourselves, or if self-compassion might be a necessary ingredient for a more honest view of ourselves (or if something else is causing both things to happen). Either way, it is clear that humility is closely tied to treating ourselves kindly. Moving from self-knowledge to compassionate acceptance is key as we engage with the world more objectively and less defensively.

Other research supports this claim: Although stress can take its toll on well-being, several studies suggest that people who are humble fare better when adversity strikes. A large, nationally representative study found that stress is consistently related to lower levels of happiness and life satisfaction, and greater symptoms of anxiety and depression.[20] However, these negative effects were reduced for humble individuals. They were able to maintain a greater sense of well-being and mental health during periods of stress better than those who were less humble. In another study, researchers found that this buffering effect of humility helped allay doubt in one's religious beliefs.[21] Being humble can help people come to terms with the objective reality of life in a way that doesn't threaten their religious beliefs as deeply as when they are less humble. They are able to see, and accept, the world as it is and process stress more effectively.

Toward Honesty

Awareness and acceptance are some of the initial benefits of humility. When we cultivate self-knowledge (seeing ourselves and the world for what they are) and acceptance of what is, we begin to see how beneficial humility can be. If we're able to overcome our shame and avoid vanity, we can act with autonomy, set good boundaries, establish realistic goals, seek personal growth, and treat ourselves with compassion. Our default mental tendencies make it challenging to approach the world objectivity, but the first step toward humility requires an honest assessment of ourselves and our reality. This can be painful. After all, these biases developed in order to keep our positive views of ourselves intact. It certainly feels better in the immediate moment to elevate our self-view and cultivate a world that conforms with our preconceived ideas. But now we understand that the world created by our biases is illusory (not our objective world). Humility beckons us to boldly accept who we are and our place in the world with compassion and authenticity. And when we do, we can begin to live more authentic and meaningful lives.

2

—

Authentic Relationships

UMILITY IMPROVES OUR RELATIONSHIPS. We are naturally social creatures, and when people are asked what makes life meaningful, relationships regularly rise to the top of the list. Our fondest memories—the ones that persist into retirement and form the wistful nostalgia into which we are often swept away—typically involve other people. Inasmuch as our relationships provide meaning and create deep and lasting joy, many people experience considerable discord in those relationships. Some have difficulty forging deep connections with others, whereas others find themselves plagued with perpetual conflict and unhappiness (sadly, the divorce market in the United States is almost $12 billion annually; divorce rates have doubled since the 1970s). Why do some relationships flourish and others flounder? How is it that some people enjoy deep and meaningful bonds with friends and family, whereas others struggle in their close relationships? And how can we improve our relationships in the varied domains of our life?

Perhaps unsurprisingly, ego often stands in the way of healthy relationships. When we're overly focused on ourselves, we are unable to receive feedback, act persistently defensive, and don't consider the needs of others: It can spell disaster for relationships.

It takes considerable effort to protect a fragile ego, and when we do, it often comes out in ways that hurt the ones we love. On the other hand, a decade of research in psychology suggests that humility is a highly desirable quality across all types of relationships, from friends to coworkers, and family to romantic partners. When people have self-awareness and can admit their own limitations and mistakes, when they can check their ego and curb their inclinations toward selfishness, and when they think of the needs of others, research suggests we want to be in relationship with them. We're drawn to individuals like this, and our relationships with them are meaningful, important, and dynamic. Let's look at how humility can help people form and maintain authentic relationships.

How Humility Strengthens Relationships

Of all the benefits of humility, the clearest is how it transforms relationships. The *social bonds hypothesis* argues that humility helps improve our relationships with other people across time—from initial friendship and attraction, through the challenges and stress of ups and downs, to the commitment of long-term partnership. Because humble people restrain their egos and are thoughtful of the needs and well-being of those around them, their relationships flourish.

I first met my friend Kevin when I was in graduate school. A mutual friend introduced us and said that he could see us becoming good friends. In many ways, Kevin and I are quite different. He plays the drums, is the pastor at a small church, enjoys photography, and is an avid birder. Despite our different interests (although I have recently begun birding as a hobby, thanks to my wife), what helped our friendship flourish—and likely sustained it over the years—has been Kevin's remarkable humility. He genuinely took interest in wanting to know me; he asked questions about my family, was curious about my research, and regularly checked in to see how I was doing. He was a thoughtful and kind friend when my brother passed away just before my last year in graduate school, and years later, he offered a poignant poem that I read at my father's eulogy. He is empathic and considerate, and quick to admit when he is unsure, doubting, or simply doesn't know—a rarity among many in his ministerial profession. He regularly thinks of others and seeks feedback to become a better person. He is authentic and desires real connection with other people. Though far from perfect, I often think of Kevin as an exemplar of humility. And I count myself lucky to be his friend.

Of all the necessary ingredients for a healthy and happy relationship, humility would be in my top two, right alongside shared values. Psychological research shows that humility is a wellspring of positive, pro-relational features. Early research on romantic relationships suggested that people often enter a relationship with a default inclination toward prioritizing their own needs.[1] They often act independently, seeking to maximize their own happiness and satisfaction. While this may be a fine short-term strategy in temporary relationships, this approach doesn't make for a healthy and equitable atmosphere in long-term relationships. As a result, people must transform their motivation and shift from a selfish, independent focus to a relational, interdependent focus.[2] That is, they transition from thinking solely about themselves to considering their partner and the relationship, and, in doing so, begin to act interdependently—considering the needs of their partner alongside their own.

Humility helps the relationship mature. Whereas narcissists, who are markedly low in humility, engage in a game-playing style of relationships,[3] humble people approach relationships with greater authenticity, care for their partner, and concern for the quality of their connection. In addition, knowing yourself better—what psychologists call "self-concept clarity"—also significantly improves relationship quality.[4] Because humble people know who they are, they can securely interact with their partner rather than hide behind and play games.

Because humility contributes to flourishing relationships, those who are humble are often highly valued romantic partners. Humility signals to others how they're likely to be treated in a relationship. Although the brash self-absorption of narcissism may be attractive to us early on, that routine gets stale fast as the narcissistic partner turns their efforts of justifying their own superiority toward us in order to protect a fragile, overinflated ego. True confidence isn't condescension or contempt; rather, it springs from a place of honesty and security. Only those who are secure can enjoy a partner's success, admit when they are wrong, and consider how their actions affect their partner. When someone is the right size—not overly inflated and defending their ego, nor too small and shrinking in a relationship—it contributes to a vibrant, mutual, and interdependent relationship. They can accept difficult feedback about how to improve, aren't constantly seeking affirmation of an overinflated sense of self, and are willing to value their partner's needs.

Research supports this notion of humility as a signal of a desirable partner—as an indication that someone might make a good long-term mate. A large study of more than nine hundred participants revealed that humility is rated as more important in an ideal partner than every other feature of personality, including sensitivity, agreeableness, conscientiousness, and openness.[5] This pattern was found in both short-term and long-term relationships, though it was stronger in the latter. The authors concluded that trustworthiness may be the central defining feature of a romantic relationship—and humility is an indicator of whether a partner can be trusted.

Although humility improves relationships, it's not always our default approach to ourselves or other people. Many of us have built our self-worth on external contingencies, creating a fragile

ego teetering like a house of cards, waiting for the wind of criticism to knock us down. We have cognitive biases that distort how
we see the world, protect our positive self-view, and render us
unwilling, or unable, to take feedback constructively. In order for
humility to be truly transformative, we have to address the issue
of our fragile ego and our relentless defense of it.

The Problem of Ego in Relationships

Fragile egos can doom relationships. People spend an inordinate
amount of time and energy preserving an unflinchingly flattering
and overly glowing view of themselves in their own minds. But
for many people, this inflated self-view and its requisite defense
stem from a deeper-seated insecurity and fragility, which can
undermine how we interact with others. When we're unsure of
who we are without external praise or affirmation, we hustle to
collect evidence of our worthiness rather than believing that we
are inherently enough. In the process, we act defensively to maintain a positive view of ourselves, which in turn wreaks havoc on
our relationships. An unchecked or fragile ego gives rise to four
perilous patterns in relationships: selfishness, insecurity, toxic
conflict, and stagnation.

Most obviously, people with fragile egos act *selfishly*. It's not
bad to ensure that our needs are being met; in fact, doing so is
healthy. But to do so exclusively—and to the detriment of other
people in our life—is problematic. Those with fragile egos seek
only to meet their own needs. They make sure they get what they
want without regard for others' needs and don't consider the feelings of close family and friends. They are fine trampling over
others if it means they'll get ahead. They are first to accept praise
and last to take responsibility or blame, often accusing others and
shirking responsibility. A common mantra is "It's not my fault."
A friend, partner, or coworker unwilling to own up to their share
of the blame or to be held responsible for what they did is stuck in

an unhealthy pattern. This kind of selfishness elicits selfishness from others, creating a noxious cycle where each person is looking out for themselves. When everyone cares only about themselves, competition reigns and collaboration wanes. And romantic partners will quickly get fed up with this kind of immature egotism.

People with fragile egos also make *insecure* friends and partners. Because they never truly believe that they are enough, they tend to relate to others in ways that convey this insecurity. They often do not trust their partners. They might try to control their partner or act dishonestly. Similarly, they might try to conceal their true self. They act inauthentically or hide parts of themselves; after all, those who cannot love themselves for who they are find it hard to believe that others would love them just as they are. They may also relate to their partner anxiously, being clingy, jealous, or otherwise preoccupied. This may include constantly checking on their partner's whereabouts and questioning their intentions and motives. Finally, they might avoid true intimacy, keeping interactions on the surface level, seeking only casual interactions, and distracting or immersing themselves in work or other overcommitments. All these maneuvers keep them from expressing—and receiving—authentic intimacy and deep connection. Their defensiveness shields them from the sheer delight and enjoyment of relationships.

Ego also breeds *toxic conflict*. When people put their (fragile) egos first, they prioritize proving their point rather than listening to others or remaining open to the evidence. This means that in disagreements, people naturally tend to defend their position, no matter the cost, over hearing their partner or trying to see someone else's perspective. For them, being right matters more than making the relationship right. And when receiving feedback, they tend to get defensive, justifying their actions and rationalizing their behavior instead of integrating that feedback and working to change. It can be hard to admit when they are wrong or apologize for their actions. Their default tendency is often to reciprocate their partner's bad behavior. If their partner lashes out in frustration, they up the ante and snap right back. They may look for ways to find leverage or power over others, because they're afraid that their positive view of themselves might be illusory, and they need status to affirm their worth. Together, these behaviors escalate conflict. When ego is involved, people don't argue well (they care more about winning a fight than navigating a difficult situation with their partner), are resistant to feedback, fail to give others the grace they deserve, defend their position and behaviors, withhold forgiveness, and jockey for power. Such a pattern creates a toxic exchange that can be ruinous for relationships.

Finally, this can lead people with fragile egos toward *stagnation* in their relationships. They aren't willing to grow or change. They lack the insight to ask themselves where they could improve and don't know themselves well enough—or have the security or courage—to admit their own shortcomings. They focus only on their strengths and think they're doing just fine. Moreover, resisting feedback and remaining defensively entrenched prevent them from considering or appreciating new perspectives. It's hard to be curious about fresh ideas when we're so busy defending the ones we have. And so, when ego gets in the way, people don't adjust or calibrate to change dimensions of themselves in meaningful ways that produce growth. They get stuck. As other people grow, they might feel as though they are outgrowing their friend or partner.

The Transformational Power of Humility

Humility directly counters each of the four hallmarks of an ego-centered relationship. Humility involves starting from a place of security—enoughness. Humble people believe that they have inherent worth and value, apart from external contingencies, such as accolades or affirmation. From there, humility includes an accurate sense of self, regulating one's ego, and prioritizing the well-being of others. What this looks like within relationships is prioritizing mutual benefit, psychological security, healthy conflict, and growth. Relationships that emerge from ego alone and those from humility are compared in Table 3.

Humble partners are able to rein in their ego, so they want relationships that are *mutually beneficial*. They think of others' wants and needs and consider their well-being. They want interdependent, equal relationships, not ones marked by positioning for power or capitalizing on a partner's weakness. They don't worry about their own needs getting met, because they can do so in ways that consider the needs or wants of others. And when humble people believe that they are enough, they make *secure* friends and partners. That is, they have the psychological security to look inward and admit their limitations, receive and integrate feedback, and accept blame and responsibility. They trust other people. They don't smother their partner with clingy jealousy nor

Ego-Centered Relationships	Humility-Focused Relationships
SELFISHNESS: Prioritizes my needs and wants above all else	MUTUAL BENEFIT: Considers both my own and my partner's needs and wants
INSECURITY: Untrusting, overbearing or avoiding, inauthentic, guarded	SECURITY: Trusting, authentic, open, seeks intimacy and self-disclosure
TOXIC CONFLICT: Defensive, rejects feedback, denies wrongdoing, seeks power	HEALTHY CONFLICT: Open, seeks feedback, curious about others' perspectives, seeks equality
STAGNATION: Unwilling to grow or change, stuck in a behavioral pattern	GROWTH: Open to new ideas, changes in light of feedback, grows and adapts

Table 3. A tale of two relationships

avoid intimacy and self-disclosure. They can authentically engage with others to forge deep, meaningful connections.

Humble partners are not perfect, and, as in all relationships, conflict is common. But humble partners understand how to have *healthy conflict*. They don't start by defending their own views; rather, they seek to listen to others. They admit what they don't know and are eager to learn. They are curious about the perspectives of others and are willing to change their beliefs in light of new evidence. They welcome feedback and aren't constantly seeking power. Because of this, they are also likely to experience *growth*. They change based on what they learn from others and the world around them. They can embrace knowing that they will be different in the future than they are now—and that's perfectly fine. In fact, they welcome this change. When we set aside the labor of protecting our ego, we open ourselves up to new ways of experiencing love and engaging the world.

How Humility Helps Relationships

So, how exactly does humility enhance our relationships? Psychologists have been researching this question for the past decade and have produced quite a bit of data. Researchers have used different techniques to find the answer, ranging from asking people to rate their partner's humility, to measuring both partners' humility directly through self-report, to presenting people with options of potential partners who vary in humility or arrogance. Across these different approaches, the results indicate that people are more likely to want to become friends with humble people,[6] more likely to want to start and maintain a romantic relationship with humble (as compared to arrogant) partners,[7] and more satisfied with and committed to humble romantic partners.[8] In fact, research on close romantic relationships found that humility, including both self-ratings and peer-ratings, predicts higher relationship satisfaction, even when statistically accounting for other dimensions of personality.[9] Given that humility is, in part, about prioritizing the needs of others, it's no wonder why humble people are so attractive to potential friends and romantic interests: their humility is a signal for what it's like to be in a relationship with them. Of the myriad features of one's personality that contribute to a healthy and flourishing relationship, humility rises above the rest. But what might account for *why* humility is so valuable for relationships?

In order to try to explain why humility is so important to healthy relationships, my colleagues and I asked more than four hundred participants about their partner's humility, as well as how satisfied with and committed to their relationship they were.[10] The results indicated that to the degree that someone's partner was humble, partners were more satisfied with the relationship. In other words, having a humble partner is directly associated with greater relationship satisfaction. In addition, this work suggested that the positive association with relationship satisfaction comes from being more committed to the relationship. People commit more when their partner is humble. This work both supports the social bonds hypothesis and aligns with viewing humility as a signal of trust in a relationship. When our partner is humble, we're all in.

Other research has sought to identify reasons why humility makes relationships more satisfying. One study replicated the findings above, confirming the importance of commitment in explaining relationship satisfaction, but also added another potential mechanism: relational gratitude.[11] This research found that people are more grateful for their relationship when their partner is humble, and this leads to more satisfying relationships. Having a humble romantic partner can lead to a greater sense of commitment and gratitude for the relationship, both of which are recipes for satisfaction in the relationship.

One drawback of these studies is that they rely on correlations, which means we can't draw any causal conclusions. Maybe when people are satisfied in their relationships, they are more likely to view their partner as humble: After all, if things are going well, I may assume my partner must be a pretty humble person. Or, maybe as people are more committed, they act more humbly toward one another. Even still, people might be grateful because their relationship is going so well. So, the gold standard of determining causation is an experiment in which we can manipulate some features of the study and see how people respond. I led such a project under the guise of a dating profile study.[12]

We wanted to see if people really did prefer humble partners relative to arrogant ones when given a choice. We invited participants into the lab, one at a time, to take part in a dating profile study, in which they wrote a short description of themselves as they might for an online dating site. We then asked them to take a bogus personality test, which was really just a filler task to boost the believability of the study. Then, they were told that participants in the study were rating each other's profiles, so they could read and rate another profile. They read a fake profile about a sophomore student at the university who briefly described themselves in vague terms, such as "I'm fairly athletic but not overly sporty," which was accompanied by a profile with percentiles of personality dimensions supposedly generated from the test. All participants read the same profile except for one critical difference: For half of the profiles, the computerized personality test indicated their humility was in the 87th percentile, whereas for the other half of profiles, humility was in the 24th percentile.

The results were telling. When evaluating the profiles, participants who thought the target was humble rated them as more attractive, were more willing to share their own profile and phone number, and indicated a stronger desire to meet this individual in person. To increase our confidence in these results, we replicated the findings again, with a larger sample and with an arrogant profile versus a humble profile rather than different percentiles. And the results confirmed the original findings: Humble partners are highly desirable for new romantic relationships. Humble, not arrogant, partners are sought after, and people are willing to take action to make those new romantic connections.

Humility is also important in keeping romantic relationships healthy. Not only are we more attracted to humble partners, but humility can help keep the relational bonds strong. Research examining ways of keeping one's partner committed in the relationship revealed that partners high in humility are less likely to rely on tactics that include deception, exploitation, or manipulation than more arrogant partners would.[13] Because humility is associated with a sense of psychological security, humble people don't have to rely on controlling their partners or employ dishonest tactics to keep their partners from leaving. They know that they are enough and are respected as such. This sense of security permeates the relationship, facilitating honesty and mutual agreement, and reduces the likelihood of engaging in unhealthy manipulation or deception. And if both partners are humble and approach one another with the security of being enough and the willingness to accept each other's feedback, it makes for a healthy relationship that not only can weather most storms but also results in combined growth.

Showing the Real You

Our desire to belong is a powerful motivation. In fact, it may be one of the strongest drives we have—and for good reason: It's evolutionarily adaptive.[14] We need other people to reproduce and increase our chance for survival (it's easier to fight off predators or other threats in a group than alone). The fear of isolation is one of our core existential concerns.[15] Because of it, rejection stings and exclusion can feel excruciating. We hate feeling left out, abandoned, neglected, or otherwise ostracized.

Given our desire to avoid rejection, we often fail to show our "true" self to others. We hide aspects of who we are out of fear that others will reject us. We put our best foot forward, secretly hoping no one learns something about us that will cause them to leave. This deep-seated fear is not simply of being rejected but being *fully seen and rejected*. When people glimpse our true self—our authentic, messy, flawed self—and then decide to leave, it leaves lasting pain. We put on a mask or evade full disclosure out of fear. We protect ourselves.

The desire for protection can inhibit joy and keep us from fully experiencing the rich depth of love and acceptance. Because we shield who we really are out of fear of rejection, we don't allow ourselves the opportunity to be fully loved, for all of who we are. What if we find someone who actually does see us for who we are and is willing to accept us? That love and acceptance can be transformational and healing. But if we never share ourselves, we'll never know. And by hiding parts of ourselves, we may be left wondering if those who love us would still feel that way if they really knew *all* of who we are.

We put ourselves in a trap. We fear rejection, so we hide to protect ourselves from pain; but when we hide parts of ourselves, we don't fully experience love and may always wonder if another's love for us is conditional, likely to slip away if we revealed our true self. Either way, this defensive maneuvering robs us of a rich and authentic relationship, and it keeps us from experiencing the depth of love. Our guard is perpetually up, keeping out both the full range of pain *and* love.

Humility may offer insights to this protection problem. When people feel secure, knowing that they have worth and value, they are less consumed with the evaluation of others. Of course, rejection still stings, but starting from a place of security rather than insecurity can help embolden a person to risk sharing their true self. Similarly, knowing oneself well enough to share the good and the bad can help facilitate the process of authentic self-disclosure. When we know that we have something good and worthy to offer, rejection may say more about the person doing the rejecting than it does about us. And tapping into the empathic desire to reciprocate when others share their true self can elicit acceptance in return, creating a safe environment for people to come together, just as they are. Indeed, humility often gives way to authenticity.

Humility is a key feature of authentic relationships. When people feel the security to share their true self—who they really are—with others, it can lead to greater authenticity in relationships. Of course, this security in a relationship must come from both partners; a mutual humility is often key to the most secure and authentic relationships. Research has highlighted the relationship between authenticity and humility, more than any other feature of one's personality.[16] We see this kind of authentic appeal of humility across the span of a relationship. In this chapter, I'll discuss how humility helps forge new (and likely, more authentic) relationships across the relational trajectory.

Humility is helpful for forming brand new relationships.[17] In one study, my colleagues and I had undergraduate college students come into the lab to be assigned to work in small groups. Having never met one another, they were assigned to three different tasks to strain their humility. Initially, they described aloud to the group their strengths and weaknesses as a leader. Next, they participated in a group exercise where they had to imagine they were astronauts that had crash-landed on the moon more than two hundred miles away from their intended rendezvous point and had to decide how to allocate resources to make the journey. After a round of negotiating which fifteen items to bring to ensure survival, they completed their last task, which was collectively working on challenging standardized test questions, in which they could not move on to the next question until a unanimous decision was reached. These situations are ripe for displays of power and contentious debate. Participants rated each other's humility (and their own) after each activity. The results revealed two key findings. First, truly humble people don't inflate their self-reported scores, but arrogant people do. That is, arrogant people say they're humbler than other people say they are, whereas humble people's assessment of their own humility is more aligned with other people's ratings. Second, and most critically, people admire and respect humble group members and indicate a desire to work with them again in the future. Simply put, humble people are accepted and others want to continue a relationship with them. This suggests that on a first meeting—especially with a shared activity where conflict may occur—humility is an important signal to attract potential friends and teammates.

Keeping Relationships Thriving

Humility is also good for helping relationships thrive. Research has examined how humility helps serve *relational maintenance functions*—those behaviors that can keep relationships intact and healthy. Examples include having healthy conflict (arguing in healthy ways), repairing relationships with forgiveness following an interpersonal offense, reacting constructively when a partner acts selfishly, and building trust. Forming relationships is only part of the work; there is plenty to be done to keep relationships intact and flourishing.

Conflict is an unavoidable part of any relationship, but *how* we navigate conflict matters. Humility promotes healthy conflict. One study examined the role of humility in helping interethnic couples navigate arguments related to culture.[18] Sometimes, couples in which partners are of different races or ethnicities argue about cultural topics, but how they argue matters. When partners fall into patterns of ineffective arguing, in which they have persistent conflict resulting in neither partner feeling heard or understood, it erodes relationship satisfaction and commitment. However, this pattern is reversed with humble partners. Perceiving a partner as humble is associated with more effective arguing around cultural matters. Humble partners can argue in healthier ways: They share directly, listen to their partner, receive feedback nondefensively, seek to understand their partner's perspective, and treat their partner with empathy and respect. Moreover, as we've seen, having a humble partner is associated with better relationship quality. Humble individuals listen, validate, and appreciate differences of their partners amid conflict. Humility can lead to fighting better, which can help improve the relationship.

Humility can also help people repair the hurts incurred during a relationship. Sometimes, we say hurtful things or are inconsiderate to those we love. We may act selfishly and disrespectfully. Conflict and stress can give way to interpersonal offense. Humility can help us forgive. In one study, my colleagues and I compared couples in in-person (proximal) relationships with couples in long-distance relationships.[19] We asked them to recall a time when their partner offended them, and then report how much they had forgiven their partner, as well as how humble they viewed their partner. We also collected information about how severe the offense was and how forgiving the participant was on average (trait forgivingness). Even when controlling for how severe the offense was and a person's average tendency to forgive, the results revealed that people harbored more unforgiveness toward partners in long-distance relationships, except when their partners were humble. The stress of navigating the complexities of a romantic relationship over distance can lead to unforgiveness, unless the partner is humble. We're more forgiving of humble partners, who can make the challenges of a long-distance relationship a bit more palatable.

By promoting forgiveness, humility can improve how satisfied we are in our relationships. Another study my colleagues and I conducted looked at the benefits of humility in forgiveness by sampling people over time.[20] We intentionally recruited people who had been offended or hurt in their romantic relationship in the past two months. They wrote about their offense and their partner. We then surveyed them every week for six weeks, inquiring how much they had forgiven their partner for the offense, as well as their view of their partner. The results provided potent evidence for the power of humility: Over the course of the study, viewing one's partner as humble predicted greater forgiveness in subsequent weeks. Humility elicits forgiveness.

A study of women in romantic relationships who had offended their partner and took responsibility for the offense highlights the importance of forgiveness.[21] Humble partners can admit when they are wrong, take responsibility for their mistakes, and offer greater forgiveness to their partners because they know they've been wrong as well and so are motivated to take their partner's perspective. These patterns keep relationships together and help ensure both partners are satisfied.

Humility also builds trust. Humility and honesty are two sides of the same coin, and research suggests that humble individuals tend to trust their partner more; those low in humility are less trusting and often ask their friends to help ensure their partners don't cheat on them.[22] It's possible that this level of trust is because humble people are more secure in their relationship, or perhaps they perceive their partner as more satisfied. Either way, being in a relationship with a humble partner suggests a more stable and enduring relationship where trust and respect, rather than game-playing and strategizing, keep the other partner engaged and committed.

Finally, humility is also key to long-term committed relationships. Within married couples, research has found that humility increases relationship satisfaction by building trust and facilitating makeup strategies.[23] That is, married people are more likely to trust their spouse when they view them as humble, and they experience more instances of behaviors designed to repair rifts in the relationship. Importantly, one's perception of their spouse's humility was more predictive of these positive outcomes than a spouse's self-report. It's not enough to think you're humble; your partner has to perceive you that way. But when they do, it can make a long-term relationship, like marriage, more trusting and satisfying.

Avoiding Potential Pitfalls

There can be some pitfalls with a humble partner. Thinking *too low* of oneself—a type of inaccurate self-view that is not humility—can undermine relationships, since these individuals don't think of their own needs at all. Remember: A humble person has an accurate view of themselves—not deflated or self-defeating—and can prioritize the needs of others, but not to the detriment of their own well-being or the health of the relationship. For example, if someone is always giving and never considering their own needs or desires within the relationship, it can lead to blurred boundaries or risk codependency. Having clear boundaries is still a necessary part of healthy relationships. Each person should know where they end and their partner begins. Of course, *inter*dependency is the goal: I affect you and you affect me, and we care deeply about one another, but my sense of self is not tied to yours. I am differentiated. So, it is important to be clear that humility does not give way to losing oneself in a relationship. Humble people have the security of knowing who they are, and they are able to empathize and show love from that security.

A related pitfall is when humble people are exploited by arrogant partners. Most research has looked at humility on the individual level. Even when considering how humility affects relationships, few studies consider whether the humility of *both* partners mattered, so my colleagues and I tackled that issue directly.[24] As part of my postdoctoral research with forgiveness expert Everett Worthington, I focused on a study of new parents to better understand the role of forgiveness and humility in navigating stress. Dr. Worthington wanted to see if humility before a stressful event predicts better outcomes during and after the event. The transition to parenthood is one of those few unique situations in life in which (a) there is a definite "pre-stress" period where we're alerted that a big life change is coming and have time to get participants into the lab before it happens, and (b) it's a near guarantee to be rather stressful. In one such analysis, we assessed new parents in the third trimester of pregnancy (before birth), and then again when the baby was three months, nine months, and twenty-one months old (two years after the initial "baseline" assessment).[25] The study found that while most folks increased in stress over time, having a humble partner (viewing that partner as humble) was associated with experiencing less stress. A separate analysis revealed a similar pattern with a couples' adjustment from pre- to post-birth of their new baby.[26] Humility helps protect against some of the stress of a new baby and improves how couples adjust to their new life.

These results show that when both partners were humble, people reported better mental health during the stressful time after the birth of their first child, and better relationship satisfaction and physiological responses to conflict. But here's the second half of that story: These results only held up when *both* partners were humble. When one of the partners was arrogant, the effects dissipated. In the pressure cooker of parenting or consistent fights, it's possible that an arrogant partner can dominate, or even exploit, a humble partner. If one side is always giving, and perhaps even always expected to give and give in, resentment can build, and the emotional cost can take a toll. In such high-stakes situations, what is needed more than ever is mutual humility between partners. Couples in which both partners were thoughtful of the other and relatively humble experienced much higher levels of personal benefit and a stronger relationship.

This work has some important implications. For one, it's important to think carefully about choosing a relationship partner. Not only is being humble important for relationships, but having a humble partner is paramount. When the stress of life builds or couples find themselves arguing over money, sex, or (ironically) communication, having a humble partner to help navigate these concerns makes all the difference. In addition, research has highlighted how important it is to build *relational value*.[27] Relational value is when partners view each other as people of worth and allow each other to play a key role in one another's lives. They find the relationship rewarding. Their partner and the relationship matter to them. This value protects against grudges and revenge as well as exploitation. When people value their relationship and relationship partner, they're much less likely to exploit them or act dominantly over their partner. Finally, this research shows a boundary condition of humility: It cannot fix every relational ill. An arrogant partner can overwhelm, despite one's best efforts to act humbly.

As is usually the case, humility is just one of many virtues one might lean on. Wisdom is needed to know when to prioritize courage and justice. When trust has been fractured and the relationship doesn't feel safe, humility may not be the most helpful, or healthy, priority. Rather, ensuring that one's boundaries are maintained, needs are addressed, and personal well-being is prioritized may require the courage to stand up to an egotistical partner and the motivation to ensure the relationship does not fall into a pattern of exploitation. A humble response might be having the self-awareness to know when a relationship is no longer safe, and the security to move forward with a radical overhaul or dissolution of that relationship.

If we can rest in the security of humility, avoiding arrogance and self-deprecation, the potential benefits in our relationships are powerful. Creating boundaries that protect us from exploitive partners and working to cultivate value in a relationship can create a situation where both parties feel safe to be themselves and both members' achievements are celebrated and losses grieved. In a healthy relationship, a sense of equality, mutual benefit, and interdependence permeates the air. These qualities can also have a profound effect on our connections with other people.

A Hope for Healthy Relationships

Humility won't cure all of our relationship ails, but it may serve as a central organizing virtue in the constellation of strengths. Starting from security rather than defensiveness, sharing oneself authentically, prioritizing the needs of others, and engaging others with trust and respect can lead to greater commitment, gratitude, and satisfaction, as well as healthier functioning. Humble people often make better friends, coworkers, and partners. They are open to feedback and willing to change and grow. Given our increasing isolation and loneliness, finding ways to strengthen relationships is a worthwhile pursuit. Moving toward secure and healthy relationships may even help make life more meaningful.

3
—

Ambition and Achievement

CHUCK FEENEY WAS RAISED in a working-class household. After attending Cornell University, he cofounded the Duty Free Shoppers Group, which expanded to more than four hundred locations and helped him earn more than $8 billion over the course of his career. Many international travelers have seen these stores in major airports and are familiar with this brand. What is more impressive than his story of hard work and determination (and perhaps a bit of luck) is that he managed to give away nearly every penny of his wealth in his lifetime—and did so largely in secret.

It's not uncommon for wealthy people to give away a part of their fortune. However, relatively few, if any, give away *all* of it, and many do so through foundations bearing their name or in ways that recognize their gifts. Hospital wings and university buildings are commonly named after significant donors. However, Feeney was different. *Forbes* magazine called him the "James Bond of Philanthropy." It wasn't until a business dispute in the late 1990s that his connection with a generous foundation intent on donating all his wealth was revealed. *The New York Times* chronicled his accomplishment of giving away his wealth while alive, noting that he always lived a modest life, often flying in coach and eschewing fancy restaurants for burgers in small cafés. His donations often came with the condition that he would not receive credit, nor would his name be attached to any of the projects funded by his generosity. Now, he lives a relatively quiet life with his wife in a rented apartment, with $2 million remaining in savings, a fraction of his total wealth after having clandestinely donated almost $8 billion. Many consider Feeney to be an exemplar of humility, having made these donations without seeking public praise or accolades. Is it possible that part of Feeney's professional success might be due, at least in part, to his humility?

Critics of humility equate it with lack of achievement or settling for mediocrity. After all, Steve Jobs, who by all accounts was a narcissistic jerk who regularly soured relationships, helped launch the successful corporate empire of Apple, contributed useful and widely adapted technology, and made himself and his stockholders plenty of money along the way. This would suggest that ego gets the job done, right? But this argument is problematic for several reasons. First, it casts "success" in a narrow light, with a monolithic and purely capitalistic definition; neither money nor professional success are the best indicators of well-being or necessarily beneficial to personal relationships. Second, it pits humility *against* achievement. However, as research reveals, humility is a common if not necessary ingredient in groups and companies that achieve considerable success. It's a foundational element of transformational leadership. Third, such accounts misperceive humility as timidity. In the domains of ambition and achievement, ego is important but insufficient: Confidence and competence are both key for professional success, but they are often not enough. Hard-driving leaders can burn out employees, and outperforming peers often draw the ire of coworkers—unless they are humble.

As Feeney illustrates, one doesn't earn more than $8 billion from a sustained business without ambition and achievement.

But what role did his humility play in his success? And more broadly, how can humility lead to excellence and help hard-driving, ambitious individuals, groups, and companies thrive? In his seminal work *Good to Great*, Jim Collins talks about "Level 5" leaders, who combine an undeterred vision (or will) with humility. Humble leaders put the company's values and health first, rather than prioritizing their own personal gains, which often elicits a strong degree of trust and commitment from their employees.[1] Recent research has underscored the importance of humility at work and the pitfalls of being entirely self-sufficient; after all, business is inherently dependent on relationships.[2] This has led scholars to characterize humility as a key virtue for leaders and managers, and a highly valued trait for any employee.[3] Humility is often associated with better customer service, more satisfied employees, and greater organizational resilience. Even so, it's often overlooked in corporate settings,[4] an oversight that can be costly.

Humility in Power

Humility is often the most necessary where it is most challenging to practice, as in positions of power. The *social oil hypothesis* argues that humility helps protect against the wear and tear of relationships in which there is a power difference or high potential for conflict. This can be seen clearly in the nature of leadership—after all, leaders are often in positions of considerable power with a clear hierarchy, where conflict is a consistent possibility. But what might humble leadership look like? Empirical research suggests that a humble leader is one who balances competing goals of *service* (being able to stand back) and *taking action* (empowering others, enforcing accountability, and allocating resources).[5] It looks a lot like standing behind people as one moves them forward. Critically, this research revealed that humility is most important in situations where leaders have the most power. The

greater the position in the hierarchy, the stronger the effect
humility had on an employee's energy, dedication, and involvement at work. Put differently, in situations of considerable power,
humble leaders are especially effective.

Humility helps people focus on the needs of others, making
them better leaders. And humble leaders are attuned to their
followers' needs and can calibrate their responses to promote a
healthy work environment. They recognize the importance of
accepting the blame and sharing the praise, as well as receiving
feedback on what they are doing well and what needs to change.
In high-conflict situations or when there's a significant power
difference, we're often concerned with protecting our ego at all
costs. We may want to make sure we get noticed and receive
credit, and that our views are validated—even if it means going
behind our peers. Sure, validation and fair allocation of credit
and resources are important. But in high-stakes situations,
threats to our ego are heightened, because we feel that there is so
much on the line. This can leave a trail of carnage in our relationships. Adopting a stance of humility can go a long way as a
counterweight to ambition. In tandem, they are a powerful
combination.

Humility often balances out problematic features of a leader's
style or an ineffective organizational structure. Supervisors who
are seen as both humble and agreeable are less likely to be
viewed as abusive.[6] Similarly, humility in a leader results in
greater empowerment among their followers (or employees), and
this relationship is stronger among both leaders and followers
who generally accept the power dynamic of a hierarchical organization.[7] When an individual has power, humility helps keep
them in check.

A clever research study confirmed the important role of humility to balancing power. Using an economic game that created
power asymmetries—the dictator game, in which participants

decided how to split money between themselves and a fictional partner—researchers found that humility was associated with less exploitive behavior.[8] When in positions of absolute power, humility was associated with greater generosity than a proclivity to think only of oneself. Power is a thorny issue, and people in positions of power can easily exploit others or burn bridges; humility helps them avoid such costly mistakes.

From Me to We

A humble leader moves from thinking about *me* to thinking about *we*. Researchers have argued that humility is a key ingredient to charismatic leadership, in part because such leaders are less focused on themselves and more open to the perspectives of others.[9] In fact, along with forgiveness and integrity, humility is a key characteristic that facilitates transformational leadership—a style of leadership that inspires followers, encourages personal growth, and often yields exceptional outcomes—and enhances people's willingness to follow that leader.[10] Humility broadens one's perspective from thinking merely about oneself to considering the needs of others and the larger organization or community.

The shift of humble leaders from *me-to-we* has demonstrable effects on employees. Under humble leadership, employees are more likely to share constructive challenges and innovative ideas for improvement—using their voice—largely because they feel as though this engagement is part of their role as followers.[11] Having a humble leader is associated with employees reporting a greater sense of personal power, which leads them to using their voice to speak up and speak out.[12] Under humble leadership, people feel empowered to use their voice and know that doing so is encouraged (if not expected). What is the result of this empowerment? Teams are more proactive. In a study of more than fifty leaders and three hundred followers, research found that when leaders were rated as humbler by their followers, there was greater psychological empowerment among employees, which, in turn, was associated with greater proactive behavior.[13] As humble leaders demonstrate, sharing the power benefits everyone in the relationship, leading to stronger teams.

The advantages of humble leadership are most evident under stress. My colleagues and I conducted qualitative research that detailed the benefits of humility among leaders of humanitarian organizations, who often work amid crises that follow disasters.[14] These leaders—who were described as open, teachable, aware of their humanitarian context and calling, and virtuous—shared the credit, admitted their mistakes, and were focused on others. This resulted in cascading benefits to their employees and partners, organizations, and beneficiaries. Humble leaders found the work to be more meaningful, employees had greater buy-in and did higher-quality work, organizations were healthier and had less burnout, and, critically, the people they were serving felt as though they mattered.

In stressful situations, leaders fall into old, reliable patterns of thinking, which saves time and effort but can lead to serious mistakes. We're less likely to seek out, or even notice, new information, which can result in simply confirming what we've always believed and doing what we've always done—even if that result is largely ineffective. Under stress, we can get stuck. However, humble leaders are able to get different results and are more effective, because they seek out and wrestle with more objective data when making a decision—something researchers call *balanced processing*.[15] They demonstrate an openness to feedback from every angle, including their employees, peers, and bosses. When they are inexperienced, arrogant leaders become rigid and closed-minded, whereas humble leaders are flexible and open to new ideas—they can overcome their inexperience through seeking, learning, and listening well.[16] They set aside ego for the sake of the organization and get better results.

This openness comes out in different ways. A study of business leaders reveals that a *growth mindset* and a *relational identity* are both features of those who are humble.[17] The former refers to viewing one's characteristics and traits as malleable or changeable rather than static or stable. Someone with a growth mindset might say, "I'm not skilled at that right now, but I can learn." The latter refers to viewing oneself as interconnected with others and valuing the health and functioning of the larger collective, whether that's a two-person relationship or a large group or organization. Humble leaders view their traits and abilities as something they can develop, and they know that they are part of—and accountable to—something bigger than themselves. In turn, followers report more energy for relationships and less emotional exhaustion, which is associated with better performance at work, both subjectively rated and objectively measured. People have more capacity to do good work when their leaders are humble.

What Are the Benefits of Humility at Work?

We have seen that humble leadership can produce better outcomes for employees, but what about the organization? Research has found that with humble leaders, people report greater job engagement, higher job satisfaction, greater orientation toward the team's goals, and less voluntary turnover.[18] People want to work for humble leaders. After all, humble CEOs ensure greater pay equality in their top management teams, which leads to better financial performance for the organization.[19] By spreading the wealth, humble CEOs are actually generating more of it by earning their companies more money. And humble leaders not only share the wealth but are also more likely to engage in shared leadership—a collaborative way of interacting in which team members rely on each other, are mutually influential, and collectively decide how to move toward the organization's goals.[20] Humble leadership is good for business.

Let's take a look at some of the key outcomes of inviting humility in one's work. Keep in mind that because work is inherently relational, themes similar to those discussed in chapter 2—on how humility improves close relationships—will appear. Critically, this research has been conducted in the workplace setting, with an eye toward effective leaderships. Here is a bird's-eye view of the research findings.

Humility leads to authenticity and sincerity. A series of studies found that when leaders are humble, followers feel safer and less threatened, and are more likely to feel and act authentically.[21] Humility is not only important for leaders; employees benefit as well. One study found that humble individuals avoid "impression management"—or behaviors used to manipulate others.[22] Those high in humility were less likely to report self-promotion (bragging or exaggerating), ingratiation (endearing oneself to others in order to be liked), exemplification (appearing to be hardworking by going "above and beyond"), intimidation (trying to appear powerful or making threats), or supplication (announcing one's weaknesses to appear needy and elicit pity). From this, we can conclude that in the workplace, humble individuals are *sincere*.

As in interpersonal relationships, humility fosters trust in the workplace. A study of more than 275 work pairs found that followers trust humbler leaders, unless they think the leaders are acting humbly as a form of manipulation.[23] And trust is critical both within and outside of an organization. In my own work, we've found that people perceive humble leaders as more trustworthy, which leads them to donate more money to their causes.[24] Part of what people are weighing when they evaluate philanthropic giving to organizations such as nonprofits is whether they can trust the leader (and organization) with their hard-earned donation. Humility signals trust.

Humility breeds innovation and creativity. A study of more than 150 people found that humble leaders are likely to elicit greater innovation from their employees.[25] Another study high-lighted how humble leaders positively affect employees' creativ-ity.[26] This greater creativity comes about because people feel safer to share information and end up sharing more, which leads to new and different ideas.[27] When people communicate more and offer each other more feedback, especially in more diverse teams, it leads to a wider realm of ideas.[28] Humility allows the space for people to share their ideas without judgment, provides room for communication, and capitalizes on a team's diversity of thought by encouraging all to brainstorm freely.

Humble leaders develop resilient, growth-oriented teams. Both field studies and experimental research suggest followers report more resilience when their leaders are humble.[29] This is especially important in organizational settings where people feel as though there are high-stakes organizational politics at play.[30] Such environments can be toxic, but humble leadership can reduce any negative effects by helping people become more resilient. Not only that, but these leaders can cultivate expan-sion and growth.[31] Down the line, this can lead to greater adaptability, which can positively affect a company's bottom line.[32] Creating a culture where people can overcome hardships by adapting to stress allows organizations to be nimbler and better positions them to tackle new challenges as an organization.

All these benefits lead to better performance at work. A meta-analysis of the association between personality factors and work outcomes analyzed seventy-seven studies consisting of more than 22,000 participants; the results revealed that humil-ity was reliably associated with less counterproductive work behavior and positively associated with better organizational citizenship.[33] These effects were above and beyond other dimen-sions of personality, intelligence, and even integrity. There is something unique about being humble that allows us to work more effectively and be a better team player. Other work has shown that humble leadership helps followers feel more engaged and is associated with greater psychological safety.[34] When employees aren't worried about retribution for their mistakes and their leaders model openness, admit when they are wrong, and remain teachable, it creates a feeling of greater safety for people to more completely lean into their work.

Finally, humility within organizations is contagious. A survey of more than two hundred employees from thirteen organizations in China revealed that followers of humble leaders reported greater job satisfaction and work engagement; they also self-reported being humbler, suggesting humble leaders may lead to humble employees.[35] This association was stronger for highly effective leaders. Another study of more than eighty teams found that humble leaders foster humbler teams, and the team's humility leads to greater effectiveness at work.[36] Humble leaders not only improve work conditions for followers but also help foster a sense of humility among them. Humility breeds humility.

Let's discuss a few caveats. It can be frustrating when there is a mismatch between an employee's humility and their supervisor's humility, and people feel worse when they are humbler than their leader.[37] This makes good sense: Who wants to work for an arrogant boss when one is trying to cultivate humility? It could be a recipe for exploitation. Therefore it is critical that those in leadership cultivate humility. Second, although humility is valuable—and currently *undervalued* given all that we have learned about its effects—it alone is not sufficient for professional success. One must also have skill, vision, and a strong work ethic. Humility cannot remedy a lack of investment in a project or an underdeveloped skill set. It's not a panacea. Rather, it's likely that a balance is needed.

Striking a Balance

Humility does not run counter to competence. Similarly, a healthy sense of self is not antithetical to being humble. Surely, confidence and conviction are often important ingredients for professional success—societies need people with big aspirations and a desire to make a lasting difference in the world. Ego can be healthy. A research project in China sampling more than two hundred CEOs and eight hundred managers found that humility can offset expressions of narcissism in leaders, resulting in greater innovation due, in part, to greater charisma in those leaders.[38] Another study in the United States found similar results: tempering a leader's narcissism with humility led to positive organizational outcomes.[39] In short, balancing ego and humility is key. Humility helps harness that strong ambition. An unchecked ego, much like a closed-minded conviction or unflinching commitment, can be harmful. The key is to counterbalance the sure-mindedness and strong motivation for success with an openness to new perspectives, the willingness to listen and learn, and a broader consideration that prioritizes other people. Humility helps keep us grounded when we set our sights on a grand prize.

Can a leader can be *too* humble? Some research suggests that a leader's humility is beneficial only up until a point; at excessively high levels, the benefits wane, largely because such leaders are perceived as less competent.[40] In the minds of many, humility and competence appear to be at odds. However, let's focus on three critical points: First, the level at which humility stops helping and starts hurting organizations is still rather high (think of scoring greater than a four out of five on humility); leaders can and should express humility to improve their workplaces and the experiences of their employees. Second, ensuring a leader's competence is critical. When leaders were also competent, the penalty for extremely high levels of humility is reduced. This means developing competent leaders who are also humble is key. And third, organizational context matters. Supportive organizations can lessen any potential drawbacks. Balancing competence and humility is a recipe for the best work-related outcomes.

The other pitfall that humble leaders need to avoid is that of false humility. If followers perceive that a leader is not authentic but is instead hypocritical, then perceived humility is associated with *poorer* outcomes.[41] That is, if a leader's humility is seen merely as a form of manipulation, employees will readily react negatively against that. Humility must be authentic and consistent to be transformative—to inspire people to experience personal growth and achieve exceptional success. Moreover, when a non-humble leader tries to express humility, they often experience emotional exhaustion.[42] It's tiring to be something we're not.

What messages are we to take from these lines of research? That humility is (a) seen as an authentic feature of a leader, (b) expressed equally to and perceived uniformly by all followers, and (c) part of the supportive organizational culture. When organizations can build humility into their core values, they reap the benefits. Similarly, as we approach our own work—whatever our role or capacity might be—humility can help.

A last word on the interplay between humility and competence: Although the two are not in opposition, in some cases, humility can help compensate for lower competence. In situations where there is some doubt about the leader's competence, the process of asking questions when a leader doesn't know—which conveys their humility—increases trust of that leader.[43] In fact, researchers couldn't identify a particular situation where a leader asking questions resulted in looking foolish or compromising a sense of competence (though they were hesitant to say that no such situation exists). Instead, it helped make up for lower competence. When leaders don't know, those who are arrogant press ahead without soliciting feedback, to their detriment; those who are humble understand their limits and ask for insight from their teams.

Embodying Humble Ambition

Humility allows us to pursue ambitious projects and strive for big change without some of the social costs or potential myopic tunnel vision associated with grand achievements. So, what might it look like to embody humility while pursuing an ambitious goal?

First, we have to develop a mission or vision for our work. One of my mentors, Everett Worthington, had his professional mission written on his desk to consider daily: "to increase forgiveness in every heart, home, and homeland." Every decision he made was filtered around this directive. When he was asked to join a new project, take on new responsibilities, or assume a new role, he asked himself if it furthered his mission. If it did, he accepted; otherwise, he politely declined. This laser focus kept him aligned with his values. His mission had nothing to do with him. It didn't say "to become famous" or "to be the top forgiveness researcher in the world," though these came to him by focusing on good work. If his mission was self-focused, he would have pursued momentary vanity projects rather than developing a rich and meaningful program of research that has changed the lives of many and given hope to countless others. Notoriety and professional accolades were by-products. Humility moves us to think beyond ourselves to something greater.

Second, we must know our strengths and weaknesses and plan accordingly. The first part of humility is knowing ourselves. Understand the assets we bring to our professional and creative endeavors and lean into them. Similarly, we have to admit our weaknesses and get help to address those, whether by working to improve them deliberately or by arranging a team with other people whose strengths can counterbalance and complement our limitations. Everyone has areas for growth. It's not shameful. Rather, these are places to work on improving over time.

Third, we need to listen. Although a commitment to a mission and vision is important, we should never be so convinced of our own opinion that we stop listening. Even if we feel a strong conviction, we should still listen; if others are confused or don't understand, this is evidence that we need to be plainer. It's up to us to communicate clearly. If there are disagreements about the best way to proceed, we owe it to ourselves and whomever we disagree with to consider outside perspectives. Countless examples of groupthink highlight the dangers of never questioning a dominant opinion. We're not the only ones in the room, or necessarily the smartest. We need to welcome questions, seek feedback, and open lines of communication. We'd be wise to listen, and to listen well.

Fourth, invite and insist on healthy collaboration. Most work requires getting along well with others, often in collaborative teams. Other perspectives are valuable, and other people bring skills that likely complement ours. We're more connected and interdependent than ever. Rather than resist others or compete with them, consider collaborating. And once we're in a collaboration, we must prioritize maintaining those relationships. Conflict can be common when the stakes are high, but the humble response is one in which we don't lose sight that people are more important than progress or products, and in which we apologize when we've made a mistake and offer forgiveness when someone else has. Keeping these relationships intact through forgiveness can go a long way.

Finally, humility suggests we serve. This is not to say that we become subservient or that we forgo proper credit or recognition. Rather, because we're considering the needs of others and broadening our perspective beyond our own, an effective way to work collaboratively is to show others their value through acts of service. From small gestures to large initiatives, showing others that we care by doing something for them goes a long way in building trust and fostering a collaborative work environment. And once it's built into the culture of a group or organization, it creates an environment that rewards service. Make service the norm, not the exception.

Surely, there are other ways to express humility in our ambitious pursuits and creative expressions. The list I offer here is merely an invitation to consider the various ways in which developing a self-awareness (knowing yourself), a modesty (checking yourself), and a care for others (going beyond yourself) might transform how we work.

The Freedom of Humility

So many life-giving advancements in human history have required ambitious goals and teams of people who work together toward a common good. Humble people don't have to run from opportunities to change the world. Rather, we need humble leaders at the helm of technological advancements, advocacy movements, and medical discoveries. We need those who value asking questions, are open to feedback, and can consider the well-being of a larger collective to work toward a better global society. And when people don't know, they need the humility to bravely ask questions and admit their shortcomings, the courage to make things right when they've failed or gotten it wrong, and security to realize the most important lesson in this domain: *we are not what we produce*. As important as our work and professional contributions may be, they are not us. Our value in this world extends far beyond what we create. Humility grants us the security to know that we have inherent worth and dignity apart from our success or achievements.

This realization of our inherent self-worth gives us the freedom to aim high—and fail. If our rejections, failures, and mistakes at work are simply a reflection of our work, and not of us, two transformational things happen. One big shift is that we take more risks to go big. Why not aim for the very best? What do we have to lose? If we're truly unafraid of failure because we realize that any such rejection is not a rejection of us but rather of our work, we can take that as information to improve and craft a better contribution in the future. Another large change is that we become free from the *personalized* pang of rejection and failure. This is not to say that it won't hurt when our idea is rejected, when our creation isn't appreciated, or when we fall short of our goal. That is frustrating and can be demoralizing. But it's not a reflection of us as people, despite what cultural myths we might have been told, and we can remain secure in knowing that our worth is not contingent on the approval of our work. When we do reach that goal, we might just realize that the biggest thing holding us back was our own fear. It's time to let go of that fear and rest in the security of knowing that we're already enough.

Just as being arrogant narcissists will inevitably ruin our relationships, having a fragile ego will impair our ability to set and reach desirably high goals. We need a thick skin to succeed—not an approach that is characterized by an inability to listen or an unwillingness to take advice, but rather one that is open to new voices and ideas precisely because we know that any dissent or opposition is not personal. This security is a perfect blend of confidence and willingness to grow and change as well. When we remove ourselves from the proverbial center of the universe and realize that not everything is about us, we free ourselves to do the real, important work that we're passionate about in the first place. And it can make all the difference.

Humble Ambition

We don't all have to be secret agents for charity like Chuck Feeney. We're not required to give away all our earnings or hide in order to be humble. But Feeney's example of avoiding the philanthropic spotlight and seeking to do right without garnering public praise and attention is admirable. It helps remind us that living according to our values is more meaningful than the pursuit of vanity or affirmation. It's a testament that a strong drive can be coupled with humility without sacrificing success. In fact, we now know that humility can help us achieve things we previously thought impossible. We can seek to empower, collaborate with, and listen to those around us to accomplish extraordinary goals. Nothing great was ever accomplished alone—humility helps us navigate demanding situations when the pressure and the stakes are at their highest.

PART II

Cultivating Humility

4

—

Seeking Feedback

O N NEW YEAR'S DAY in 2019, I registered for my first triathlon: a half-Ironman distance, which includes 1.2 miles of swimming, 56 miles of biking, and 13.1 miles (a half marathon) of running. My wife had become interested in triathlons and signed up for a few to take place during the upcoming summer, and I thought that it might be fun to train together. I was on sabbatical, had previously run a couple marathons, and recently hiked across the Grand Canyon and back, so I felt that the half-Ironman distance was the perfect challenge. There was only one small obstacle: I didn't know how to swim.

When I was seven, my parents signed me up for swim lessons at the local pool, but I was a poor enough student during a week's worth of afternoons to be the only one to fail the swim class. A few years later, during a family vacation to Arizona, my parents enlisted the help of a hotel staff member to try to teach me how to swim, but success continued to elude me. By the time I reached adulthood, I had concocted some form of synchronized flailing while holding my head above the water to slowly propel myself forward. I needed some professional guidance.

For my birthday in 2019, which was only a few weeks after my decision to commit to this triathlon, my wife bought me four swimming sessions with the top triathlon swim coach in the state. She informed them that I was going to complete a half-Ironman the coming summer. And so, on my birthday, I drove over an hour through snow to meet this legendary coach, who was quick to point out all the banners hanging in the natatorium signaling championships and state records held by his students. I felt a mixture of excitement and nervousness, but I knew I needed help if I wanted to accomplish my goal of swimming 1.2 miles in open water.

After our brief introduction and a quick history lesson of his coaching prowess, he told me to get in the pool and swim to the other side. When I clarified that I didn't know how to swim, which was precisely why I enlisted his services, he ignored my retort and told me to start swimming. Two strokes in, he screamed, "Stop!"

In utter disbelief, and through the most creative use of vulgarity I've experienced in my life, he asked what I was doing and told me that what I was attempting wasn't swimming. I affirmed his observation that I did not, indeed, know how to swim, which is both why I signed up for these lessons and what I was trying to tell him earlier. I needed his help. It soon became clear to me that he thought my wife had hired him to help me become a faster or more competitive swimmer at the longer distance. He assumed I was a collegiate swimmer or had substantive swim experience. Completely frustrated by my lack of ability, the next hour of my life alternated between profanity-laced berating and disingenuous praise for having not drowned under his watch. At the end of the hour "lesson," he suggested that we weren't a good fit and that I should seek services elsewhere. And he made it quite clear that my only chance of achieving my goal of completing the water portion of a half-Ironman would be through the aid of a motorized water vessel.

On the drive home, I fluctuated between thinking that I had made a terrible mistake by signing up for something so colossally outside of my comfort zone and wanting to prove that smug jerk wrong. Although I felt outmatched, I was angry. I was determined. I wanted this more than ever before. But I still needed help. I couldn't do this on my own.

I figured I would call the local recreation center to see if I could sign up for their group swim lessons. They informed me that I was in luck—a new class was about to start; but when they inquired how old my child was that I was hoping to enroll, I sheepishly admitted it was for me, at which point they clarified that their group classes had age restrictions and said that I would need to sign up for private lessons. Luckily, they could arrange it with one of their teachers. Melissa was a swim coach at a local middle school, and she agreed to give me six lessons while supervising swim team practice in an adjacent pool. She was patient, kind, and very honest: She was clear that I would certainly not be the fastest (or even in the top half of my group), but it was possible for me to finish. She provided direct feedback and incisive criticism when I needed it. At one point, she called over her star middle schooler, who couldn't have been more than twelve years old, to demonstrate how to swim and alternate breathing while keeping one's head in the water.

Melissa's lessons were peppered in between my own practices at my college's pool. I tried to incorporate all her advice, from how to position my head, to what proper arm strokes looked like, to what to do with my dragging legs. Over the course of several months, I kept at it. Slowly, I could get across the pool and back. With time, I could string together a few laps before having to rest. This progression built ever so slowly, and I was eventually able to swim more than 5,000 meters in a session. In August 2019, I completed the half-Ironman, swimming the 1.2 miles in open water, and I texted Melissa on the way home to thank her for her belief and investment in me. I couldn't have done it without her help.

This could have gone very differently. I could have never sought help to begin with, hoping to figure out how to swim on my own. I might have thought that my form of synchronized flailing would be sufficient and that I had no room for growth or improvement. Or I could have become mired in shame and embarrassment at any point in the process: when the highly touted swim coach berated me consistently and mocked my dreams, when I took lessons from a local middle school coach, or when a twelve-year-old kid was made to look like an Olympic swimmer in comparison to me. I could have arrogantly held on to my pride and refused to accept instruction.

Seeking and accepting feedback changed my life. It allowed me to accomplish a significant feat that I'll always treasure. Without feedback, I would have never experienced growth or been able to achieve something so difficult. The experience transformed how I approach tackling challenging situations in which I lack knowledge or ability, or in which I feel ashamed (I figured most adults know how to swim). But who offered that feedback—and how it was offered—mattered greatly. Being verbally accosted by an insecure tyrant was never going to help me learn. The kind, trusting, and honest feedback from a thoughtful and empathic swim coach, though tough at times, was welcomed and powerful. Melissa's feedback was a large part of why I was able to finish that race. I have found that accepting feedback is a crucial part of humility.

Humility helped me accomplish a feat I previously thought unattainable. In order to acknowledge my aquatic limitations and ask for feedback—and perhaps be a bit more to be open to accepting such feedback from an unlikely source—I had to be humble. Without that feedback, I wouldn't have learned how to swim and certainly couldn't have completed the triathlon. I could've let pride stop me from receiving lessons from a middle school swim coach or one of her students, but, truthfully, that was the level of training I needed. I didn't have the skill required to be instructed by a drill sergeant masquerading as a post-collegiate swim coach. And if I had tried to learn on my own, the 1.2-mile swim in open water would have been dangerous, if not disastrous. If we really want to build a life of humility, we need to seek and remain open to feedback.

A Lesson from Radical Transparency

Ray Dalio, founder of the successful hedge fund Bridgewater Associates, has achieved considerable financial success through methods that are innovative and provocative. One of his core values is "radical transparency," or a countercultural emphasis on blunt honesty, acceptance of criticism, self-improvement, and accountability. Imagine: After a presentation, your colleagues tell you exactly what they think of your pitch, without a filter; everyone's salary is public knowledge; you address any conflict with coworkers directly; if someone felt you were slacking, they'd let you know (and you could do the same). It's both terrifying and exhilarating. Conversations would get real quickly, and there would need to be a deep level of trust and mutual respect for the work of radical transparency. It might initially be hard to hear unflattering feedback or accept criticism. But you wouldn't spend your time second-guessing what people thought of you. You'd know. If you had a concern, you could bring it up and hash it out. It would cut out a lot of the unnecessary hoops we all jump through just to get through the day, allowing more time to do the important work at hand.

Of course, there are mixed responses to this approach, and not everyone thinks radical transparency is a good idea. Nor do I want to suggest anyone take up this mantle with friends and family—especially without announcing the intention to do so or make it a unidirectional flow of criticism. But imagine being so secure and eager to grow that you seek out raw, honest feedback:

you lean into your limitations and make active changes; you care about overcoming your biases; you really want people to tell you the truth.

Receiving feedback is the first step to cultivating a life of humility. If we refuse to hear ways that we're hurting others or falling short, we're going to continue hurting those whom we love and become entrenched in a myopic and egocentric view of the world. We need people in our lives to help us see ourselves as we are and the world as it is; people who can help us know ourselves better. And when they offer us feedback, we need to graciously accept it.

Feedback can be terrifying, and some feedback can feel threatening or downright mean. But if we're careful about which people we solicit input from, we can begin to move away from the powerful currents of narcissism and ideological homogeneity and get closer to a life of humility. Orienting toward feedback requires a significant shift from how we've likely always lived: For many of us, we're resistant to feedback that could be unflattering, even when it's necessary for us to hear it. This shift takes courage because it requires us to override strong cognitive tendencies that we humans developed to protect our egos. But this bravery is worth it—when we deny the opportunity to welcome feedback, our life becomes increasingly smaller, and we become enamored with our own views of the world, often to our detriment. Without feedback, we stagnate and stop growing.

So, let's look at what we're up against and how we can work to welcome healthy feedback in our lives in an attempt to know ourselves better, learn from our mistakes, and grow into the person we want to become.

Seeing the World as We Want It to Be

The reason we need feedback is because we are all motivated to see the world in a particular light. Because *knowing yourself* is a key feature of humility, we need help gaining insight and transcending the biased tendencies that cloud our thinking and perception—and that's precisely why seeking feedback is so critical. Far from being honest detectives, we're more like ambitious lawyers, seeing what we want to see in the world and emphasizing particular aspects that align with the argument we've already made in our mind. At any moment, a host of motivations are at play, shifting our perspective and obscuring our ability to see ourselves accurately. Each of these views serves an important purpose but also comes with a set of limitations that make feedback so important.

Perhaps the strongest adversary in our quest to know ourselves better and cultivate humility is our desire to view ourselves positively. In fact, this motivation is so strong, we often forfeit other important aspects of our lives and incur significant psychological costs.[1] Researchers Jennifer Crocker and Lora Park highlight the considerable toll a relentless pursuit of self-esteem may exact on us when we pursue positive self-views above all else. This is not to suggest that confidence or an appropriately sized ego is problematic. In fact, it's healthy to think favorably of ourselves. Instead, Crocker and Park detail the costs of putting this goal over all others. First, we give up our autonomy. When we seek high self-esteem by trying to meet the high standards of a culture or place our sense of worth or value in the hands of other people, we forfeit control over our own life. Without autonomy, we no longer have freedom or the ability to do what we want. Instead, our actions are dictated by external standards and expectations. We become consummate people-pleasers, wracked with the anxiety of meeting the needs of others so that we can feel good about who we are. Conversely, pursuing a life of humility unlocks a life of a freedom. We are unshackled from the narrow cultural expectations of what it means to be successful, attractive, rich, or worthy. We begin to live with the confidence and security of knowing that we're already more than enough: Our sense of adequacy does not depend on shifting cultural expectations but is inherent in who we are. We decide how to spend our time, what to invest in, and who is in our network. We take back control of our lives.

A second cost to pursuing self-esteem is forfeiting our desire and ability to learn. It's hard to learn something new if we're worried about looking foolish or concerned with being judged for not getting things right the first time. Everyone is a novice at something, and it takes effort to learn a new skill. When we place too much of our self-worth in being good at something, such as schoolwork or job performance, we're more likely to take short-cuts or engage in unscrupulous behavior in order to maintain that pristine image. Think of the person who puts all her self-worth in her career, only to receive a negative evaluation at work. Rather than admitting that there might be areas of profes-sional development that could be addressed, she might feel a strong pressure to cut corners, make unethical decisions, or get ahead "by any means necessary," in order to regain her supervi-sor's favor. Rather than accepting feedback and working to change, we lose our ability to grow when we're fixated on high self-esteem.

Third, relentlessly pursing self-esteem damages relationships. Those who fixate on high self-esteem need constant reassurance, are overly sensitive to rejection, and may be either clingy because of a fear of abandonment or emotionally disengaged because of a fear of intimacy. They might do things to attract or retain a part-ner that violates their values, such as spending lavishly on expen-sive dinners when they really desire to pay down their debt. This is a recipe for unhealthy, unfulfilling relationships. Rather, when people enter a relationship from a place of security, knowing that they are already enough on their own, they are more likely to have healthy, mutual relationships where both partners feel supported.

Finally, there are costs to our health. Both physical and mental health might suffer when our primary goal is to pursue self-esteem. When people place their sense of worth in the approval of others and meeting exceedingly high (and increasing) standards of value, they may be willing to do whatever it takes, including behaviors that are unhealthy. For example, they're more likely to drink excessively, smoke, and practice unsafe sex. They may also seek out plastic surgery or other cosmetic procedures, start extreme fad diets, or inject their body with steroids to meet cultural benchmarks of beauty. And if they fail to meet these high standards? They may experience depression or engage in unhealthy coping behaviors to soothe themselves. In short, getting caught in the game of high self-esteem has no winners. It robs us of our autonomy and does more harm than good. And it shades the whole way we see ourselves and the world around us.

Another enemy in our quest for humility is a motivation that directs our attention to align with our preconceived view of the world, what researchers call *confirmation bias*.[2] We have a tendency to seek out information that confirms or aligns with what we already believe. In fact, we store information that is consistent with how we see the world differently than information that runs counter to beliefs so that it's more easily accessible.[3] Our brains are wired to better accommodate information that fits with our schemas (or mental frameworks) about the world. Because of confirmation bias, we see the world in ways that affirm our previous expectations. For example, consider two people of differing political views watching a heated electoral debate in which both candidates make compelling points but also make serious mistakes or misstatements. Objectively, the debate might have been a close draw. However, the conservative viewer would think that their candidate won the night, whereas the liberal viewer would be confident that their candidate was the victor. When presented with mixed evidence, we see more of the evidence falling in line with our views.

A clever study tested this tendency by asking two rival sports fans to report what they saw when watching the same game.[4] In 1951, a contentious college football game between Princeton and Dartmouth resulted in numerous penalties and several injuries for both teams. A pair of researchers, one from each university, had students watch the same game film. The Princeton fans "saw" the Dartmouth team commit twice as many penalties as the Dartmouth fans recognized. Sports fans from each team are seeing two different versions of the same game. And just like committed fans, we "see" the world as we want: in ways that confirm what we've always believed. To revisit our previous lawyer-not-detective analogy, we draw our conclusion and then start assembling the evidence. This also means that we might stop looking for information once we get the answer we want. We foreclose early on a decision with minimal evidence and cease investigating information that contradicts what we believe.

Taken together, we have a strong desire to seek high self-esteem because we've bought into a cultural myth of conditional self-acceptance, *and* we're committed to seeing the world in ways that keep our positive self-view, and other prejudices, intact. This is hardly a road map to humility. It means we're likely to ignore any feedback that suggests we're anything but outstanding and that we'll get stuck in an insular loop where we seek out and only pay attention to information that confirms how good we are. As it turns out, we're naturally bent toward narcissistic self-aggrandizement. In our quest for humility, we have our work cut out for us.

Tell Me What I Want to Hear

We may not naturally be truth-seeking individuals or value unblemished honesty. We aren't always noble in our motivation to perceive the world accurately and don't always want people to tell us like it is. Sometimes we want to hear the truth—but more often, we want feedback that aligns with our purpose or a preconceived view of ourselves. We become so enamored with an idea, convinced we are right, or set on hearing positive feedback, that we eschew the pursuit of truth for positive reinforcement that will make us feel better or more certain of our preexisting view. We become so committed to one view that we're unwilling to consider an alternative. In fact, researchers have identified four different motives for the self-evaluative feedback we seek.[5] Let's look at each one and how it either helps or hinders our quest to cultivate humility.

First, we seek information that is *self-enhancing*. We seek information or feedback that protects our ego and makes us feel better about ourselves—that which is flattering, meant to boost our self-esteem, and will maintain our positive view of ourselves. We might go after it deliberately or inadvertently, and we might discount any view that conflicts by criticizing the source, making an excuse for why it isn't true, or simply not paying attention to it to begin with. We like to feel good, so we seek out feedback that reinforces the positive and avoid any intimation of the negative. We're especially vulnerable to self-enhancing feedback when our ego has been hurt, we feel threatened or insecure, or we're anxious. If we're preoccupied with feeling good, we close the door to honest feedback about ways to improve. Avoiding any negative feedback leaves us hollow and immature. The desire for self-enhancement skews our ability to engage the world accurately and is a major impediment to cultivating humility.

We also seek *self-verifying* feedback from others. We look for assurance that our preconceived ideas are correct. When we have deep commitments (think of politics and religion), a public identity, or when we're already certain about our place in the world, we want people to confirm that we're right. We're often looking for an extra nudge of affirmation, even for negative beliefs: If we think less of ourselves, we're more likely to internalize perceptions that align with our pessimistic self-view. For those who have a strong need for certainty or who are anxious about uncertainty, this might be a comfortable pattern of thinking. Here, too, being entrenched with a particular view of ourselves, others, or the world leaves no space to consider new ideas, counterexamples, or dissenting voices—even when such views are uniformly more positive or broad than those we currently hold. Desperately seeking certainty will cause us to foreclose on ideas too quickly, settle for suboptimal solutions, silence those who disagree, and curb our ability to grow.

Both of these motives—the desire for self-enhancement and self-verifying certainty—can easily overwhelm our other motivations and can be the default modes in which we operate. That's the bad news. The good news is that there are other motives for seeking feedback that can encourage growth and help us engage the world with more humility.

When we're judging our progress toward a goal, we'll likely seek out *self-improving* feedback. We look for this kind of feedback when we have a desired change in mind, and we solicit input as to whether we're closer or farther from our destination. Imagine that you're training for a race, and you'd like to run a 5K in less than 30 minutes, which is a bit quicker than a 10-minute-mile. You go for a jog the first day of training and record your time as 10:15 per mile. Each Saturday morning, you check your mile time again; after a couple of weeks, it descends to 9:53; the following week, after skipping two workouts, it bounces up to 10:02. After increasing your water intake and adding in some speed work, you get it down to 9:49 and finally 9:38 a few weeks later. As you try to put it all together for your race, you're collecting feedback on whether your approach is working. We do the same thing in many areas: When we perceive some shortcoming, we seek accurate feedback to make up for these limitations or deficiencies. We might draw from objective information (like a running watch) or subjective information (like someone else's comments), depending on the circumstance. Looking for this kind of feedback requires (a) knowing the areas where we're limited and have potential to grow, (b) being open to receiving such feedback, (c) seeking feedback from reliable sources, and (d) consistently checking back with those same trusty sources to see how much progress we're making. In areas where we know we're falling short, we can work hard to close that gap.

Finally, if we are open and eager yet don't truly know something about ourselves, we'll likely seek out *self-assessing* feedback. The motive is to obtain accurate information, which grants us a great deal of certainty and helps us know where we stand and what others thinks of us. Those looking for this kind of information prefer detailed and diagnostic feedback, which will be helpful down the line. Because this feedback is so useful, it is best solicited from someone we trust or who has expertise in the area (or both). For example, we want our cardiologists to tell us the truth about our heart health; it might not make us feel better about ourselves or confirm what we previously believed, but it's incredibly valuable information. With it, we can decide if we need to cut down on our salt intake and intensify our morning exercise regimen.

Let's look at an example to see how these four motives play out. Imagine that you're preparing a presentation for an important meeting at work later in the week, so you ask your colleague for feedback. You might be feeling insecure about the upcoming meeting, in which case you'd want self-enhancing positive feedback that the presentation is terrific. Or you might be feeling confident that the main content is solid but wondering if the opening hook needs work, in which case you'd want self-verification feedback, confirming what you already believe and affirming your decision to spend the rest of the workday fine-tuning the first five minutes of the presentation. Or you might be looking for self-improving feedback from a trusted colleague on how to improve the presentation and commit to showing them a revised version before your meeting. Or you might just want to know the honest truth, plain and simple, without other motives at play: What do they really think of this presentation, and what needs to change?

What do all these motivations have to do with humility? First, it's helpful to realize that we're not always looking for honesty. Sometimes, we want people to flatter us or tell us what we want to hear. The problem is that such feedback—while it feels subjectively pleasant—won't help us overcome shortcomings or improve as people. Instead, it strokes our ego and deludes our biased thinking even more. Second, it's important to identify trusted sources from whom we'd like to hear raw feedback. I know I'd rather hear some less-flattering things from someone I trust, though it might be painful if my spouse were the one to fill that role. On the other hand, if an uninformed stranger said something unflattering or contradicted my preexisting beliefs, I might disregard it outright. It's important to build trusting relationships with people who can offer honest feedback and with whom we can be vulnerable to receive it. Finally, these motivations show how important feedback is in any growth process. We can't develop humility alone. We'll need support, encouragement, and, sometimes, a brutally honest friend or two, who can let us know when we've fallen short and when we're making progress.

How Do We Typically Handle Unflattering Feedback?

Given that feedback is so important, how do we handle it when people share feedback that isn't flattering? The short answer is not very well. Our cognitive tendencies and self-evaluative motivations are sneaky and hidden, operating outside of our conscious awareness, if we're not careful. In fact, they can be so strong that we'll willfully ignore information we don't want to hear. We simply don't remember feedback that we perceive as threatening.

My former doctoral advisor, Jeffrey Green, is an expert on self-protective memory, a field of study that examines how we don't remember threatening information about ourselves.[6] Extending other researchers' work on selfish biases to one's basic memory functions, Green studied *mnemic neglect*, which is essentially strategic forgetting of negative information relevant to ourselves.[7] His basic research study looks something like this: Participants are given a list of behaviors that range from positive ("would keep secrets when asked to") to negative ("would make fun of others because of their looks") that describe something either important (central) or unimportant (peripheral) to how they view themselves, and that was referring either to them or someone else. Sometime later, the researchers ask participants to recall as many of these behaviors as they can. They found that people are much more likely to remember being told that they're someone who "would follow through on a promise made to friends" than someone who "would make an obscene gesture at an old lady." This is because positive descriptors of being trustworthy or kind are more aligned with our glowing view of ourselves than are descriptors that depict us making vulgar hand motions at the elderly. So, we remember the ones we like and forget the ones we don't.

The results of these studies are shocking: We literally forget information about ourselves that we don't like. Our selfish biases reside at the level of our perception and distort what we encode into memory and what we retrieve. Further research clarifying the boundaries of this phenomenon highlight that memory repression occurs for those behaviors that we think are most central to our self-concept.[8] In fact, researchers have found that we mentally separate threatening feedback from other information about ourselves.[9] This means that we're especially likely to ignore, or forget, information that is most important and relevant to our sense of self. This bias resides exactly where it can do the most damage: The feedback that is the most critical is often most neglected.

The Liberating Power of Honest Feedback

Despite our typical response to unflattering feedback, it is critically important to invite it into our lives from trusted sources and work hard to integrate it. In fact, research has found that we're more likely to accept and remember feedback from people we love or care about than from strangers, highlighting the importance of seeking such feedback from close members of our network.[10] When we overcome these biases, it can helps us identify areas for growth and may compel us to engage more authentically with others. I found this to be the case in my own life.

In late Summer 2018, I met a few of my college friends at Rocky Mountain National Park. The four of us had shared formative parts of life: We roomed together in college, stood in each other's weddings, met each other's children. This trip was a treat. We planned for three full days of camping in the mountains, playing euchre, drinking whiskey, and catching up. We cooked meals, laughed, reminisced, and played a lot of cards.

The second evening, my close friend Dan abruptly turned the conversation on its head.

"What are we doing here?" he asked. Seeing this as an opportunity to audition my comedic prowess, I replied with something sarcastic about playing cards at high altitude, which only elicited a more serious reply.

"No, I mean, *why* are we here? Are we really just going to sit around telling stories of the past, giving each other a hard time, and simply *playing cards*? We left our families behind for this trip and we haven't seen each other in years. And this is how we're spending our time? If this is it, consider it my last time."

At the time, it felt harsh. Why couldn't some old college friends get together to indulge in collective nostalgia and keep things light while playing a hallowed Midwestern card game? But he was right. We were hiding. It was safer for us to reflect on the past than share the present. It felt more comfortable to rib each other than be vulnerable. And it was easier to focus our attention on a card game than on our lives. By that point in 2018, I was a mess. My dad's health had been failing for four months and I knew he didn't have long to live, my personal life was strained, I was reeling from devastating health news, I felt isolated and overwhelmed and was taking this trip to sort out my emotions. And here I was, with the golden opportunity to share with people I love and who know me well, and I hid where it was safe.

Dan's feedback pierced me with its stinging truth. And after my snide retort, I realized, through teary eyes and a sense of guilt, his question wasn't an indictment but an invitation. He was asking us to open up, to be real—and he was telling us, however bluntly, that we weren't.

That moment was the turning point of the trip, and perhaps in how the four of us continue to relate. We literally laid all our cards on the table and shared honestly. It was messy and hard, and beautiful and sad. Out of respect for my friends, I won't share more details, but Dan's brave act to call us in to authenticity was healing and transformed our connection, even though it hurt like hell. And I'm so grateful he spoke up.

Feedback can be powerful and liberating. At first, I hated receiving Dan's feedback—but I needed to hear it. My initial reaction was to clam up, defend my actions, and build an emotional wall. But if I hadn't course-corrected quickly I would have missed the opportunity to share honestly with my friends, hear about their lives, and experience an authentic connection with people I care about. I wouldn't have realized the tendencies I had developed to avoid painful emotions or tried to cultivate more vulnerability. I would have wasted the trip. When you ignore feedback, you miss out on the full spectrum of life experiences.

It takes courage to offer feedback and bravery to listen and accept it. Most often, when your trusted sources offer feedback, it's because they care about you and want to help you improve or access a more expansive life experience. Often, they're doing it out of care, concern, and love.

Just think of the different areas of life that might be improved by inviting feedback. As discussed in chapter 1, part of humility is an honest understanding of our strengths and limitations, which we often need others to help us see, given our biases. And if we can define our abilities without assigning value judgments, it helps us know ourselves better and will eventually allow us to improve. Knowing our strengths lets us build on them, and owning our limitations helps us develop into the people we'd like to become.

Cultivating Humility: Opening Your Eyes

So how we do we avoid implications of shame, soften our defenses, and start accepting feedback? If we're going to live a life marked by humility, we need to know ourselves honestly. We need an accurate assessment of our strengths and weaknesses. The research is clear that it's an uphill battle: We're biased in how we see the world, we selectively forget critical information, and we look for confirmation of what we already believe. But there is hope: There are reliable ways to welcome feedback.

Adopt a growth mindset

Shifting how we think about our own traits and skills can encourage feedback. According to research by Carol Dweck, people tend to hold different *implicit theories* about themselves and the world around them: Some hold what are called entity theories, which are beliefs that people are fixed and do not change, whereas others hold incremental theories—also called a growth mindset—which are beliefs that people can grow, develop, and change.[11] For example, those with entity beliefs may assume that some people are naturally more talented or skilled than others, so when they encounter a setback or obstacle, they might presume that the demands of the situation exceed their abilities. In turn, they might give up, admitting that they've reached their limit. Those with incremental beliefs, on the other hand, might view such an obstacle as a challenge, understanding that people are malleable and can grow, in which case they would seek ways to build upon their skills, develop new abilities, and overcome the demands of the situation.

A meta-analysis of more than a hundred research studies (including 28,000 participants) on implicit theories highlighted the importance of these different mindsets.[12] Those adopting incremental theories or a growth mindset were more likely to value learning rather than performance and are less likely to report negative emotions when working toward their goal. In fact, they see their efforts as an attempt to gain mastery over a new area. On the other hand, those with an entity mindset—who believe that people and traits are fixed—focus more on performance rather than learning and may feel helpless when struggling to achieve a goal.

Mindsets matter in a wide range of situations. For example, a colleague and I conducted a set of studies where we told some participants that happiness was a fixed trait and told other participants that happiness could be changed.[13] Participants who were told happiness could change more readily adopted growth-related beliefs and, in turn, reported greater well-being, which spilled over to satisfaction with their relationships, health, and job. Another meta-analysis of more than seventy studies (and over 17,000 participants) revealed that growth mindsets are mildly related to less psychological distress and a stronger ability to cope.[14]

What can this research teach us about accepting feedback and cultivating humility? Prior work suggests that it's beneficial, and perhaps psychologically healthier, to embrace a growth mindset. It's admirable to value the process over perfection. When we take the stance that we're learners and prioritize process over performance, feedback isn't threatening—it's useful. Feedback is essential to growing into the people we want to become. Because we selectively forget negative information about ourselves (the mnemic neglect paradigm), when we receive feedback about traits that we believe to be modifiable, we don't engage in strategic, self-protective memory: We don't selectively forget feedback about things that we *can* change.[15] Rather, we retain that information, likely because we'll need to improve our future self. Believing that we can change reduces our defensiveness and takes the sting out of criticism.

Prioritize self-improvement

A second way to welcome feedback is to prioritize selfimprovement. One of my earliest research projects with my doctoral advisor, Jeff Green, was an investigation into what might reduce our tendency to selectively forget self-threatening feedback. Given the pervasiveness of self-protective memory, we looked at what circumstances might compel people to process criticism more deeply and be less likely to dismiss, and forget, negative feedback. In the first study, led by Green, half of the research participants were primed with words related to self-improvement (such as *aspirations*, *gain*, *improved*) and the other half were primed with neutral worlds (such as *announced*, *heels*, *tours*).[16] Those who were primed with self-improvement words did not demonstrate the usual strategy of selectively forgetting self-threatening feedback; they recalled it just as much as positive feedback.

As it turns out, prioritizing self-improvement can increase how deeply we engage with feedback, even when it's negative.

After all, if we're ever going to improve, we need to hear and accept difficult feedback. Approaching a situation with the intention to *improve* can open us up to welcoming feedback and increases our retention of the comments or criticism we receive. The work for self-improvement is the other side of the growth-mindset coin; we first have to believe that we can grow and change, and then we can do something about it.

Ask a trusted source

When I was learning how to swim, I was much more open to receiving instruction from Melissa, a coach who I could tell cared about me and my success, than from the dictatorial instructor who hurled commands and insults at me seemingly for his own amusement. I didn't trust him. To me, the person who offered the feedback made a big difference.

Research confirms my experience. Jeff Green and I investigated whether the source of the feedback matters. We wondered if feedback from a close relationship partner would be more welcomed than feedback from a stranger. After all, given our strong need to belong and to maintain harmony within relationships, it would be advantageous for us to pay closer attention to potentially negative feedback from a partner, spouse, or friend. We wouldn't want to ignore information that could jeopardize the relationship or create a wedge between us and those we love.

In our study, sets of participants came in with a close friend or partner, arriving at the lab in two pairs, and were sent to separate rooms to work on a set of memory tasks and a bogus personality test. All four participants received the same set of materials, but one pair was told that the feedback they were receiving was from the friend or partner accompanying them, whereas the other pair was told they were receiving feedback from a stranger (one of the other two participants at the study session). As predicted, people engaged in the usual self-protective memory strategy of forgetting negative feedback about themselves when they thought a stranger provided it, but this effect disappeared when they were led to believe it was delivered by a close friend or partner. We're more likely to deeply process, and remember, feedback offered by someone we care about.

This demonstrates the importance of soliciting feedback from someone we trust and care about—and who presumably cares about us. Because we're motivated to maintain a good relationship with them, we're more likely to listen to and remember that feedback. This applies even when it's uncomfortable, because we believe that the feedback is for our own good. And we're more likely to heed this advice because we are highly invested in maintaining the relationship. It takes courage for them to share and vulnerability for us to listen.

It's worth noting that it's beneficial to gather feedback from a variety of trusted sources, all whom know we well. Because humility is contextualized in different relationships, it's possible that we're humble with our partner but less so with our friends or at work. Or perhaps the reverse is true: Everyone at the office admires our authenticity and willingness to learn, but our family sees us as a know-it-all who won't listen. In either case, it's valuable to solicit feedback from people in various areas of life, and with whom there are varied power dynamics. At work, asking for feedback from a variety of people that includes supervisors, peers, and employees would be critical to gathering insight into how you lead, listen, and learn. Similarly, asking family, friends, and a romantic partner is key to obtaining a richer and fuller picture of ourselves.

Start from a place of security

Many of us have developed *conditional self-acceptance*,[17] having bought into the cultural myth that self-worth is based on success, appearance, wealth, power, or fame. We've come to believe that we're only worthy *if*—if we look beautiful enough, if we have enough money, if we have the right job title, if we have an enviable travel résumé, if we have a large-enough social media following. The list is endless. By shifting our sense of worth or value into other people's hands, we allow these contingencies to steal our freedom and redirect our time and attention toward vapid and hollow pursuits that don't add meaning to our lives or help us contribute to the world. And they certainly won't make us any humbler. When we invest in the misplaced belief that we have to earn our acceptance from others and pursue unflinchingly high standards of esteem, we seek fake goals and will undoubtedly end up unfulfilled. The truth is that we're already worthy, already enough.

It's one thing to acknowledge the logical plausibility of these self-affirming claims and entirely another to really believe and live them out. For some of us, it's safer to think we're not inherently worthy, which protects us from the pain of disappointment or rejection. We tell ourselves that it's what we deserve. We think it shields us from pain, but in reality, it prevents us from living a full and authentic life. Others of us seek the affirmation that we might not have previously received elsewhere and that we don't give ourselves. Perhaps we were ignored or dismissed, and so we never learned that we hold the power to validate our own experiences and never became comfortable enough to rest in our own worth and value. When we start from a place of insecurity, we desperately care what others think of us, and any intimation that they might not like us is devastating and debilitating.

This lack of security is most evident in the combination of high and fragile self-esteem. It's not that thinking well of ourselves is bad. In fact, it's good to have self-esteem. Rather, the trouble comes when this high view of ourselves is *fragile*—that is, dependent on others and unstable. When our self-esteem is fragile, we're likely to lash out with aggression when we feel as though we're being threatened.[18] Research has clarified that narcissism, marked by feelings of entitlement and perceived superiority, is related to greater aggression following threatening feedback.[19] Healthy self-esteem, on the other hand, is largely unrelated to aggression; it's when our view of ourselves becomes *overinflated* that we lose our sense of security and tend to defend it strongly.

Consider the context

Finally, a host of small, sometimes invisible, factors can play a role in how receptive we are to feedback. For example, think about your surroundings. In what context are you asking for feedback? Do you feel safe? Are you comfortable? Is this a place that feels welcoming and inviting, or is it associated with conflict, power, or negative emotions? Environments matter for how we process social information, so we need to take time to cultivate a place that feels safe and welcoming for inviting feedback.[20] Also, requesting feedback feels safer than receiving uninvited feedback when we're not ready to process criticism or suggestions.

When setting aside time to invite feedback, we must consider our inner state. We're probably more receptive when not tired, hungry, or otherwise preoccupied. When stress is high or we feel other pressures, we might be more defensive toward feedback.

Finally, we need to think about the power dynamics at play when seeking feedback. If we are in a position of power, someone might not be comfortable sharing honestly about areas that need growth. We should also consider the relationship with the trusted source offering insight. Reassuring a trusted source that we welcome their insight and will commit to being receptive (and not vindictive), can go a long way in soliciting honest feedback that we can use. Incisive feedback can be powerful and help us implement dynamic change. It's the first part of knowing ourselves more clearly—but we have to welcome it.

Into the Deep End

Seeking feedback changed my life. Although it might seem cli-chéd to say that completing a six-hour endurance race is life-changing, it was an important moment for me. I have a strong family history of heart-related concerns, to which I've lost my grandmother, my brother, and my dad. I often thought that cer-tain goals were simply too ambitious and only achievable by other people and not by me. Throughout my life, I learned to sell myself short. Signing up for a lifelong goal without knowing how to swim was intimidating and overwhelming. And so, achieving that seemingly far-fetched goal was truly empowering. I learned that the limitations I perceived were largely a construction of my own mind, that I could do hard, seemingly impossible things, and that I should live fully in each moment rather than in fear of the future. None of this would have been possible if I hadn't admitted my limitations and sought the feedback necessary to learn how to swim. I'm willing to bet that in your own life, there's an area where you see potential to grow, but that the thought of asking for help provokes anxiety. Take it from someone who understands your fear and who continually works to conquer his own shame: Jump into the deep end. You'll be glad you did.

5

—

Reducing Defensiveness

YEARS AGO, I HAD my first media interview about my research on humility, which centered on romantic relationships. At the end of the interview, the journalist thought it'd be interesting to see if someone who studied humility was actually humble in real life (and in their romantic relationship), so she asked me to have my wife rate, on a scale of one to ten, how humble I was. I thought this was a terrific idea and agreed to email the journalist the results of this mini-experiment. After the call, I left the home office in our basement and went upstairs to pose the question to my wife, Sara. Secretly hoping that my years of research in humility would pay off, I envisioned a high number that would affirm the spillover of my professional life into the personal. I wasn't greedy; even an eight would do. So, I asked her.

"On a scale of one to ten?" she echoed. "I'd say you're a four."

I gulped hard.

"Really, a four?"

"Wait, is ten low or high in humility?" she clarified.

"Ten is high," I responded, with sudden hope that a misunderstanding would at least put me over the midpoint, so I could rest assured that I was better than average at humility. (At the time, the irony was lost on me.)

"Oh, that's what I thought. Then, yes, a four."

I was crushed. I felt like a fraud. How could I study humility for a living but be viewed as not very humble by the person who knew me the best, and whose opinion mattered the most? How could I simultaneously be an authority on the importance of humility in romantic relationships and yet act so arrogantly in my own? I was mortified to have to email the interviewer with the results.

Embarrassment gave way to defensiveness, which is never a recipe for humility. I was genuinely perplexed—why wasn't I humble? I tried, counterproductively, to make a case for my humility by listing my humble attributes and actions (again, the irony is thick) but quickly realized I was trying to bail out a rowboat by bucketing water *in*. After taking a bit of space and time, I asked Sara why she gave me that rating.

The morning of the interview was a beautiful, sunny summer Friday in Michigan. One of the few rewards for the overcast and sunless days of winter in the Mitten State is the remarkably beautiful weather from May until October, and June and July are simply spectacular. We live about fifteen minutes from Lake Michigan, where there is a wonderful, sandy beach inside of a state park. Our plan for this particular Friday had long been to go to the beach together, enjoy a picnic lunch, and unwind from our busy week during the afternoon. We set a plan to leave by 11:00 AM, in time to guarantee a good spot before the crowds arrived, and so we agreed to make lunches together and pack up around 10:30. Knowing this, I took the interview at 10:00 but didn't emerge from the basement office until nearly 11:15. Sara was ready and waiting; the lunches were packed, the towels and sunscreen ready, and the beach reading material was organized. She had done all of this on her own and was patiently watching the precious minutes of sunshine tick by. Then, in a colossal moment of selfishness, I asked Sara if she'd be OK driving to the beach on her own to meet me, while I ran there (we lived about seven miles away), so that I could get in a training run for my upcoming marathon. Finally, and after all of this, I casually asked her to rate my humility so I would be able to follow up with my interviewer.

It's no wonder that I fared so poorly on even the most rudimentary assessment of humility. I had prioritized work over my commitment to my wife. I shoved the responsibility of readying for the beach onto her plate, then made us late, *and* I had the audacity to ask her to lug everything to the water and set up on her own so I could be efficient with my time and squeeze in a workout by running there.

Come to think of it, four was a generous rating.

I couldn't see my own lack of humility. And when given honest feedback, I responded defensively. I marshaled every reason I had about why I was probably pretty humble; after all, I'd been studying it for years. I just gave an interview about it! But all those factors simply made my blind spots bigger. Even an expert in humility needs to work hard to open his mind and reduce defensiveness.

Diagnosing Our Defensiveness

In chapter 4, we talked about the importance of seeking feedback. However, that's only the first step to cultivating humility. When you receive that feedback, you have to be able to handle it nondefensively. Overcoming your defenses is a critical part of *checking yourself.* Our default reaction is often to put up walls and make excuses: When I sought feedback from my wife, I didn't like what I heard, my ego was bruised, and my natural reaction to defend myself kicked in. Feedback isn't helpful if we immediately disregard it. We're not listening when we are defending our point. If we're going to make any progress in becoming humbler (and opening our minds), we must learn why we're defensive and closed-minded, and how to overcome this tendency in order to respond openly and graciously.

There is a deeper psychological reason why we're often so defensive: Research has underscored the power of *existential realities* in shaping human thought and behavior. Previous scholars have suggested that each of us must come to terms with the fundamental limitations of being human and wrestle with recurring existential questions about making choices in an uncertain world, feeling isolated from one another, revising our identities, confronting the reality of our eventual death, and crafting a meaningful life.[1] These realities have the potential to create overwhelming anxiety.[2] In order to deal with this potential terror, we create and adhere to *cultural worldviews*, frameworks for understanding the world and creating meaningful notions of reality. We all have beliefs about how humans came into being (the Big Bang, evolution, divine activity, emergence), how humans should act (morals, customs, laws, proper behavior), what happens to people when they die (reincarnation, afterlife, nothingness), and what makes for a meaningful life (charity, good works, success). We invest in culturally validated ways of understanding human life and death as an avenue to meaningful existence and keeping existential dread at bay. We tell ourselves stories that manage our anxiety.

The problem is that because the psychological stakes of our worldviews are so high, we often perceive that if *any* part of our narrative is wrong, we could be wrong about *everything*. And being wrong about how to live or whether there is an afterlife can generate a considerable amount of fear and anxiety. This means that our existential concerns can cause us to become defensive about most things, including how we see ourselves. Hearing that I was acting selfishly ran counter to my positive view of myself and revealed that my self-perception in that moment was wrong; so, what else might I be wrong about? Rather than consider the fallibility of my views, I responded defensively.

Many research findings support this existential approach to defensiveness. In fact, more than three hundred experiments conducted in more than two dozen countries suggest that the defense of our cultural worldview is a reliable response to reminders or challenges to cherished beliefs.[3] These defenses often operate unconsciously, on autopilot, while we're consumed with the daily hassles and enjoyment of life. If we don't think about death or the meaning of life unless reminded by a tragedy or prompted by a friend, then our defenses are working pretty well.

Cultural worldviews vary greatly and carry with them many other beliefs, such as nationalism, tribalism, moral attitudes, views of humanity, stereotypes, prejudices, religion, and ideas about reality, truth, knowledge, and humanity. It's a one-stop shop for your ideology, transmitted in successive generations and socially validated. Many people simply take their cultural beliefs as "given." We usually assume that our way of seeing the world is the best—if not the only—way. And when we encounter people who don't share our cultural worldview, we tend to get defensive.

Not only do we perceive direct questions as an attack on our views that must be defended, but the sheer existence of other people with differing (and exclusive) views suggests that one of us must be wrong. Given all that is at stake, we think: It's not me. So, we naturally assume that others are wrong. And when we allow the mere presence of their views to unhinge us, we begin to act to eradicate those views, beginning with persuasion. We try to change other people's minds while holding fast to our own beliefs and opinions. When that tactic is ineffective, as is often the case, we resort to criticizing, denigrating, or ostracizing those with whom we disagree. We may even consider their existence to be a threat and thus feel the easiest way to eliminate opposing (threatening) views is to eliminate the person who holds those views, sadly, by lashing out with aggression or violence. Defending our views can lead to ideologically motivated violence.[4] We go to great lengths to prove we're right.

Because our beliefs help us make sense of the world, we default to reacting defensively, even about issues that are not directly related to our beliefs. It's a bit like a house of cards—if we pull out one card, the whole structure crumbles. We scramble to find meaning, and the assumptions we held about deeply important human concerns, like death, are suddenly unsettled. So, it often feels safer and easier to practice defensiveness, keeping a tight grip on our beliefs, holding them with the utmost of certainty.

This process is a major obstacle to humility. The existential function of our beliefs makes it difficult for us to admit when we're wrong or to revise our beliefs. Because our beliefs keep potential anxiety at bay, learning to respond humbly requires tolerating some psychological discomfort as you revise your beliefs or rethink your position on an issue. And when we admit that we could be wrong about one (or several) of our beliefs, we must endure the distress of uncertainty. In many circumstances, the desire to manage this existential angst keeps us closed-minded and sure: a recipe for conceit.

Desperately Seeking Self-Esteem

A second and related way we manage our existential fears is by pursuing self-esteem at nearly all costs.[5] We often need to imagine that we are significant contributors who make a meaningful difference in this world. We tend to see ourselves in an extremely positive light, despite how little empirical basis there might be for this representation. According to researchers, a primary way of achieving this self-esteem is by living up to the standards of our cultural worldview. Religious people strive to uphold the values of their faith, many citizens seek to be outstanding patriots, and each of us tries to live up to our society's standards of wealth, beauty, fitness, and intelligence. When we live up to these standards, we feel good about ourselves. When we fail to meet them, we feel ashamed or excluded from our group.

We chase self-esteem in several ways. Explicitly, we love to receive praise and adoration, we seek the approval of others, and we like it when others think well of us. We chase Instagram followers, Facebook likes, and retweets—indications of positive affirmation and inclusion that confirm to us that we are loved and valued. Implicitly, we find worth in the easily quantifiable and comparable, such as the size of our bank accounts, homes, or salaries, or our recognitions or awards. We often seek to improve our own self-view by comparing ourselves to others who are in worse positions than we are and by justifying social-dominance hierarchies that keep subjugated groups under oppression. We are programmed to confirm our own significance and importance, even if it means devaluing others by these metrics.

When we seek self-esteem—especially in ways that are contingent and fickle—it becomes a constant challenge to ensure that we are enough. We attempt to find worth in an ever-changing set of cultural standards. When we pin our sense of worth and value on factors outside of our control or determined by other people, we are left with a fragile self-concept, scrambling to make sure that we're better than others. True humility is only possible from a place of security, and because the constant attempt to prove our own worth causes defensiveness stemming from insecurity, it's a massive obstacle to practicing humility.

The combination of rigidly adhering to our worldview and seeking self-esteem contributes to our default defensiveness. On the one hand, we protect our worldview at all costs. On the other, we regularly chase affirmation that we're living up to cultural standards as a way of gaining significance and worth. This combination creates a stronger penchant for fighting than forgiving—and we seek to be right rather than to understand. If we operate under these conditions, humility seems elusive, if not impossible, to practice. It's hard to admit your weaknesses and value the opinion of others when you're defensive, and it's challenging to reel in your ego when there's existential pressure to meet cultural standards of worth. Unless we can address our defensiveness, we'll be mired in narcissism and stuck in ideological narrow-mindedness. But a third component might offer a potential way out of the quagmire of defensiveness.

The Meaning Motive

Perhaps the most basic principle of being human is our unique desire to create meaning. Researchers agree that we are natural meaning makers.[6] We easily—and automatically—create narratives that give meaning to our lives. Meaning transforms the mundane into the magnificent, giving routine events in our life special significance. Importantly, we can find meaning in several areas, and when any one source is threatened, we shift to other wellsprings. For example, if your presentation at work goes poorly and your self-esteem suffers, you may find yourself reaching out to a friend to confirm your sense of belonging or connection with other people. Or if you are feeling rejected by your partner, you might seek out other ways of feeling certain, such as checking on your 401(k) balance to provide a sense of security for the future. All these domains provide a sense of meaning, and we naturally, or *automatically*, compensate for areas that might be threatened with other sources. Our desire to create and defend meaning is both fluid (we can shift our focus) and automatic (we engage in these processes even when we're not aware of it). We're wired for meaning.

So, what is meaning? Meaning can be understood as having three parts[7]: a sense of *coherence* when things make sense, a feeling of *significance* that we matter, and a *purpose* that directs us to something bigger than ourselves.[8] Our desire for coherence looms large. We naturally make sense of events in everyday life, and we typically (though not always) expect those events to be more positive than negative. This is why events that are unexpected or negative are so disrupting—in fact, they can seem downright meaningless. We rely on predictability for coherent sense. Over time and with experience, we develop schemas, or frameworks for interpreting and organizing information, which help us know what to predict and how to make sense of the world. We know that our romantic partner is kind, our boss is supportive, and our running buddy is chatty. When our partner acts rudely, our boss is critical, or our running buddy is silent, we immediate want to understand why. Anything that violates our schemas commands our attention. When we notice a discrepancy between how things usually are (for instance, Peter usually carries on a lively conversation during our typical seven-mile loop) and how they are now (Peter is aloof and quiet), we seek to understand the source of it. Sometimes, we simply incorporate this discrepancy into our existing schema (Peter was internally processing a problem from work, so we are still good friends who chat on runs), and we maintain our way of seeing the world. Other times, we have to change our schemas altogether (Peter is emotionally pulling away, so we might not be as close as I once thought).

Because schemas are so incredibly useful for providing a sense of coherence, we are hesitant to change them. Research has found that even when people are presented with information that should cause them to change their schemas, they are reluctant to do so.[9] In a classic social psychology example, researchers infiltrated a cult group whose leader prophesized that world would end on December 21, 1954. The leader told her followers that only their small group would be spared from total annihilation by being picked up by visitors from space. Once it became clear that the leader's prophecy about the end of the world was false, rather than admitting that she was wrong, she claimed that the faith of the small group—whose commitment included, for some, leaving their families and jobs—saved the whole world.[10] The evidence was clear and damning, but the followers' beliefs remained strong.

It's hard to change our mind, even when evidence suggests we should. We desire a constant, consistent understanding of the world, which makes the process of incorporating new feedback difficult and often ineffective. This resistance is driven in large part because we want to hold on to our particular narrative about the world, which helps us feel meaningful. Because we're motivated for meaning, we try to make sense of nearly everything, and we do so more as soldiers defending our way of seeing the world than as archaeologists searching to uncover the truth.

In addition to coherence, we also desire feeling significant and having a strong purpose. Significance is when we feel valued and loved, as though who we are truly matters and what we are doing is making a difference. It's the feeling of worth that we experience when we contribute something important to the world or those around us. Purpose is having a clear direction or orientation toward something larger than ourselves, such as our community or an important cause. It's what motivates us toward a long-term goal. We work hard to create each of these three components of meaning.

Research has found that we defend our sense of meaning unconsciously.[11] In one of my earliest research projects, we brought participants into the lab and had them complete a word-pairing task. While participants were focused on determining if target words were either colors or numbers, smaller "priming" words were presented for less time, approximately fifty milliseconds, in rotating corners of the computer screen. These momentary flashes in the periphery of people's visual field were either words that threatened their meaning (such as *chaos*, *empty*, *futile*) or neutral words (such as *chair, echoes, furnace*). Although they did not notice these words (confirmed by our post-study interviews), participants whose meaning was threatened unconsciously went on to rate life as more meaningful across several dimensions: They reported higher self-esteem, greater certainty in life, greater belonging with their friends, less religious doubt, and greater self-reported meaning. When their meaning was impugned without their awareness, they doubled down that their life was indeed meaningful.

Defensiveness Is Our Default

A harsh truth about being human is that we're naturally defensive. We also hold a strong fear of uncertainty: We don't like "not knowing," and our culture treats any lack of knowledge as inherently bad. It's a hard pill to swallow. Some of us acknowledge that we may have defensive tendencies, but then we quickly begin assembling evidence for the ways that we're not that bad or that other people are worse, which is just a different version of the same defensiveness. This tendency runs deep.

Our defensiveness comes out in a few ways. First, we have a desire to be right. We want our views about the world to be validated by other people. Usually, this means that we become friends with people who share our beliefs, and we tend not to surround ourselves with people who hold different opinions than we do.[12] When we're wrong, we seek ways to prove that we're right, even at the cost to our relationships. And we twist evidence to confirm that we're indeed correct (recall all of the biases we discussed in chapter 1?). Our drive to be right makes it hard to receive feedback.

We also desire certainty. The world is unpredictable, and it's advantageous for us to know what's coming next. Because humans are intelligent and have the capacity for self-awareness, we're able to mentally "project" ourselves into the future—that is, we're able to envision different possible futures. This mental simulation can be a powerful source of meaning.[13] We can imagine ourselves in different places, enjoying myriad experiences, with various people, in a host of different contexts. But we're also aware that life does not always go as we imagine, and we can live with a high degree of uncertainty about those possibilities. We know that we could be struck down with a terminal illness, run over by a bus, attacked by a stranger, caught in a natural disaster, abandoned by our partner, or fired from our job. Psychotherapists suggest that our lack of control in the world—and the human burden to have to make decisions despite the absence of any one clear best choice—is a primary source of anxiety and other mental illness.[14] We desire certainty in an uncertain world. So, we cling to certainty when we can and avoid uncertainty whenever possible.

Finally, and as mentioned before, we act defensively because we interpret the world in ways that are consistent with our own schema—we see the world precisely as we want to. We're so adept at ignoring inconsistencies with our beliefs and at seeking—and paying attention to—only the information that affirms our preexisting beliefs, that we often don't realize when we're acting defensively. It's hard for us to see how truly closed-minded we are. When we do experience events that threaten our worldview, we're quick to shift to defending our meaning in other areas. This compensatory response offers an important clue to how we can start to become less defensive and more open-minded: If our defensiveness arises from challenges to meaning, then building meaning should help us feel more secure and be less likely to respond out of self-protection.

Opening Your Mind: How to Reduce Your Defensiveness

Once we understand that we're meaning-seeking animals who flourish best when things make sense (and when we feel like we matter and have a purpose), we can start to discover how to open our mind to new ideas without our natural defensive reactions. We're about to explore four ways to help cultivate humility by reducing defensiveness: affirming areas of meaning, acknowledging limitations, diversifying social investments, and seeking to prove yourself wrong.

First, working to *affirm areas of meaning* can inoculate you from threats against your own views and help reduce defensiveness. Research suggests that the ways we find meaning (such as relationships, self-esteem, certainty, values) are somewhat interchangeable.[15] Finding ways to reinforce your sense of meaning can make you more receptive when other areas of meaning are challenged.

Second, it's important to *acknowledge your own limitations.* Humility involves an accurate perception of both strengths and weaknesses. Admitting that you have some flaws will help reshape the ideas and self-perception you have about yourself, which will make seemingly challenging information less threatening. After all, if you know that you have limitations and can own them, when you receive feedback that contradicts the way you see the world, you can fit it more neatly into how you make sense of the world. Admitting that you are often wrong makes it easier to be wrong, because it's less unexpected to be wrong.

Third, it's important to *diversify your social investments.* Because our defenses are often sharpened by people who share our beliefs, you need a network of friends, family, and colleagues who hold different ideas from yours. By weaving together a rich tapestry of voices in your life, you will engage with divergent viewpoints, which should reduce your defensive responses by familiarizing you to different ways of seeing the world that are held by people you like. Acknowledging that other people hold different perspectives and appreciating your shared humanity with them make you less likely to respond negatively to future perspectives that run counter to your own.

Finally, and perhaps most challenging, you can develop an open mind by intentionally seeking to *prove yourself wrong*. This counterintuitive approach involves going out of your way to find information that goes against some of your most deeply held beliefs. Learning to argue against yourself and seeking opposing views are tools to avoid falling into the trap of closed-minded defensiveness and are markers of wise decision-making.

Affirming areas of meaning

The way that we see the world provides us with one of the most enduring and pervasive senses of meaning. In fact, we suspect that *our* reality is the *only* reality, and we take many of our assumptions for granted. How else could other people see the world than the way we see it? And if others see it differently, certainly they're mistaken. Because our view of the world is so deeply ingrained and difficult to change, encountering information that runs counter to this view is inherently threatening. But the good news is that there are many other ways we can find meaning—and research suggests that when those areas are brimming, we might be more willing to loosen the tight grip on our view of the world and entertain the possibility of revising our beliefs.

Research suggests that we experience various sources of meaning interchangeably with one another: A threat to one domain leads us to seek meaning in another domain. But this interchangeability is not simply a reactive reflex. It means that we can preventatively work to affirm meaning as a strategy to reduce defensiveness in the future.

A long line of research on *self-affirmation*—a broad term that refers to ways people feel that their sense of worth or value is highlighted—has revealed that people respond much less defensively after they affirm what they value. This work was pioneered by Claude Steele, who suggested that having people affirm their values increases their sense of authenticity and integrity, which makes them more secure and less likely to act defensively.[16]

Self-affirmation can take several forms, such as reflecting on our core values or thinking about a meaningful relationship. Our existential fears are a strong provocateur of defensiveness—can self-affirmation reduce our defensive responses to this threat? One set of studies had some participants affirm their core values before reminding them that they were eventually going to die, and then having them read different essays that either confirmed or challenged their core views.[17] The researchers found that after having people reflect on their own mortality, they were more defensive and rated the essay (and author) that challenged their views more negatively, unless they had affirmed their core values. Affirming their meaning left them more open-minded in the wake of threat.

My colleagues and I sought to replicate and extend these findings several years ago.[18] I had students come into the lab, where they were instructed to write an essay about their most cherished beliefs and why they held those beliefs. They were told that they would be exchanging essays with another student, and while they were waiting for their partner to finish writing, we randomly assigned them to the self-affirmation task: We had a third of the participants write about their important values, another third write about their three most important relationships, and the last third write about their plans for next week (as a control condition for comparison). Because most of these students were religious, we set up the study so that they would read an essay from their "partner" who was strongly anti-religious. This essay went into detail about the peril of religion as a poison to society. We focused only on those participants who were religious, because we wanted to be sure that this experience would be sufficiently threatening to their worldview. After they read their "partner's" essay, they got their own essay back, with

feedback suggesting that their own writing was poor and illogi-
cal and that they were immature and biased. Finally, they had
the chance to provide their own feedback on their "partner's"
essay and rate their partner's ability to write. We found that the
participants who affirmed their relationships were the least
defensive: They gave their antagonistic partner the highest ratings. In our study, the relationship-affirmation condition was
the most effective in reducing defensiveness, followed by the
self-affirmation task, and finally, the control condition. The previous research suggested that focusing on affirming *one's self*
would reduce defensiveness, whereas our study revealed that
affirming a *different* source of meaning, such as a cherished relationship, also works to reduce defensiveness following criticism
from someone with drastically different values. When we
remember the people in our life whom we love, it lessens the
sting of criticism by a stranger because we're able to maintain a
sense of meaning in other areas.

We don't like to be challenged, and we often respond defensively, but we can override this tendency. By reminding ourselves of the different sources of meaning in our lives—our
loved ones, our core values, our career, our pets—we can inflate
our sense of meaning and enhance our feeling of authenticity
and integrity, taking the edge off future threats. Being secure in
our areas of meaning allows us to open our minds to change.
It's a balance between security and growth, and we need the
former to achieve the latter. So, the next time you feel like you
want to respond defensively by arguing, putting other people
down, discounting the views of others, or doubling down on
your way of seeing the world, take a moment and remind yourself of what you find meaningful. A small reminder might go a
long way in recentering you, providing you with a breath of
safety, and allowing you to be open to new and different ideas.
And perhaps, this different way of seeing the world, though

scary at first, might be more meaningful than you could have imagined.

Acknowledging your limitations

I hate to bring this up, but you have some pretty big flaws. I know I do; I just don't like to dwell on them. It still pains me to relive the memory of my wife rating me as a four out of ten on humility. I'd rather not think about my shortcomings, and it stings when other people see them (or point them out). If you're anything like me, you don't like talking about your flaws either. We'd rather focus on what we're good at than the areas where we're lacking. I'd rather talk about the marathons I've run or my accomplishments at work than deficiencies in my relationships or my tendency to never throw out old food or donate old clothes. And I certainly don't want to talk about the various ways I might be wrong.

We already know the perils of confirmation bias: We stop searching for information when we find what we're looking for. And when we're presented with information that could be interpreted in different ways, we pay most attention to the information with which we agree and walk away thinking that our views are justified and supported, conveniently forgetting about the counterpoints (in a process called *attitude polarization*). But we're not doomed to this pattern of intellectual closed-mindedness.

We can break free from this defensive approach to new or differing information. Recent research suggests that acknowledging—and owning—our limitations will help us open our mind.[19] In the twenty-first century, most people's lives are made possible by interdependence. We need each other. I couldn't be writing this book if not for the thousands of people who made it possible for me to find a job I did not create, write on a laptop I did not design, live in a home that I did not build, eat food that I did not grow, drive in a car I did not manufacture, and wear clothes I did not sew. From an evolutionary perspective, humans have helped solve collective problems and made it easier for us all to survive collectively through the division of labor. And as we've become more specialized, we realized that we're not able to do it all; there are things we're good at and areas where we're lacking. Similarly, we can turn the acknowledgment of our own limitations into a grateful realization that we're all in this together.

Nobel Prize–winning researcher Daniel Kahneman explains that we have natural tendencies toward these self-biases—what he calls System 1 thinking.[20] This type of thinking is quick, unconscious, involuntary, emotionally driven, and intuitive. If left unchecked, it's our default way of thinking. However, when we're motivated and have the mental capacity (such as when we're not distracted or stressed out), we can shift to System 2 thinking, which is slower, more rational, conscious, and deliberate. We can pause and overcome our natural defensive responses. When we realize that we have limitations—and seek to acknowledge our flaws—we can begin to slowly and deliberately override our natural and more arrogant defensive reactions.

Diversifying your social investments

For most of us, our social lives mirror our interior lives. We pick partners who share our values, select friends who share our beliefs, and find communities that share our interests. Most people want to spend time with other people who are just like them. Early social psychology research found that it's uncomfortable to be in a close relationship with someone you disagree with, especially when the topic is really important.[21] As a result, we either change our attitudes or opinions, or we change the relationship. When my wife and I first started dating in college, she was a fan of the TV show *Survivor*. She had been watching the series for several years, since the pilot episode, and was committed to watching it each Thursday night (when it aired back then). I stopped by her house one Thursday evening to ask her if she wanted to go out for dinner, only to be rejected and told that she had plans to stay in and watch the show. Each week played out similarly, until I realized just how important this show was to her. So, I began to watch it with her. It became part of our weekly rhythm. I started wearing *Survivor* T-shirts, discussed the show between episodes, and even—honest to God—played a season or two of *Survivor* fantasy, in which players gain points for what show contestants do in each episode. In no time flat, I was all in.

And while that might be a cute story about the lengths that some people may go for those they love, it's not at all uncommon. We all start integrating aspects of our partner into our own lives and sense of self. Disagreements cause tension, so we are quick to align our attitudes with our loved ones, especially if they feel more strongly about those opinions than we do.[22] When two people both feel strongly, they might change the relationship, create distance, or break it off altogether. The same process works with wider social circles. We pick friends with whom we agree, and we distance ourselves from people who are different. Unfortunately, this leads to insular echo chambers, where we form one-sided opinions that are validated by others and we distrust people who are different. We create our world to confirm the stories we tell ourselves, and we develop prejudices toward those who challenge our beliefs in the slightest.

And that's a problem—for our relationships, our neighborhood, our work, our society, and our world. We shouldn't simply become insular and ignore or judge those who are different. This divide perpetuates closed-mindedness, prejudice, hate, and violence. It also creates false beliefs about people who are not like us. One of the surest ways to avoid insular thinking and help reduce prejudice comes from psychological research on the *contact hypothesis*.[23] When we have regular interactions with typical members of a group that are either neutral or positive, over time we become less prejudiced: We start seeing "the other" as a human, just like us; we develop empathy and compassion; and we seek to better understand their perspective, which should widen our own. We can dislodge our unchallenged beliefs by interacting with those who hold a wider set of beliefs.

In each college course that I teach, I implore my students to find people who are different from them, get to know them, become friends, and start diversifying their social networks. They should seek out friends of different ethnicities, religions, cultures, economic classes, political parties, or in different stages of life; these could be people who like different music or TV shows, have different hobbies or interests, or come from a vastly different background. In one class, I assign my students to attend at least one service from a faith tradition different from their own (and for some, this is *any* place of worship). If we don't get uncomfortable by getting to know people different from us, we'll stop learning and growing, and we'll be stuck in our entrenched ways of thinking and behaving. So, finding different voices is an important part of reducing defensiveness.

But beware: People often make exceptions when they have a positive interaction with someone who is different. They think that one person is a "special case," and it doesn't really apply to the whole group. Avoid this trap of making an exception (a "sub-schema") and instead, realize that just like your newfound friend, other people who are different are often just as kind, friendly, and interesting as they are. Diversifying your social circle will help you reduce your knee-jerk reaction to vigorously defend your beliefs.

Proving yourself wrong

Proving ourselves wrong can also mitigate defensiveness. Recall our discussion of confirmation bias, which is our natural tendency to seek out information that will confirm the beliefs and attitudes we already hold. For example, when we think our friend is being stingy, we look for the ways that they fail to act generously and ignore the times when they offered to buy our meals or pick us up from the airport. Our oft-mumbled retort is "I knew it!" and we quickly amass evidence that we were right along, handily ignoring the mounds of facts and data to the contrary. We see the world the way we want to see it. This proclivity obscures our own interpretation of the world, plus it can run us afoul when working in groups by poisoning our decision-making process with groupthink, which includes (among other features) the desire to only look for information that is harmonious with the group consensus.

Because this tendency is so natural, you have to actively work against it. A surefire way to do this is to intentionally seek to prove yourself wrong. This can be accomplished by actively criticizing your beliefs. What evidence is there that you might be incorrect? Who are knowledgeable people about this issue whom you've previously disregarded—and what do they have to say about the topic? What are some counterpoints to your arguments? Simply put: Why might you be wrong?

Consider one of your deepest-held beliefs—perhaps your religious beliefs, political opinions, view on climate change or immigration policy, interpretation of the Second Amendment, or stance on the free market. It's natural to protect your most cherished beliefs by treating them as "untouchable," free from direct inquiry or too much scrutiny. We hold them unquestioned. But when we are enamored with an idea and begin to protect it at all costs, we close our minds and forfeit our search for truth. If we're going to "prove ourselves wrong," we have to courageously begin considering alternative views. Begin by arguing against yourself. What weak spots might you have in your argument? Where have you not yet searched for facts or evidence regarding this topic? Why might motivate you to have this belief, and in what areas might you have blind spots?

The goal of this exercise is not to simply add more ammunition to your defense (so you can better argue why your original opinion or belief is correct). Nor do you have to change your cherished beliefs and switch political parties or religions. Rather, the point is to realize that other smart, decent people believe differently than you do, so it's possible—even *likely*—that you're wrong about a few things. We can't know everything, and none of us is right all the time. Seeking out ways to keep yourself grounded in that reality will help you to be less defensive when your views are challenged. You're already aware of your own limitations and can then acknowledge that your views may be at least partially wrong.

Putting Humility into Action

All this talk about defensiveness might be making you, well, rather defensive. You might be a bit irritated, or perhaps think these are good suggestions *for other people* but don't really apply to you. After all, you're pretty good at humility; it's those other folks who could stand to be humbler. But just as I fell prey to thinking I was open-minded and humble because I had been studying humility for years, you might think that your own need for humility is not as great as others'. However, this, too, is just a well-crafted defense to keep your self-esteem high and your beliefs intact. Hiding behind our defenses inhibits our growth. Finding strategies to be less defensive is important as we work to be better people.

I still struggle with being defensive, because I'm human. Even still, I try to listen to different voices. I seek out perspectives that are different from my own. I try to establish friendships with people from different backgrounds and who have varied interests from my own. And I attempt to own my flaws. I'm sure I'll mess up again—though hopefully not on a Beach Friday—and when I do, I hope I'm quicker to admit guilt, take responsibility, ask for forgiveness, receive honest feedback, and commit to change. It's not easy work. And I'm actually not terribly good at it. But I'm committed to trying, because it sure beats the alternative.

6

—

Building Empathy

S EVERAL YEARS AGO, I had two very different interactions within a few months that helped me better understand why some relationships flourish and others flounder. The key difference between these two exchanges was how much empathy was brought to the situation. After all, as we'll soon see, building empathy is critical for cultivating humility.

Our friends the Wilsons invited my wife and me to meet their good friends the Maxwells.* Their hope was that the six of us—we three couples—would hit it off. The Wilsons dreamed that my wife and I could develop the kind of depth and connection with the Maxwells that they had, and in turn, we'd all have more rich relationships. They were excited. We had high hopes going into dinner, which was at one of our favorite restaurants. It's always exhilarating to think that you could meet new people who might be in your life for years (or decades) to come.

As we were waiting for our drinks to arrive, Mr. Maxwell asked us what books we were reading. My wife, a voracious reader, began to list a few recent authors she'd read. She got no further than two or three authors in, before he interrupted.

"Ah, I see. I now know all there is to know about you."

*Their names have been changed.

We were shocked. Mrs. Maxwell looked mortified. The air was sucked out of the room. While someone tried to make an awkward joke to relieve the palpable tension and I devised a plan to order a second round of drinks before the first round arrived, my wife turned to me and mumbled, under her breath, "And now *I* know all there is to know about *him*!"

It was stunning to see his lack of empathy on display. He didn't care to get to know my wife or her intellectual interests, didn't ask what she thought of the author or that particular book, in fact, didn't gather any more information about her at all before rendering his verdict. He prejudged her—everything about her—by his interpretation of why she had read a book.

The rest of the night was clunky and strained. There was a missed opportunity for empathy. We weren't able to recover from that flagrant display of arrogance. Needless to say, we didn't become lifelong pals, and our hopes for shared vacations were dashed before the appetizers arrived. It soured what might have been a decent shot at building a friendship. We went our separate ways, but my wife and I still talk about that disastrous dinner.

A second event couldn't have been more different. A few months later, a student came by my office hours. She nervously entered the room and closed the door, asking if she could share something with me. I invited her to have a seat and asked what was on her mind.

With tears welling in her eyes, she said, "Dr. Van Tongeren, I'm here today because I'm hoping you'll be able to help me. I heard from some people that the college is considering arming its campus safety officers. I want you to know what a terrible decision I think this is. I think a lot of people feel the same way I do. I've been sharing my opinion with everyone, but no one seems to listen to me. So, I figured that I'd reach out to you . . .

"This isn't easy for me. As a Black woman, I am programmed to fear White men like you. So just to be here is taking all the courage I have. But I figured that you might care. We've talked about race, violence, and prejudice in your class, and so I thought that you might understand. I remember the research we covered about prejudice and discrimination, and figured that you might be open to hearing from me about this issue. I'm so incredibly scared that if this policy change happens, I will no longer be safe. My friends feel the same way. But we need someone to listen to us, to talk to the administration—to do *something*. Can you help me?"

Tears immediately overwhelmed me, and for the first time in my professional career, I sat sobbing in my office with my student. I was overwhelmed by her vulnerability to share her concern with me, and I can only imagine how much courage it took to confront her fear and ask *me*—a White male professor—for help. I told her that I was honored that she came to me and promised that I would raise her concern with the decision-makers, that her voice would not go unheard. We processed for a few minutes before heading off to class. She talked about feeling vulnerable, and how much courage it took to share honestly with me. I named, plainly, the power differential that she felt and helped me see. I felt dismayed that she was afraid of me and grateful that she trusted me. And we both felt as though the situation had left us raw and tired—and agreed it was good and necessary work for us both.

The courage demonstrated by my student overwhelmed me with empathy. I could perceive her fear and vulnerability, as well as her strength and conviction. I sought to better understand her perspective and how this decision affected her. I tried to listen well. And then, I took action. I sent emails. I had meetings with the officials making decisions. In the end, the college decided against the policy change. I followed up with the student to let her know that I shared her concerns with the administrators, who listened and responded. Her courage was rewarded. Change happened.

She couldn't believe it. She was relieved and surprised that I would follow up; not only to the administration, but then again to her, to close the loop. And I shared how grateful I was that she had trusted me with her genuine concern. When she came to my office, I could have dismissed her worry or assumed that someone else would help her. Yet I was so grateful that I responded empathically. I can't say that my actions, or even her story alone, changed the administrators' minds, but they helped. Not only did these actions transform the larger community, they transformed both of us in the process. Another aspect we experienced was racial healing; she felt like she could trust me, and I started to see my power and privilege, as well as how my presence affects others. In that moment, the hard, good work could only be done with courage and empathy.

In the quest to become humbler, perhaps the biggest step you can take is to cultivate a deep and real sense of empathy. Empathy is defined as having two parts: the ability to see someone else's viewpoint, and feelings of compassion and warmth toward other people; this, in turn, leads people to help comfort or soothe the person who is in distress.[1] Said differently, empathy involves both opening your eyes (taking another person's perspective) and your mind (reducing defensiveness) by *opening your heart*—becoming attuned to the emotional experience of other people. Empathy allows you to prioritize the needs and value of other people. It's addressing the third component of humility—*going beyond yourself*—that can lead to cascading changes across all areas of your life.

Social Animals

It's a well-established truism in psychology that humans are fundamentally social creatures with a strong need to belong. We thrive when we feel accepted, as though we fit in, and when we're in the welcoming and accepting company of other people. From an evolutionary perspective, the need to belong makes a lot of sense: It's easier to survive in groups than alone, because of the advantage offered by others in fending off predators or hostile groups, and we need to find a partner to generate offspring. This powerful motivation is so ingrained in our psychological makeup that rejection can feel debilitating; some even turn to aggression after being excluded.[2]

One element that helps us develop, cultivate, and maintain lasting positive social relationships is empathy.[3] Research has established that our brains are designed to perceive, and mimic, the feelings of those around us.[4] We possess mirror neurons that activate the part of our brain responsible for emotional responses to emulate the emotional experience of those around us. When we see someone in pain, we *feel* it. In a parallel fashion, our brain is equipped with mechanisms to help us see someone else's point of view; we're able to *see* things as others do. And together, this emotional concern and perspective-taking should compel us to turn our efforts toward prosociality—helping those we see in distress.

Why Is Empathy Important?

Some of the most fascinating early research on empathy suggested that it was crucial to getting us to transcend egoistic motives and enabled us to be more altruistic. This research settled on age-old philosophical questions: Does pure altruism exist? Can we ever be truly *unselfish*? When we help other people, are we reaping personal or social benefits that feel good or somehow offer us an advantage? Do we help others just to boost our own self-esteem or provide us with some downstream benefit? Or are there situations in which our desire to help others arises from a nobler and more compassionate source and is not motivated merely by selfish interest?

Researchers sought to answer a basic question: What motivates us to be altruistic? Empathy emerged as a strong candidate.

Dan Batson and his team of researchers long contended that true
altruism does indeed exist, and empathy is its core mechanism.
Using clever studies, such as alerting participants to a fellow participant's need or allowing some participants to reduce the number of electric shocks ostensibly (but not actually) delivered to
another participant in the lab, Batson's work has consistently
pointed toward the role that empathy plays in reducing the distress of others and motivating us to help those in need.[5] Batson
also ruled out competing accounts that suggest other selfish
imposter motives might be at play, such as gaining personal
rewards (self-esteem or praise) or avoiding social punishments
(guilt or shame).[6] Empathy is critical because our selfish motivations are so pervasive; we desperately need it to go beyond ourselves and help those in need.

When it comes to our relationships with other people, one
notoriously sneaky motivation to help others is *moral hypocrisy*:
when people appear to others and themselves as moral without
incurring the costs of having to behave morally. Batson and his
colleagues engineered experiments to offer critical insight into
the inner workings of our hypocritical minds. In one study, he
told participants that they were in charge of assigning themselves
and another participant to different experiments: One of them
would complete a task for a chance to earn a raffle ticket for a
thirty-dollar prize for each correct response, whereas the other
would complete these tasks for no chance of the reward at all.[7]
Clearly, the former option is preferrable to the latter, and most
participants agreed: Given this dictatorial power, most participants gave themselves the favorable option, even though the
majority of them thought assigning the other participant would
have been the morally right thing to do. In a follow-up study,
participants were given the option to flip a coin to assign the
tasks. Obviously, this would be much fairer. Only half of the participants decided to do this (the other half just assigned based on

their own decision), and of the half that did, nearly all still assigned themselves the positive task. They flipped the coin to *be perceived* as moral, although 90 percent of participants—much higher than chance—gave themselves the beneficial outcome nonetheless. They disregarded the outcome of the coin toss and decided to do what they wanted anyway. And to rule out the possibility that participants were just deceiving themselves by selectively misremembering which side represented which person, another study used a coin labeled with "self" and "other" to remove all doubt and found, once again, that even among those who flipped the labeled coin, participants overwhelmingly assigned themselves the positive task.[8] We want to give the impression that we're moral without having to do the hard work of actually being moral.

Here we see the intersection of two of Batson's lines of work: The link between empathy and altruism, and the nagging thread of moral hypocrisy obstructing our motivation to be moral. Empathy compels us to do good when our penchant is strong to appear moral without having to sacrifice anything. It helps us overcome our selfish motives and actually help those around us. But we need to be wary of deceiving ourselves into thinking that we're being moral when we're simply looking for ways to send that message publicly. Moral hypocrisy is a dangerous trap, similar to *virtue signaling*—ensuring one is sending visible messages of aligning with a preferred worldview without any personal costs— and *slacktivism*—voicing public support for a cause without making any actual sacrifice or real effort. We look like we're moral to others, and perhaps ourselves as well, but aren't actually doing any real work.

Cultivating empathy gets us to move beyond our proclivity toward selfishness in the guise of selflessness. When we truly perceive and feel the distress of others in need and work hard to take their perspective, we can't help but be compelled to act morally, in ways that will benefit others. Empathy helps snap us out of selfishness.

Empathy Is Central to Humility

Empathy doesn't just help us be *social* animals, it makes it possible for us to be *moral* animals. It helps us tune in to the suffering of others and work to reduce their distress or any harm they're experiencing. Researchers have found that empathy is key in several relational virtues, including forgiveness. By understanding how it functions in forgiveness, we can gain insights into how empathy is crucial for humility.

You might imagine that revenge is an effective response to keep people from hurting you—after all, if you establish a reputation as someone who will respond with payback, you would think that people would steer clear. However, retaliation only gets you so far. Matching, or elevating, every offense within a tight-knit community with swift revenge can quickly unravel the social fabric. Some of my own work with colleagues revealed that we do more of a "forgiveness calculus": We consider how much the relationship means to us and whether we're likely to be exploited again in the future. Combined, the value of the relationship and low exploitation risk lead to greater forgiveness.[9] From this we learned that forgiveness is a positive response in the wake of a transgression that helps keep close and treasured relationships intact and healthy.

Empathy—as a mechanism for forgiveness—helps transform revenge and avoidance into compassion and ultimately resolution.[10] This change toward forgiveness only occurs when we're able to consider what the person who hurt us was likely thinking. When we're hurt, we turn inward and tend to our own emotional wounds, to ensure that we're safe from future pain. This behavior is a healthy way to protect ourselves. Just as we pull our hand away from an open flame, we often need to recoil when we're stung by the transgressions of others. Those who get stuck in a patten of repeated offenses (and are always quick to forgive) risk being exploited and often lose their self-respect and sense of who they are.[11] But when we offer forgiveness only when we're ready, we can put ourselves in the shoes of the person who wronged us and ask what they were thinking and if they were trying their best. This practice of empathy helps us go beyond ourselves and consider others, making us more likely to forgive.

Empathy is also central to humility. It helps people improve their social relationships. My colleague Don Davis found that humility is reliably related with empathy.[12] Other research findings have found that empathy is consistently associated with positive outcomes, such as enhanced relationship satisfaction.[13] People are more satisfied in relationships in which they feel understood by their partners.[14] What's more, within couples, empathy boosts future relationship satisfaction.[15] Researchers randomly assigned couples to an empathy intervention or a waitlist control (where participants wait to be part of the intervention until a later time, to isolate the effects of the intervention), and then participants worked through five sessions designed to build empathy. In the first session, they learned what empathy was. In the second, they learned that empathy involves being emotionally sensitive toward others, watched a video of a couple relating, and discussed how to be more emotionally sensitive by monitoring one's own emotions and listening. The third focused on communication, including how to listen well to your partner. Session four focused on empathic checking, which involved partners giving feedback as to whether efforts to be more empathic were working well. The final session focused on situational factors that affect empathy and practical next steps. This empathy intervention improved relationship satisfaction six months later, after these changes had time to settle in and take effect.

A consistent finding in the empathy research is that we can't think of others when we're preoccupied with ourselves. When we get too self-absorbed, we lose sight of other people, as confirmed by research on narcissism—which is the near opposite of humility. Narcissism is marked by traits such as perceived superiority, self-admiration, and entitlement.[16] As you might imagine, and as research confirms,[17] narcissists lack empathy.[18] There's only so much attention to go around, and it's hard to think of others when you're enamored with yourself. In turn, self-admiration ruins relationships.[19] Mutual respect is lost as narcissistic individuals engage in rivalry and competition.[20] When you're looking for every opportunity to stroke your own ego, you will lose most of your relationships along the way.

Opening Your Heart: Building Empathy

You may be wondering: How might you build more empathy in your own life? As we've discussed, researchers have developed interventions to help couples be more empathic, and other work has shown that parents can foster empathy in their children by modeling it and by encouraging them to take the perspective of others.[21] We *can* become more empathic. Recall that empathy is a mix of having an emotional experience related to the well-being of others, considering different people's perspectives, and being motivated to prioritize the needs of others by acting on these feelings and shifts in perspective. Now here are four potential strategies that can help you cultivate greater empathy.

Attuning your emotional connection

If you are emotionally unavailable or disconnected from your own emotional experiences, you won't likely be able to experience a strong sense of empathy for other people. That is, if you aren't attuned to when *you* feel angry, sad, happy, or confused—or acknowledge the emotional experience occurring in your own body—it will be harder for you to connect with the emotional experience of *someone else*. For that reason, the first step to cultivating greater empathy for others is to tune your own emotional connection.

Emotions are our body's way of communicating changes in the environment. They usually alert us to something that needs attention. We have to first *experience* the emotion, then *identify* the emotion, *express* the emotion, and then *use* the emotion. Let's look at each of these steps.

Thanks to evolution, the experience of emotion is fairly easy for most neurotypical folks: Our body will give us feedback about something in our environment that should direct our attention and marshal our resources. We have emotional experiences with regularity, even if some of those emotional experiences are relatively low in intensity (such as feeling pleasant). It becomes harder for some folks when we're trying to identify the emotion. At times, it's clear: someone cuts in front of us in line, and we're angry. Or we're nearing the end of *Sophie's Choice*, and we're aware that we're sad. But other times, we're not as sure; emotions like shame, embarrassment, and confusion can be expressed in ways that are harder to identify. We may be short with others, ignore our feelings, be resistant to sharing honestly, or feel so overwhelmed that we are emotionally numb. We know we're feeling *something*, but we're too scared or ashamed or confused to determine what that might be.

When we're unable to identify our emotions, we have a hard time expressing them. They get a bit stuck. If we're stewing in anger toward our parents but never express that, it may come out in harmful ways, such as resentment or frustration toward our partner or close friends. Moreover, we can't use those unidentified emotions for anything helpful. Anger helps us realize that it's time to be assertive: A boundary has been violated, and we need to stand up for ourselves. But if we don't realize that we're angry, we don't know that we should act.

Understanding this process can be incredibly useful for cultivating an empathic connection with others. By consistently practicing this kind of emotional attunement in our own lives we can
be more aware, and attentive to, the emotional experiences of
others. On the flip side, when we're emotionally unavailable, it
usually results in a lack of empathy. So, we need to practice these
steps to foster our own emotional connection. Sometimes, the
work of tuning in to our emotions requires the assistance of a
therapist. In any case, being intentional in cultivating our inner
emotional life is beneficial to ourselves and others.

Practice perspective-taking

Next, consider the perspective of others. By taking the viewpoints of others seriously, you shift yourself out of your own myopic vantage point and implicitly concede that you might be
wrong. Honest perspective-taking is more than just a thought
experiment in which you allow the vague possibility that someone else might have a valid point. Thorough and honest
perspective-taking looks more like (a) admitting that you have
limitations and blind spots and are not completely right, (b) welcoming the opinion and viewpoint of others as valid and important, (c) granting that the other person is trying their best, and (d)
respecting the inherent worth and dignity of the other person.
We're not very good at practicing this kind of rich
perspective-taking; instead, we desperately seek affirmation of
our own views. Often, we can barely wait for someone to stop
sharing their opinion for us to tell them exactly what we think
and why we're right. And in interpersonal disagreements, we
work harder to present our airtight case, justify our motives, and
vindicate our actions than we do to really listen to someone else's
lived experience and see their humanity. We dismiss their viewpoint, deny their experience, denigrate their worth, and dehumanize them along the way.

To gain a sense of what this might look like, and how tough it might be, let's peek at a related field of inquiry: forgiveness. Forgiveness researchers found that having people take the perspective of their offender helped victims work toward forgiveness.[22] In fact, this empathic perspective-taking is often *the* critical step in forgiving those who wronged us. Consider for a moment that kind of empathy. Imagine the biggest emotional transgression or offense someone has committed against you—and then put yourself in the shoes of the offender to consider their perspective, what they were thinking, and how they might really have been trying their best. It will certainly shift your perspective and often motivates forgiveness. And it's why researchers and therapists have said that this kind of empathy is like giving an altruistic gift: You don't have to do it, but doing so is selfless. You have every right to seek revenge or avoid that person. But when you do engage in an empathic response, it helps facilitate forgiveness and repair the relationship. That's the kind of real perspective-taking that can change relationships and lives.

Developing the ability to take someone's perspective in this way takes practice. I don't have a silver bullet to offer that will help you perfectly overcome any default tendencies to want to defend your own viewpoint, but one strategy that might make it easier is to reflect on your own shortcomings. You don't need to ruminate on your missteps or mistakes; wallowing in shame or self-loathing is not productive. Rather, consider the ways that you might have let others down, hurt other people, or made a pretty big mistake. Were you offered forgiveness? If so, how did that feel? If not, how transformative would that have been? Realizing that you are fallible and prone to mistakes might allow you a bit more understanding, patience, and grace when others offend or misstep. Of course, this is not a justification to allow people to take advantage of you, but reminding ourselves that we've let people down in the past and could extend the same kindness and compassion to others, will go a long way.[23]

Learn active listening

Another way to build empathy is to think about what you didn't know and had to learn—often by listening to others. Some of us learn our limitations the hard way. I used to stubbornly refuse to eat sushi, out of the mistaken fear that I would not like it. For several years, my wife enjoyed sushi when out with friends or coworkers, while I would avoid it at all costs. Despite her opinion that I would, in fact, find sushi delicious, I stubbornly held on to my negative attitude. One night, my graduate school advisor organized a big dinner at a Japanese restaurant to celebrate my successful thesis defense. At a table surrounded by colleagues and professors, and to my absolute horror, the decision was made to order the large sushi platter for us all to share. I was between the rock of public embarrassment—who didn't eat sushi by the time they were in their twenties?—and the hard place of my certain belief that raw fish was unpalatable. After imagining how feasible it would be to escape through the bathroom window and never see this group again until graduation, I gave in to social pressure and joined in the feast. And I loved it. I had obstinately held on to my position, and I was wrong. For years, I'd been missing out on what is now one of my favorite meals. Whenever I'm quick to judge someone who refuses to try something new, I try to remember that I was once hesitant, too.

The same reluctance to change permeates our beliefs. Often, once we change our viewpoint, we can't imagine why other people would be so foolish as to believe something different—even when we were those very same people in the recent past. Religious converts denigrate their pre-conversion self.[24] Ex-smokers harshly judge those who smoke. Those who shift their ideological commitments roll their eyes at the ignorance of those who hold their previous beliefs. How quickly we forget how much we've learned, and how different we are now from what we once were. I can only imagine how incredibly annoyed I would be at myself ten, fifteen, or twenty years ago. And I hope my future self will think back on who I am now with acceptance. May we strive to do the same with others.

Active listening, which involves reflecting back what you've heard and affirming the meaning with the person who shared, is an art worth developing—and it requires work to listen to others without judgment. So often we come to conversations thinking that we already know all we need about someone or something; and when we do, our own arrogance obstructs us from learning something new and forging new connections with those around us. Resist the urge to allow your preconceived notions of people, such as relying on stereotypes or judging others without knowing much about them, shade how you interact with them. Instead, work to learn their perspective by having them share it themselves—and by engaging in active listening. To practice active listening, echo back what you hear and check to ensure that you're understanding correctly. Affirm that you're listening through active engagement and reflection. Summarize what they've shared and ask if there's anything else they'd like you to know.

Putting empathy into action

Another way of building empathy is to think of the needs of others, which comes easier to some than others. There's a continuum from those who think only of themselves to those who care, perhaps too much, about the needs of others. I tend to fall more sharply on the people-pleasing side of the continuum. I enjoy making sure other people are comfortable, cared for, and happy—sometimes to my own detriment. I can forget to ask myself what my own needs are and how to care for myself when I'm helping others. While that makes me incredibly attentive toward others during stressful times, it means that, if I'm not careful, I'll let my own needs slide and will suffer as a result. For some of us, thinking of others comes naturally.

For others, it requires a bit more effort to consider how your actions will affect other people and what they might need in tough times. If this describes you, try a simple thought experiment and ask yourself: What would I want or need right now if I were this person? Now go beyond the thought experiment and put it into action. Similarly, try asking others what they need and then following through. By going out of your way to help others, you will come to value their needs.

One of strongest hesitations that people have about adopting an empathic approach and considering the needs of others is the fear of being exploited. Although we may not say it in so many words, we are afraid that if we prioritize or value the needs of others, our own needs will go unmet. Operating from a mindset of scarcity, we worry that there will not be "enough" to go around—whether that is enough attention, love, respect, admiration, praise, or affirmation. The concern is that caring so strongly for others means that we will suffer. But if you have established a healthy level of humility with appropriate boundaries, this will not be the case.

Helping others never precludes setting clear boundaries and doesn't erode our self-respect. This is why humility is so important to empathy: Humble people are able to think of the needs of others precisely because they are firm in the belief of their own worth and value and don't ceaselessly chase the conditional love and affirmation of others. Knowing our abilities and limitations is central to the self-awareness dimension of humility. Truly humble people can set healthy boundaries, knowing what they are able to give and where they need to say no. In this way, humility is liberating: It affords us the self-knowledge to determine the best way to care for others without losing ourselves.

From Security to Strength

True humility doesn't require you to lose your sense of self or your needs in order to value the needs of others. Remember, humility comes from a place of security: Your worth is not dependent on the approval of others, so you can make decisions that value your needs alongside theirs. You can think of others when you aren't continually thinking about yourself. We humans are all in this together, equally small yet significant. We are enough, even when we are misunderstood, imperfect, or unsure.

From this humble security comes the strength to care for and value others. This strength takes on many forms, depending on the situation. Sometimes, it might look like compromise: accepting that we cannot (and shouldn't) always get our way, and that healthy relationships are marked by mutual respect and equity. Sometimes it's the acknowledgment that we make small sacrifices for a bigger benefit to others. For example, the humble acknowledgement that our minor inconveniences—such as sorting the recycling or reducing our energy consumption—might be a slight annoyance, but the benefits to others will accumulate. In relationships, remember that humility does not mean becoming smaller; it means allowing others to be fully themselves and encouraging them at every success. This humble strength might be the courage to sit with others who are experiencing pain and emotional distress, even when it's uncomfortable. By bringing your whole self, you can show up fully for others and support them in their time of need.

Empathy Expands Your World

Whereas selfishness shrinks our sense of self, empathy expands our world. When we only consider ourselves, we turn inward and are ultimately left feeling lonely. On the other hand, valuing the needs of others and considering their perspectives are not only central to a life marked by humility but can open us up to more fully appreciate the world around us.

Research on positive emotions, such as joy or happiness, has revealed how important they can be in our self-expansion and growth. Negative emotions, such as anger or fear, elicit a narrow set of responses to alleviate us from potential peril. We usually fight, flee, or freeze: we start swinging, running, or hiding. We're just trying to survive. Positive emotions, like empathy, are different. Rather than shrink our world, they enlarge it. These emotional states are affectively positive (they feel good) and increase our thought-action-repertoire; that is, they help us see the world as larger and offer a wider number of viable responses of how to interact.[25] When we're not simply trying to survive, we have a richer set of behaviors at our disposal. We can live more fully. We can appreciate others and the world around us, understanding that it's not just all about me.

If you've ever been to the Grand Canyon, you've experienced this type of "enlargement" from positive emotions. Standing on the rim of this majestic spectacle can overwhelm us with feelings like awe, appreciation, and gratitude. We feel small and safe, happily insignificant yet wonderfully meaningful.

My friend Nathan invited me to the Grand Canyon after my camping trip with my old college roommates. I drove down to meet him and some of his extreme running buddies to attempt a double-crossing of the Grand Canyon. He was an ultramarathoner, an athlete who completes distances greater than a marathon, and this particular excursion was known as the Rim-to-Rim-to-Rim. We would run down the South Rim of the Grand Canyon, across the canyon floor, and up to the North Rim, just to repeat it in reverse the next day. (We gave ourselves a night's sleep in a bed in between crossings; other runners do it all in one day.) As one of the few non-ultramarathoners in the group, having completed only two measly *regular* marathons, I was nervous. This was an august group who had completed treks across the Sahara Desert and through Death Valley and did 100-mile races like they were 5K Turkey Trots. I felt misplaced and outmatched. But those feelings all melted away when I saw the canyon for the first time, and by my first step down the descent, I couldn't stop smiling. I was overwhelmed by its sheer size and beauty. I felt awe. I felt small. I was grateful to be alive. And this helped motivate me to complete the two-day trek, feeling well and finishing strong, and make memories I won't soon forget.

That's what empathy can do. Just like other positive emotions, it moves you to a place where you can feel smaller—maybe, in our culture of self-aggrandizing, just the right size. And not only does this this right-sizing help make life feel richer and more meaningful, it invites others in, where they don't have to shrink and can be their full selves.[26] You create the room for others to be who they are, and you embrace them where they are at.

Quick to Listen

Empathy can make or break our relationships. I think back and wonder what would have happened if that late summer dinner with the Maxwells played out differently; if our new acquaintance had expressed genuine interest and curiosity to get to know my wife rather than searching for the lowest common denominator to fill out his preconceived notions of who she was by her taste in books. If he had followed up his initial question about her literary interests with another question and then simply listened—setting aside his assumptions and seeking to learn from her perspective and get to know her—could we have developed a friendship? I'll never know because his comment soured our experience and betrayed his unwillingness to get to know us. Indeed, that was really all *either* of us needed to know to realize that this wasn't the kind of relationship we had hoped it would be.

I also think back to the bravery of my student in voicing her concern about the school's safety policy. I remember her vulnerability and courage in sharing with me about a delicate topic. I still remember what I felt and how it shaped the whole conversation, and how my emotional expression opened new pathways of communication and fostered a sense of trust between us. Her authenticity called out mine, and it was a moment that changed us both.

Empathy resided at the center of both of those interactions: a lack of empathy in one, and mutual empathy in the other. And that empathy can make the difference between relationships that flourish and those that flounder. Let's commit to practicing empathy to improve our relationships, even when it feels like hard work.

7

—

The Importance of Self-Regulation

CULTIVATING HUMILITY IS A bit like training for a marathon. It takes hard work, practice, and persistence. It requires effort and consistency. It can't be done in day or even a week; there's no quick fix or "life hack" that can get you to be humbler faster. You have to put in the miles, so to speak. In the quiet, lonely places where only you know your motives, it will prepare you for the race day of real relationships and authentic living. Sometimes, you mess up, stumble, or have a bad day. It's hard, but it's worth it. And it helps us build a humility that lasts.

Developing a Humility That Lasts

Let's extend the marathon metaphor as a helpful framework for developing a strong and authentic humility that can weather adversity. Just like signing up for a 26.2-mile race, if you're serious about developing humility, it'll take a strong investment. We've already discussed how our minds are wired to be self-focused, we live in cultural currents that reward narcissistic self-aggrandizing, and we filter information to show us the world we want to see, rather than how it actually is. We have our work cut out for us. But it is possible to rewire our brains if we have a training plan. We need to have a sense of where we're heading. Let's look at some strategies that may be helpful.

First, cultivating humility should be *comprehensive*. Humility needs to permeate your entire way of approaching life: how you handle new situations, receive feedback, engage with other people, and treat yourself. Trying to be humble at work without attending to your relationships at home can be troublesome, as can ignoring feedback or failing to work on developing your own self-awareness. Think about the four kinds of humility: relational, intellectual, cultural, and existential. Ask yourself, in what ways am I

- working to be humbler in my relationships?
- being open to new ideas, insights, and perspectives?
- seeking to learn from others and appreciate their culture?
- appreciating the expansive nature of the world and feeling grateful for my smallness?

I think of these four flavors of humility as mutually reinforcing. Just as preparing for a race requires not only a lot of running but also eating right, hydrating, and cross-training (such as biking and weight lifting), humility will be more sustainable if you develop it across these different dimensions.

Second, you should strive to develop a humility that is *resilient*. Setbacks happen. Just as one might pull a muscle or twist an ankle while training, you'll struggle in the journey to becoming humbler. It will be harder at times to practice humility than at others. Some days, selfishness will come through, insecurities will lead you to brag or react defensively, or you'll start doubting that you're making any progress at all. You may even question whether putting in the effort is worth it at all. For instance, during a race, the people enjoying themselves in the crowd seem a lot smarter (and happier) to me, while I'm laboring through a race I paid to complete; but those moments are fleeting, and I can reorient myself to staying focused on the larger goal.

When it gets hard to practice humility, that's precisely when you need it the most. Conflict in relationships or clashing views may draw out your urge to react defensively, act selfishly, and stop listening and start shouting. You might find it particularly challenging when you receive negative feedback or are overlooked, when others are praised, or when the desire for external validation is strong. You can also endure by trusting that you are in the place you need to be, and others are exactly where they need to be. Humility allows you the confidence and security to know that your choices are suitable for you, and that others are making choices that fit them best. This is when humility shines. Anyone can be humble when it's easy, but a lasting and authentic humility persists even when it's hard.

However, no one gets this right all the time. Everyone messes up, and when you do, it's helpful to *treat yourself with kindness*. Withhold harsh self-judgment or negative self-talk. The goal is progress rather than perfection. Ask yourself if you're working to get a little bit better each day than the day before. Know that you will fall short—and it's understandable. It happens to me regularly. Perfect humility is unattainable. Just as not every training run is perfect or even better than the prior one, on average you're making progress toward becoming humbler.

Finally, a lasting humility becomes *habitual*. When you engage in humility comprehensively throughout all areas of your life, strive to be resilient in the face of hardship, and give yourself a pass when you don't get it quite right—it'll start to become second nature. In this midst of the long slog of training, lacing up your shoes and getting in a run becomes ingrained in your thinking, especially when juggling other commitments. I often ask myself, when can I get my miles in today? Some days are easier than others, but I rarely miss a run. It's just part of my regular routine. Despite poor weather or previously agonizing runs, I have kept at it—and it got better. Humility is the same way. It may never be easy, but with practice, it gets better until it becomes part of your posture toward the world.

Researchers have argued that we can make virtuous behaviors such as humility more habitual through "nonidentical repetition"—or, put plainly, practicing humility in different contexts, with different people, and in different situations.[1] We become better runners when we train on different terrains, for different distances, and at different speeds. So, giving yourself a wide variety of chances to practice humility will help you develop a lasting and enduring humility. And, like any skill, the more you put it into practice, the more it develops. In fact, learning how to do the hard work of acting virtuously despite its difficulty may be a common thread in building a life of meaning.[2]

The Importance of Self-Regulation

If I had to nominate one skill that would improve your life, I'd put forward self-regulation. In simple terms, self-regulation is our ability to do hard things. More scientifically, self-regulation is roughly analogous to self-control and relates to our ability to exercise control over ourselves—our impulses, default reactions, natural responses—in order to align with some standard or goal.[3] For example, perhaps we want to reduce how much we use our cell phone; we may feel as though it's natural to check our phone whenever we're bored, anxious, lonely, depressed, or simply experience a lull in conversation. Perhaps checking the phone has become habitual, a kind of soothing comfort. Over time, when feeling uncomfortable or anxious, this urge may compel us to reach for the phone, but we can self-regulate by exerting control over this impulse and sitting with our feelings. We hold a particular goal in mind and bring ourselves in line with that goal.

Evidence of self-regulatory failure is widely evident in our culture, where addiction, obesity, violence, and mental health concerns loom large. Of course, each of these is more complex than mere lack of self-control (which would be akin to victim blaming), but self-regulatory processes do play a role: When we're overwhelmed and stressed out, do we pour ourselves a second drink or reach for a pleasure-producing and pain-alleviating substance? Can we eat in moderation and select healthier foods rather than the delicious yet unhealthy options? Are we able to moderate our response to insults or divergent views without lashing out with aggression? Do we engage with the hard work of caring for our mental health when easier options to escape or avoid are available? Self-regulation helps us overcome strong, perhaps natural, urges to accomplish something difficult but meaningful, such as tackling a lengthy and challenging project at work or completing courses necessary for a degree or promotion.

When it comes to humility, self-regulation is the key to inhibiting our default selfish responses, allowing us to respond humbly—even when everything inside screams otherwise—by considering the needs of others. When we desperately want to brag or we get jealous at the praise others are receiving, practicing self-regulation helps us overcome these strong, arrogant urges. It's the mechanism that enables us to make the hard decisions and persist despite challenges. But how does self-regulation work, and just how do we enhance our self-regulatory skill?

There are three pillars to self-regulation: setting a standard or goal, monitoring progress, and building the strength to engage. First, self-regulation involves *standards* or a goal toward which we're hoping to shift our behavior. For humility, as previously discussed, this target might look like having an accurate view of ourselves, keeping our ego in check, and thinking of the needs of others. In each three of these features—knowing yourself, checking yourself, and going beyond yourself—it's important to be clear in our own mind what a modicum of success would look like. To know ourselves well means understanding our strengths and weaknesses, owning our limitations, and regularly seeking feedback; it can also mean admitting that we have a certain biased way of seeing the world and need help appreciating different viewpoints or going beyond our default interpretation of the world. To check ourselves includes reining in some of those self-aggrandizing impulses, sharing the praise, accepting our part of the blame, and remaining open, rather than defensive, when criticism or conflict bubble up. To go beyond ourselves means cultivating a sense of empathy toward others, considering the needs of those around us, and understanding our connection to something larger than ourselves, whether that's other people, nature, or spirituality. As these are the markers of a humble life, they serve as the road map for our journey toward living humbly. We can orient ourselves toward these characteristics so we don't lose our way.

The second pillar of self-regulation is *monitoring* or checking our progress toward these goals. Setting goals or having standards is important, but if we're not assessing how well we're doing in aligning our thoughts, emotions, and behaviors with those goals, it is largely an exercise in futility. It would be like carefully charting a cross-country trip on a map and then jumping in the car, tossing the map in the backseat, and driving vaguely east. Without regular points of self-reflection, we won't know if we're staying on course. Knowing how to live a life marked by humility is the first step, but it's not enough. We need to move past intellectual curiosity about being humble and toward an evaluation of the ways that our life aligns (or doesn't) with these different goals. We might start with a self-inventory, realizing that we're probably more than just a little biased in our own introspection, and we're likely to overestimate our own humility (as I have done and regularly do). But whatever areas of improvement we can identify may be glaring to others. After this, asking for consistent feedback from a trusted source will help us assess how close or far we are to aligning with some of these aspirational goals. Finally, making both self-reflection and seeking feedback a regular and consistent practice will help ensure we're working toward developing a lasting humility. Just as we need to continue to check our map when on a road trip, or listen to electronic devices dictate turn-by-turn directions, continual check-ins are important to see if we're making progress toward becoming humbler.

The last pillar of self-regulation is *building the strength* or ability to engage in these efforts. Being humble is hard. It can feel difficult to hold our tongue when we want to brag about a recent accomplishment or respond defensively when offered criticism. It can be tiring to continually think of the needs of others, especially in a world obsessed with image and self-enhancement. But just like other skills that are challenging at first, we can develop the stamina for acting humbly. Over time, with practice, our endurance for doing the work of humility will grow. Part of this progress is getting the conditions right. Just as a cool day, flat road, and plenty of hydration can help us run farther (and faster), our situation plays a role in how much strength we have to act humbly. If we're feeling stressed, distracted, or overwhelmed, or if we don't feel safe, our default reactions of selfishness and self-protection will be terribly hard to overcome. Because it takes effort, other cognitive or emotional demands can reduce our ability to be humble. Being thoughtful about cultivating space in our life that feels safe, allows for rest, and grants us the attention and effort required can be incredibly beneficial. Of course, we can't always pick our perfect settings to be humble, and often when the conditions are the worst is when humility is most needed; but relying on the practice we've put in when the weather is good will better prepare us to act humbly when conditions are bad.

Finding a Motivation

Developing self-regulation is critical to our well-being. One study, which followed children from birth to age thirty-two, found that self-control predicts better health, greater wealth, and lower crime, even when accounting for intelligence and one's family background; and self-control during one's early life (three to twelve years of age) predicts future successes on these dimensions.[4] Some have argued that self-control is so important, you probably can't develop too much of it.[5] Others have suggested that helping children tolerate delayed gratification helps them learn self-control.[6] In a world where acting on our impulses is easier than ever—think of forty-eight-hour shipping on many products, the convenience of drive-through fast food, or a near endless compendium of TV shows and movies to binge-watch—improving our self-regulation can help not only our humility but nearly every aspect of our lives.

One of my friends and colleagues, Nathan DeWall (from the Grand Canyon adventure), conducted extensive research on self-regulation, which translated from professional knowledge to a personal transformation: He went from being a sedentary academic to an ultramarathoner. Unhappy with his lifestyle, he harnessed his understanding of this important skill to learn how to run *really* long distances in some of the most grueling conditions on the planet. I met Nathan when he visited my college during his yearlong sabbatical, a time in which he completed several 100-mile races as part of his application package for the Badwater 135, which has been named the world's toughest footrace. In order to prepare for this 135-mile trek from Death Valley (the lowest point in the United States) to Mount Whitney (the highest point in the United States) in July, he also completed a six-day, 250-kilometer trek through the Sahara Desert and a 500-kilometer run over nearly a week across several states in the summer. He assembled a world-class running résumé to complete some of the most demanding runs in the world using the power of self-regulation.

Fortunately, as Nathan can testify, there are ways to get better at self-regulation. We might not run through the scorching heat of a desert, but we can improve at doing difficult things that require attention, focus, and determination—largely through practice. For example, researchers have studied the effects of randomly assigning people to complete difficult tasks for a two-week period, such as striving to maintain excellent posture, consistently trying to improve their mood, or keeping a food diary.[7] After two weeks of practicing one of these different forms of self-control, participants performed better on a self-regulation task when brought back into the lab. Similar results were found in a separate two-week study in which people were assigned to practice physical exercise (squeezing a handgrip twice a day for as long as they could) or avoid sweets.[8] Another study assigned people to use their nondominant hand for two weeks and found that people responded less aggressively when provoked or threatened.[9] Practicing difficult things can train our mind and body to better persist in future tasks that require effort.

Another line of scientific research investigates our motivation for pursuing a particular goal or avoiding temptation.[10] Sometimes, we act because we really *want* to; we're intrinsically motivated, and accomplishing the goal aligns with our values or is personally meaningful to us. Other times, we act because we *have* to; we feel extrinsic pressure to fit in or pursue a goal, either because of what we can gain (such as the approval of others) or because of what we're avoiding (such as shame, embarrassment, the judgment of others). Not surprisingly, when we're motivated to do something because we genuinely *want* to, we're less tempted to act impulsively and encounter fewer obstacles in our quest for self-control. In addition, this motivation can change our implicit responses: Having a motivation that is directly aligned with our values makes self-control more automatic and natural. When it comes to humility, *we have to want to change*. We can't embark on this journey begrudgingly, or because our friend or partner is making us, or because we feel like a failure if we don't. True, lasting change in humility must come from a genuine desire to make ourselves better, humbler people precisely because it's something we actually want.

Most directly related to humility, some researchers have argued that activities that "shrink" ourselves are helpful to building self-regulation.[11] For example, meditation, mindfulness, focusing on the present moment, and reducing how much we think about ourselves may all contribute to better self-regulation. These exercises help us get our mind out of the way. By ridding ourselves from the center of our world, we may, in fact, better control ourselves. I imagine that this is because doing so helps "right-size" us back down to where we have a broader appreciation for nature, other people, and the cosmos, where we feel appropriately small. When we shift the focus away from ourselves, we paradoxically might get better at overcoming our selfish impulses and controlling our behavior.

The culmination of all this research is this: If we're serious about increasing our ability to do hard things, we should start doing hard things more often. Practice leads to persistence. When our own urges and cultural messages point us toward arrogance, it can be hard to willingly choose humility, to resist the temptation to brag or respond defensively to criticism, or to think of others when we feel underappreciated. Just like going for a morning walk or carving out time for meditation can become habitual, cultivating self-awareness, checking our ego, and thinking of others will become second nature. But we won't get there quickly, without the effort or right motivation. So, it's important to ensure we have (a) a healthy *motivation* for why we're developing humility, (b) consistent *practice* at trying to be humbler, and (c) persistent *patience* as we try (and occasionally fail) to live more humbly.

The Self-Control—Humility Loop

Humility and self-control might be mutually reinforcing. The research on shrinking our ego and developing self-regulation suggests that as we practice more self-regulation, we develop greater humility, which in turn can help facilitate better self-control. It's as though there is a positive loop of humble self-control—not only can self-regulation help us do the hard work of humility, but humility can help us do hard things in the future.

In one set of experimental studies, people were randomly assigned to a humility condition, recalling a time when they felt humble, or a neutral condition, recalling a mundane activity. They were then tested on a range of tasks requiring self-control. The results were striking: Participants in the humility group persisted longer on a strenuous handgrip exercise, were less likely to consume M&M's (and ate significantly fewer) left out by the researchers, and continued to solve difficult cognitive problems longer than participants in the neutral group.[12] Reminding people of their own humility causes them to act with greater self-control in the future.

Other work has examined the link—and benefits—between self-control and humility in the real world. Researchers found that humility predicted less substance use over time in a sample of college students, as well as less substance use among those arrested on drug-related charges in a prison facility.[13] Another study found a positive link between humility and self-control on leadership outcomes among a sample of more than two hundred US Air Force officers: Only when these leaders exhibited self-control did the positive effects of humility translate to more ethical leadership, better performance, and greater overall flourishing.[14]

Putting It into Practice

You may be wondering what is there for you to learn from all of this research, and how to put it into practice. Here are some tangible steps. To start, let's think of the three pillars of self-enhancement (standards, monitoring, and strength) and how we can align an intention to cultivate humility with these areas. First, think about your standards:

- How do you want humility to look in your life?
- What are some of the behavioral indicators of a humble life that you want to embody?
- How do you desire to respond to criticism or receive feedback?
- What would it look like to know yourself better?
- How can you think of others more considerately or empathically?

We've discussed these in detail in previous chapters, so you might find it helpful to make a list with three columns, one for each of the dimensions of humility: knowing yourself, checking yourself, and going beyond yourself. Under each heading, jot down a few aspirational behaviors you'd like to lean into as you work toward becoming humbler. You can draw these from what we've already covered: You can seek feedback from others, or you might imagine a person who really exemplifies humility whom you'd like to emulate. For example, you might write: "Meet with a friend once a week to seek honest feedback about ways I can grow" (knowing yourself), "Pause and think about someone else's perspective before responding" (checking yourself), or "Consider what someone else might need in a situation" (going beyond yourself). These actions will serve as your standard or goal. Much like trying to complete a marathon in under four hours, this target will help keep you oriented.

Next, think about how you're going to monitor your progress. What regular check-ins will you need? Schedule them into your calendar. Just like you'd make time to run each training day leading up to a race, you need regular checkpoints to assess your progress.

Then, think about how to get appropriate self-improvement feedback. Remember, you might be biased about your own progress; you might think you're doing better than you actually are. When I first started running, I would often think I was running faster than I was; but my watch told me the cold reality. Even if I tried to make an excuse for my time, it would rarely work. The objective feedback offered by my digital companion was grounding. It told me how much progress I had made and how much work was left to do. Similarly, you'll want feedback that is as objective as possible. Asking a wide range of trusted people—friends, family, peers, a partner you trust—and perhaps allowing them to respond anonymously in some cases, can help immensely. When you do this regularly, you can be proud of your improvements, knowing that it's not just people telling you what you want to hear.

Now, remember the importance of strength. Being humble is hard work and can be tiring. But cultivating an intrinsic, *want-to* motivation is key. When you're trying to develop humility because it aligns with your values and you're authentically convinced that it is good and right to do, you'll be much more successful at it than when forcing yourself because you feel like it's something you have to do. In this case, the carrot is much more motivating than the stick. Framing your journey toward humility as seeking the positive, rather than avoiding the negative, will sustain you when your practice of humility becomes challenging. Most runners run because they enjoy doing it. Many could engage in other exercise regimens, or perhaps skip working out altogether, but are intrinsically motivated to run—they choose it because it either aligns with their broader goals and values or because they genuinely like running, not because they feel undue pressure or expectation from others. One of my good friends loves working out at his local gym but doesn't really enjoy running. I love to run but would loathe his gym-based workouts. Aligning your motivation with your behavior can buoy you to do the hard work.

Once you've thought through your aspirational standards, monitoring plan, and building up strength (especially through motivation), practice generously—in many different areas of life: at home, with friends, at work, and when you're by yourself. Remember, developing a humility that lasts should permeate all areas of your life.

Practice over Preaching

This chapter talks a lot about running, but in my life these days, I don't bring it up much—maybe because I know plenty of people who are faster or run farther, or maybe because I've realized that the true joy of running is how it changed me personally, showing me how much I had previously limited myself and how far I could push myself. In the same way, you'll find people who are humbler or have more practice restraining their ego, but don't let that discourage you. Your journey is about how it changes you, not how quickly you get there. Now, I enjoy slowly plodding along, whether I'm training for a race, running with a friend, or just taking in the scenery. I've allowed running to change how I approach life, knowing that hard work is good and produces changes that are worth making. I've been grateful to meet friends who run and share their stories, to be able to move and value my own health. And I've learned that it's more important how I act than what I say. As with running, cultivating humility takes practice and persistence. When you put in the work and train consistently, you will begin to notice changes in your life and reap the benefits of your investment.

PART III

How Humility Can Change Your Life

8

—

Bridging Divides

HUMILITY HAS DIFFERENT TYPES or expressions. We can be humble in relationships, about ideas, or about questions greater than ourselves—and we can be humble about our way of life and how we see the world. This last kind of humility is known as *cultural humility*, which is marked by an openness to other people and their unique cultural perspectives.[1] People tend to assume that their worldview—their cultural lens—is naturally superior to that of others. After all, if we thought we were wrong, we'd change our minds. Instead, we believe that our ways of thinking, feeling, behaving, or relating are the best. Though we might not explicitly state it, it's a commonly held assumption. The problem is that when we encounter a different cultural worldview, it's difficult for us to understand that perspective. We see others' lives through our lenses. People high in cultural humility work against these ingrained biases: They realize that their personal view is not inherently superior to anyone else's and that each person has an equally important and worthy way of seeing the world, and they demonstrate a curiosity to learn and openness to change. They realize that knowing *something* about a person doesn't mean knowing *everything* about them. They invite respectful, collaborative relationships with people offering diverse viewpoints, and work to broaden the circles of inclusion.

Culturally humble people appreciate the unique nuances of different relationships. They are able to check their ego and don't assume that previous interactions with members from a group will seamlessly transfer into a relationship with someone else from that group. Rather than taking a "one-size-fits-all" approach, culturally humble people understand that every person's story and cultural background is nuanced and personalized, and they seek to learn about that specific person. They work hard to combat their own prejudices and are curious to learn from people who see the world differently. In practice, cultural humility enables them to approach people from a different culture or who hold distinct ways of understanding the world with respect and curiosity, seeking to learn from them and appreciate their diversity as a strength.

More than ever before, technology has increased our ability to engage with other people who share our same beliefs and has shaped the news and information we receive based on algorithms determined by our online behavior. For example, people who frequent Fox News will receive more news stories that present conservative perspectives than those who click on articles from CNN and are given more liberal perspectives. Our information consumption has been tailored to our behavioral patterns, as well as to the patterns of those around us. Of the myriad problems posed by this kind of curated media diet is the enhanced likelihood for *group polarization*, which is the tendency for like-minded groups to become more extreme when discussing issues about which they agree.[2] For example, when a group of people get together to discuss why recycling programs are important, these folks may not only learn more arguments that make them more convinced than ever that they are right for holding these beliefs, but they may also adopt a more extreme version of their original position in order to be more distinctive from others—*I want to show my friends that I really care about the environment, so I get even more passionate and feel more strongly about my position.* When people can find groups, online or in person, that share their beliefs, discussions cause them to become more emboldened and extreme in their opinions. The result: The middle ground evaporates, and we're left with two camps on nearly any issue.

Research has documented the extent of our prejudice toward dissimilar groups. We hold strong negative feelings, based on both explicit and implicit reports, toward those who hold different political affiliations.[3] We are prejudiced against people who don't share our religious beliefs, leading us to put down alternative views and attack those who hold them.[4] This pattern is most pronounced when the discrepancy between our beliefs and the beliefs of another is the greatest, largely because we view those who hold opposing views as threatening. One clever study showed how reactive people can be to threats against their worldviews.[5] After reading a passage ostensibly written by someone holding opposing political beliefs that assailed the participants' own ideological convictions, participants were given the opportunity to act aggressively, by doling out hot sauce as part of a separate food-tasting study, after learning that the one who would have to eat it detested spicy food. When feeling threatened, participants allocated more hot sauce as a means of aggression. We think, feel, and act in ways that dehumanize those who aren't like us.

This pattern is troubling but unsurprising. Some of the most consistent findings in the field of social psychology center around *ethnocentrism*, or the preference we hold for our group's identity— whether that's nationality, sex, gender, religion, or politics. Researchers have come up with numerous reasons that this strong prejudice exists. For example, throughout our evolutionary history, groups may have been competing for scarce resources. If my group needs access to food, which is in limited supply, I may develop negative attitudes toward the other group that also wants access to that scarce resource. In the battle between groups, my survival depends on my group prevailing, so, other groups are seen as threats.

Another compelling theory for such intergroup conflict is that our self-esteem is tied closely to our group membership—my group has to be the best because I am a member, and any group that isn't my group is naturally the *other* group, which, by default, must be inferior in some way to my group, as a way of preserving my exaggerated sense of self-esteem. The positioning of my worth, value, or esteem on my standing relative to someone else is precarious; it constantly requires me and my group to assert dominance over other groups to maintain a sense of superiority, which breeds intolerance, prejudice, and hate. It's a recipe for perpetual conflict.

Cultural humility is also about understanding how people's various identities play a role in their lives, including issues of gender, sexual orientation, political allegiance, religious identity, and racial identity, among others. Having this humility includes the confidence to know that these different viewpoints can strengthen relationships, organizations, and communities. When we act out of a place of cultural humility, we can appreciate how diversity enriches society, business, and relationships.

Some research has explored the precursors and outcomes of cultural humility and suggests that it is expressed not only by the three keys of humility—self-awareness, regulating our ego, and being open to and supportive of others—but also by self-reflection and critique.[6] Regularly asking how we can do better will help us become more culturally humble. We can foster cultural humility by diversifying our social circles, being attuned to power imbalances, and engaging in the work of social justice. Putting cultural humility into practice results in mutually respectful and collaborative partnerships. Cultural humility is not something we achieve; it requires constant nurturing and attentiveness to cultivate a continued appreciation for those who differ from us.

In this chapter we'll explore common domains where we can see the importance of cultural humility and how it can help us work toward collaborative relationships in which we've historically seen strife and contempt. We'll take a closer look at several areas in desperate need of an authentically humble response: society, politics, and religion. We'll discuss what the research says and how we can embody a greater degree of cultural humility.

A Few Considerations

Humility is important, and listening is key, but a commitment to cultural humility does not mean abandoning our values or giving up the fight for what is right. Humility is not passivity. Scholars such as Ignacio Martín-Báro[7] and Paulo Friere[8] argue for the importance of liberation in healing social divides and pioneered the study of liberation psychology, which helps people identify the oppressive structures in their social and political world and work to challenge them. Understanding the perspective of others, especially those who have been historically marginalized and oppressed, is critical for seeking to heal some of the deep social wounds in our world. Here, we see that humility is key to this process: Listening to the lived experience and seeking to understand the viewpoints of others are necessary components in this liberatory work. In fact, engaging in active listening can enhance humility.[10]

Humility is central to this process: Recall that a humble response is one in which we see ourselves as the right size. For those with identities or in positions of power and privilege, that likely means reducing your inflated sense of self or perceived superiority to realign with a more accurate view of reality, right-sizing *downward*, in which our common humanity is a unify-ing feature. For those with marginalized or minority identities, that means stepping into the fullness of ourselves, knowing that although culture has told us to shrink or take up less space, we have a security that arises from a confidence in our inherent worth and value that compels us to take up our rightful full space—right-sizing *upward*. And by cultivating self-awareness, we know our worth and hold it with confidence when encountering those who would tell us otherwise.

The work does not stop there. Humility must be coupled with courage and wisdom: courage to continue to seek out and dis-mantle the oppressive structures that are causing these deeply painful social divides, and wisdom to know when and how to assert confidently for the cause of justice and healing. Resis-tance to oppression may not appear to be humble, but it is drawn from the secure conviction of knowing what is right after listen-ing to those who have been marginalized, empathizing with their pain, seeking to understand their perspective, and viewing them as equals: All of this leads us into action. And it arises from the security of knowing our inherent worth and dignity and resisting those who would seek to oppress us by attempting to put us down.

Humility does not require us to abandon our values. A will-ingness to listen does not presume that all viewpoints are equally meritorious or just. Humility enables us to work together to root out racism, sexism, homophobia, transphobia, ableism, and other oppressive prejudices that exclude, "other," and marginalize individuals and groups. Humility does not require that we set aside the fight for belonging and inclusion; rather, it motivates us to act on them. When we see our own self-worth and the worth of others, we can rest in the confidence of knowing that our pursuit of justice and fairness is sufficiently good, even if those around us won't validate our work to bridge divides.

Anchoring Humility

Any discussion about humility—especially cultural humility—must include a discussion of equality. Viewing others as equal is prerequisite to developing humility of any kind. Anyone who views themselves (or their group) as superior, and another person or group as inferior, cannot, by definition, be humble. We must acknowledge and respect the personhood and humanity of every other individual we interact with, even if we strongly disagree with their viewpoint. The problem is that many of us can resort to dehumanizing others as a way of justifying morally reprehensible behavior. We don't talk about people; instead, we talk about "the left" or "the right," or "them" or "the others." Our language betrays our othering, in which we protect ourselves from the full weight of holding despicable beliefs about others. We stop remembering that they are children or parents, siblings or friends, partners or employees—that they are real humans, made of the same stuff as you and me, just as alive and precious and beautiful as we see ourselves. By creating a psychological distance between ourselves and those with whom we disagree, we falsely think we can justify hateful words or hurtful actions.

Part of that psychological distance comes in the form of moral superiority. We think we're right and have the moral standing to hold our ground. At best, we pity them for not knowing what we know and try to convert or persuade them; at worst, we put them down and treat them as subhuman. Whether we're operating from a savior complex or from a place of moral defense, neither approach affirms the humanity and dignity of the other person or group—which is precisely why any effort toward cultural humility must be rooted in the deep belief that we're all inherently equal. And we must live by that belief in our daily lives.

On Society

Culture saturates each aspect of our social world and gives us meaning. It's so ingrained in how we see the world that we often assume our cultural worldview is both *normal* and *correct*, which, by extension, suggests that other views are *abnormal* or *incorrect*. The message is clear: *Their* way is inferior to *our* way. It's an implicit message about their worth as humans—and this message may give way to thoughts, feelings, or actions that convey that they're subhuman and don't deserve the same rights and respect as we do.[11] In turn, we may begin to treat others who are different with anger and fear. And when we dehumanize others, we might try to force them to start seeing the world our way.

True cultural humility is motivated by a genuine desire to respect and learn from others. Some of us may flaunt an inauthentic cultural humility that is expressed as virtue signaling, making sure people see our culturally endorsed values, as a way of building credibility or enhancing our ego without embodying those values in our daily lives. It's the near opposite of humility and is tantamount to narcissism: going out of our way to let everyone know how accepting we are and condemning viewpoints that our culture may find distasteful. Those of us whose humility is inauthentic don't live by the values we have signaled or do the hard work of addressing our implicit biases and prejudices. Virtue signaling commodifies a faux cultural humility, in which our primary motivation is the ego-feeding attention that comes from gaining the approval from the in-group. Posting a tweet or social media story does little to raise the awareness of a hundred or so followers; sometimes it's a way of showcasing values just enough to alleviate the psychological pressure to do any work toward justice and equity. It's a mental trick to reduce cognitive dissonance that is all style and no substance.[12]

Inauthenticity may also look like cultural consumption, in which we think we're appreciating and valuing others, but we're really using them to advance our own agenda or assuage our own guilt. This covert narcissism may seem like respect for others, but it's missing any consideration that our viewpoint is not superior (and is likely flawed) or any attempt to modify our beliefs in any way. When we don't seek feedback from other people or actively try to integrate their perspectives, we stop seeing the worth and inherent dignity of others and implicitly assume that we're better—or, perhaps, that we're doing them a favor, falling into a savior complex. We secretly think that we're so great for helping out the "disadvantaged."

We can tell that behaviors like virtue signaling and cultural consumption are not expressions of humility because they are *transactional*, not relational. Rather than considering the needs of those who are oppressed, such actions fail to appreciate the humanity of other people. They're all about what "I" can get from these exchanges and degrade people into the utility they can provide. And it couldn't be further from humility. Humility is inherently about relationships.

Cultural, Racial, and Ethnic Identity

Both experiencing and acting on cultural, racial, and ethnic prejudice and discrimination often results in traumatic wounds that we carry with us. Author and trauma specialist Resmaa Menakem argues that people—both oppressors and oppressed—hold this racial trauma in their bodies.[13] This trauma changes the ways our brains respond to events and causes us to react reflexively even when our actions elude rational explanation. For example, people who have experienced trauma may act aggressively out of fear even when there is a no justifiable reason to be afraid. When we have embodied trauma, it alters how we process information and make decisions. Likewise, for those whose group has historically been in power, we see how strong a prejudiced reaction might naturally be—and the need for humility to help counteract some of these powerful tendencies. But this personal and collective healing can only happen once we start to do the work. For those of us with cultural privilege, by checking ourselves, we can begin to question our initial impulses to shape our subsequent actions and bring ourselves in greater alignment with our values.

Cultural humility is vital in our relationships with people of different identities. But we often see a lack of cultural humility around race and ethnicity. Although explicit expressions of racism have decreased over the past several decades (though certain parts of the world have seen surges since 2016), implicit prejudice continues to be a problem.[14] This nefarious expression of prejudice—which has many different names, including aversive racism—is a more covert form of racism, in that the person holding these views is often unaware of their motives and would publicly deny any prejudicial attitudes.[15] However, these biased tendencies emerge in ambiguous situations that permit racist actions without culpability. For example, one study had participants compare college applicants and decide which students to admit.[16] Some had a higher grade point average (GPA) and lower standardized test scores, whereas others had higher test scores and a lower GPA. The essays were also modified to signal that some applicants were Black and others White. Participants preferred the White applicant with a higher GPA to the Black applicant with lower GPA (but higher standardized test scores), arguing that GPA is more important. Given the weight of GPA, the Black applicant with high GPA (but lower test scores) should have been chosen, but they were not. In these cases, participants argued that test scores were more important and, again, selected the White applicant. Except when the Black applicant was unanimously strong on all dimensions, White applicants were preferred; participants in the study simply shifted their rationale to appear reasonable rather than racist.

Sadly, implicit racism emerges in a variety of domains, such as in microaggressions—verbal or linguistic slights in which people betray their racist sentiments in ways that undermine the target of their speech. These can range from outright racial slurs (microassaults) to asking a person of color how they got their job (microinsults) or telling a person of color, "I don't 'see race'" (microinvalidations).[17] One study examined microaggressions that occurred in a counseling setting and its effects on the therapeutic relationship. When there was a rupture in the relationship between therapist and client, greater cultural humility led to a greater working relationship and a perception by the client that their situation improved because of counseling. Culturally humble therapists can better navigate such events than more arrogant therapists.

We have to be careful when assessing our own cultural humility. Sometimes, we get it wrong; we often think we're more culturally humble than we are.[18] Seeking feedback from a trusted source, ideally from someone who doesn't share the predominant cultural narrative, can be valuable. Understanding how others actually see us can be sobering and informative—but if we approach it with an eagerness to learn, a willingness to listen, and a desire to change and grow, such feedback will be like gold. If most of our trusted sources of feedback share our cultural identity, we need to seek out authentic relationships with people who are different along various dimensions of identity—people at work, in the neighborhood, or from a shared interest group (such as a book club or hiking group) who might not share our cultural lens. We can be intentional by volunteering at a community center as a way to meet a wider variety of people.

It's important to create space to have open conversations. Research by Robin DiAngelo highlights how White people tend to express *White fragility* when discussing matters of race. That is, White people are often defensive and unwilling to wrestle with the hard truths of how their actions perpetuate racism. They resist discussing the ways that cultural structures have been designed to benefit them and oppress people of color. They often look to others to soothe and comfort them when they feel uncomfortable or guilty for enacting racism. In fact, those in the cultural majority don't often consider culture or cultural identity. They simply assume their way of seeing the world is standard or default; that they're normal or regular, and others are somehow abnormal, divergent, or downright perverse. They signal to others that they haven't considered how their limited perspective is just one way, not *the correct way*, which is rather arrogant. The privilege of unexamined superiority is hard to overcome with meaningless gestures or trite performative signals.

The hard work of cultural humility is coming to terms with the reality that our view is just one of many; had we been born to a different family or in a different part of the world, our entire paradigm would be different. Beginning with this acknowledgement is a good first start, but it's not the totality of the work required to fight for justice, seek healing, and bridge divides. We must listen to the lived experiences of others, including and especially those who have been marginalized. And we must act. Humility enables us to take courageous steps to upend the oppressive systems that only benefit a select few.

Political Identity

We often have difficulty discussing politics with people we disagree with, and there are many reasons for this. We might naturally suppose that we're right and others are wrong, we might fail to appreciate the positive features of other people's beliefs, and we might not see anything wrong with our own viewpoint. In turn, this can cause us to avoid information that runs counter to our deeply held beliefs. A study in which people were surveyed multiple times per day for three days revealed that most people simply avoid sources of information that conflict with their worldviews.[19] We shape our lives and funnel our information in ways that confirm what we already believe. No wonder we're so stubbornly resistant to change and can be so defensive when people offer alternative perspectives.

Honing humility when it comes to discussing politics can help. My colleagues and I looked at *political humility*, especially in the context of threatening information.[20] In the first study, we found that political humility—or the ability to consider alternative viewpoints—was associated with greater openness. In a second study, we gave participants two essays to read: The first was a mixed-evidence essay on abortion, designed to test how they processed ambivalent or mixed information; the second was an essay that assailed American values, which had been previously used to generate worldview defensiveness. Finally, we gathered written responses about the participants' own views. Those who exhibited political humility were able to admit that their political viewpoint had negative features, acknowledged that other viewpoints had positive features, suggested that the mixed-evidence essay was convincing, and reported positive views toward the author of the threatening essay. On the other hand, those who exhibited high political commitment to their views identified few negatives in their own viewpoint, strengthened their attitude after reading the mixed-evidence essay, denied that the ambivalent essay offered conclusive proof, and held negative attitudes toward the author of the threatening essay. Humility, especially in the face of threat, can lead to greater honesty about our own fallible beliefs, a more honest evaluation of evidence, and more positive attitudes toward those who have strongly divergent opinions. Humility is key to finding common ground in political disagreements.

We also examined circumstances in which one person offended another when it came to politics.[21] Participants recalled a time they experienced a political conflict and completed assessments of their own political commitment and humility, as well as the political humility of their offender. They also indicated their level of forgiveness toward this perpetrator, as well as their general level of humility—we wanted to focus in on specific humility around politics, rather than just their general disposition to be humble. The results were telling: political humility, both for the participant and their offender, was associated with greater forgiveness, even accounting for different levels of political commitment. Being humble about politics makes people more likely to forgive and be forgiven following a political conflict. In addition, when political commitment was high, forgiveness was low, except for those high in political humility. This suggests that people can hold their beliefs with conviction as long as they also hold them with humility. Humility is not about a lack of commitment, but rather an openness to new perspectives and the realization that our viewpoint can be limited or wrong.

Religious Identity

Given that most world religions laud humility as a virtue, we might think that practicing religion would elicit some of the humblest responses. In a religious context, encountering people of other religious beliefs might elicit love and acceptance, but it may also provoke pity or mistrust.[22] We often see the most intense defensiveness and unwillingness to change when it comes to the matter of God. One review of the literature suggested a weak relationship between religion/spirituality and humility.[23] In my own work, I asked people to self-rate their own humility, as well as how much they valued humility, and whether they were religious. I found that religious people self-reported being humbler and valuing humility more than nonreligious people, who might have viewed humility more akin to humiliation.[24] One powerful conclusion resulted from asking people to recall a time when they acted humbly but were not humiliated—this reduced aggressiveness following a threat to one's religious views, suggesting the importance of humility. On average, the data aren't there to support that religious people are actually humbler than nonreligious folks; they may just be more familiar with and keen on endorsing the virtue.

Why might religious people value humility so greatly but be no more exceptional at practicing it than nonreligious folks? It's likely because people put so much psychological investment in religion. Given that religions promise to solve the nagging problem of death through the potential of an afterlife, there's simply so much at stake to be right. Who wants to spend several more lifetimes suffering or all of eternity in conscious torment? The promises of religions stack the deck against being open-minded, especially when so many religious views claim epistemic exclusivity—you have to believe one specific way and denounce all other ways of seeing the world. Such an approach might make for a cohesive in-group, but it doesn't foster cultural humility. Rather, it can feed aggression and out-group prejudice. With so much at stake, other commitments become more salient; for example, although humility and love are central to many world religions, under strain and pressure, people may prioritize loyalty and commitment to the group, which makes tolerance and acceptance of other groups difficult to practice.[25] When we perceive a threat from another group, we often cling more strongly to our beliefs and signal to our group that we're loyal and committed. This can make it extremely challenging to appreciate diverse perspectives.

When people *do* demonstrate humility around religion, it can open them up to greater connections with other people. When religious leaders are humble, they are better at their job. One study found that humble religious leaders held more positive attitudes toward psychology—a field that some clergy view as a competing explanatory framework or a useless (if not harmful) inferior version of the truth.[26] When clergy hold negative views toward psychology, it alienates parishioners who attend therapy and harms those who could benefit from therapy—and it can severely limit the ability of pastors to do their jobs well if they ignore a large field of empirically based findings known to improve mental health. Other work has found that considering being part of an ideologically diverse religious small group (such as Bible study) can reduce anticipated feelings of belonging and meaning in life, although this potential cost is mitigated or eliminated among the humbler.[27]

When religious communities are culturally humble, it makes all the difference. One study my colleagues and I conducted looked at how the degree of a religious community's cultural humility affected their LGBTQ+ minorities.[28] To the degree that LGBTQ+ participants reported that their religious community was more culturally humble, they also reported less minority-related stress, which in turn was associated with lower levels of depression and anxiety and greater feelings of belonging. What is even more powerful, these positive associations remained when accounting for the religious community's stance on LGBTQ+ issues (whether it was affirming or non-affirming). When a religious community can hold their beliefs with humility, whatever those beliefs are, the most marginalized in the community feel a greater sense of belonging and report better mental health. Cultural humility can transform a group into being welcoming, with cascading positive effects.

Gender and Sexual Identity

The divide around gender and sexual identity can be deep and charged, often with people on various sides of the conversation holding strong opinions. Researcher Annaliese Singh has argued that liberation psychology practices can also be used in work with gender-nonconforming and transgender clients.[29] Contending that affirmation is a necessary but incomplete start, Singh advocates that therapists address the larger systemic pressures that oppress people who don't conform to heteronormative cultural standards, working collaboratively with their clients for social change. So much of the work that needs to be done is in uncovering and reversing unconscious biases that lead to oppression and cause deep wounds.[30]

This is seen with different types of sexism. A long line of research in social psychology has found consistent evidence for sexism, in which women are viewed and treated as less than men, expressed in two main ways. Hostile sexism is when overt, aggressive statements are made, and benevolent sexism is when people believe that women are fragile and should be protected. Whereas the prevalence of hostile sexism has been largely decreasing, benevolent sexism is pervasive and often explicitly endorsed. The concept of chivalry often upholds benevolently sexist themes, believing that women need men to protect them. To be sure, such beliefs also harm men, as related assumptions include the notion that men are incomplete without women to fulfill their lives. These assumptions often go unchallenged, operating outside the conscious awareness of those who embrace them.

Beyond these binaries, other forms of prejudice and discrimination exist. Those who do not conform to gender stereotypes or hold traditional gender identities (nonbinary, gender-nonconforming, transgender) and those with marginalized sexual orientations (LGBTQ+ individuals) often suffer explicit and implicit bias, including discrimination and violence. Research has found that such hostility is often derived from the belief that the unfamiliar identity or behavior is somehow disgusting, impure, or unnatural.[31] Other research has found that people who have contact with LGBTQ+ people report more positive attitudes toward the community than those who don't, and having a closer relationship strengthens this positive association.[32] In short, getting to know someone with a marginalized gender or sexual identity generates more positive attitudes toward gender or sexual minorities in general. It's easier for people to be prejudiced toward someone they've never met, but understanding the humanity of another person often melts their negative feelings. And perhaps they see that these "others" are normal and lovely, just like they are. But it takes cultural humility to step outside of the predominant way of seeing the world to better engage with people who are different or are marginalized.

Intersecting Identities

People hold multiple identities. Cultivating cultural humility can help us appreciate and embrace people's intersecting identities.[33] Racial and ethnic identities, political identity, religious affiliation, gender identity, and sexual orientation only constitute a few of our potential affiliations. Each of us may hold different combinations, and those particular intersections may be experienced differently for each person. Because culture has been largely attuned to only one set of privileged identities—namely, cisgender, heterosexual, White, male frameworks—people whose identities do not align with this narrow intersection often suffer prejudice and discrimination. Whoever does not fit this specific definition is viewed as inferior and is "othered." Many of us adopt a singular view of favored identities into our worldview without question, but we must challenge this thinking to dismantle the systemic oppression generated from such beliefs. A powerful tool we can use to this end is cultural humility, which drives us to critical evaluation of our own beliefs and prompts change.

Often, an identity becomes salient depending on our context. For example, we may become acutely aware of our gender identity when in spaces largely occupied by those of a different gender. Or perhaps we will notice our racial or ethnic identity when interacting with those of different racial backgrounds. These intersecting identities can also play a role in how we engage others with cultural humility. Each person's identity contributes to their lived experience. If we truly want to listen to others, and if we care about expanding our worldview and not asserting our particular way of engaging the world as superior to others, we need to be aware of the identities of others and affirm them. We share a common humanity, though each person's experience of that humanity looks different. We can build love and inclusion from our common humanity without ignoring or glossing over other identities and the ways they intersect.

To work toward healing in our divided culture, we need to listen to those whose identities are most affected by a given situation. As a White, cisgender male, I can't speak for women or people of color because those are not my identities; how could I know what that lived experience is like? While I can (and should) be an ally for equality, my perspective should not be privileged over that of the people most directly impacted by any event, policy, or change. It is conceited to presume I know what is best for those who are marginalized. The onus of responsibility to listen humbly falls on those who are in positions of power and privilege. We shouldn't speak for those whose lived experiences we have not faced; we must listen and give them the platform to share their stories, seeking to understand their perspective. We need to attune to their emotional experience and, with empathy, consider what it would be like to be them. If we have certain privileges, ask why others shouldn't have the same. Aren't we all deserving of the same equal access? This empathic understanding should lead us to work for change. Here, too, we see that empathy is critical for both the development and expression of humility.

The Role of Ego

What role does ego play in working through difference? Remember, humility involves knowing yourself well enough to own your limitations and admit when you're wrong, as well as realizing that your way of seeing the world is not the only or best way. A healthy ego is good: we need to stand up for ourselves, voice our concerns, and fight for the rights of others. It's important to draw from a deep reservoir of security to do the hard work to make the world more loving and just. A strong sense of moral conviction to fight injustice is necessary to upend the systems of oppression in our world,

It's worth highlighting that cultural injustice often obligates those with marginalized identities to demonstrate the most restraint when engaging in discussions around advocacy and justice. Unfairly, those who are oppressed are often expected to act the most composed. A few years ago, my wife, Sara, co-led a group of people to urge our city to adopt a wide-reaching and fully inclusive nondiscrimination ordinance. This group presented their case to the city council over the course of several meetings spanning more than a year. At each meeting, this group—advocating for inclusion and equality—had to consistently show restraint while the opposing group spewed insults, falsehoods, offensive accusations and faulty data and engaged in bullying. These meetings were difficult, and sometimes traumatic, for those in attendance. Over the course of these meetings, as Sara's group consistently maintained composure and did not respond defensively to the baseless allegations and false claims of the opposition, the city council embraced the ordinance. The motion passed almost unanimously, and the following year, Sara and her co-leaders were awarded our city's Social Justice Award for their work advocating for this ordinance.

It's a cruel injustice that those who are already marginalized need to demonstrate such composure when they are the ones whose lives are most negatively affected by a policy or law. The problem is the overinflated egos of those in power. And this is why the primary responsibility to listen falls onto those with privilege. When we're too convinced that we're right, we stop listening. When we self-aggrandize, we lose our capacity to empathize with others and see their perspective, which gives way to narcissistic bias.

Research has linked narcissism with racism, yet humility and integrity with greater acceptance[34]: This looks like hearing others' perspectives and considering them as valid. One of the most challenging endeavors of maturing into a productive contributor to a fair and equal society is balancing the demands of fighting for causes we know to be right and just while remaining open to the reality that we might be wrong. Sometimes, we can be so convinced we're right that we don't listen to others; but what if our silence gives way to oppression? What if in our quest for humility, we drift into complacency or deference? How do we strike this delicate balance?

A good place to start is to have a diverse set of conversation partners, including those who do not agree with us and hold differing opinions. Next, and perhaps just as critically, is to grant that they are *trying their best*, working from their perspective and their own limited worldview the best way they know how—just as we are. A signal to them that we take their arguments seriously is to listen well. It is also our responsibility to offer the other person a realistic chance to share their perspective in a way that they feel heard and affirmed. We must give ourselves the opportunity to have our mind changed by their evidence and argument by being empathic, willing, and open-minded.

In the end, we might not change our mind. We might conclude that the evidence was insufficient to outweigh our perspective. But if we don't even grant others the space to present an argument, or if in this repeated process across conversations and with different people, we *never* change our mind or revise our beliefs at all, chances are that we're acting arrogantly. We simply cannot be right all the time. I certainly am not. Think of all the things we currently don't know: most of everything about the universe over all of time. Our actual knowledge is so infinitesimally small that our confidence in such knowledge should be held tenuously. In fact, if we're not learning, growing, and changing our opinion, we're either incredibly conceited or have a stunted and homogeneous social group. If we can't remember the last time we changed our mind, that's a red flag that we need to develop humility.

There are tangible benefits of cultural humility. Culturally humble leaders are often better able to lead diverse teams and demonstrate a willingness to learn from everyone on their team.[35] Therapists who are culturally humble have better spiritual and religious competence, a greater ability to work with clients holding a wide range of religious or spiritual beliefs.[36] Developing cultural humility is not only morally admirable and personally beneficial, it can help us be more effective leaders and work better with others.

What Are We So Afraid of?

Disagreeing with other people about our core commitments can expose existential valleys. In some cases, these are more like canyons. At various points, I've introduced the idea that each of us holds on to our cultural worldview as a way of making sense of the world and keeping existential anxiety at bay. We ascribe to a version of reality in which we're making a meaningful and lasting difference that affirms our significance in order to mitigate the potentially overwhelming terror of our own mortality. We seek ways to achieve symbolic immortality by leaving our mark, extending our existence in the memories of those who live beyond us, who can appreciate our contributions and benefit from our discoveries and achievements. And we must believe that this world is not simply a random assortment of meaningless exchanges and chaotic disorganization, leaving our life devoid of purpose or any more inherent worth than that of a sea slug or tire iron. Our worldview does this nicely, which is why we defend it so vigorously.

The problem is that our worldview is simply a bandage covering the deeper wound of our existential concerns. It's meant to relieve our anxiety—but only if we adhere to it and only to the degree that we can keep it intact. So many factors (such as conflicting media information, differing opinions, personal uncertainty) disrupt our cultural worldview that we spend significant mental and emotional energy defending and reassembling it in ways that preserve its integrity—even if that means distorting or denying reality. We work hard to keep these views in place.

A second problem may be even thornier. In the event that we actually do the hard work of revising our cultural worldview—in response to experiences or personal growth, or in light of new information learned from others—we might begin to rest on the idea that now we're truly open-minded. We've arrived. We may pity or even criticize our former self for ever holding those outdated beliefs. The irony is that we'll begin to defend this new worldview with the same ferocity as we did our former belief system. We haven't become any *less defensive*; we've simply changed *what we're defensive about*. Countless times, I've seen people leave a conservative fundamentalist religious upbringing, in which they were dogmatic about excluding people who didn't fit into their belief system, to join an extremely progressive or liberal viewpoint, lauding themselves for tolerance, only to quickly exclude those who don't align with these new beliefs. Before, their motivation was purity and sanctity; now, their motivation is justice and fairness. A quote often attributed to the psychologist William James summarizes it succinctly: "A great many people think they are thinking when they are merely rearranging their prejudices."

So, are we just destined for defensiveness? Is our future one in which our best plan is to adopt the most "tolerant" worldview and hope for the best? I'm doubtful—and actually more *hopeful* than that. I don't think defensiveness is our destiny. Instead, we need to honestly engage with the underlying existential realities that cause us to cling so tightly to our worldview. We have to get to the source of the problem rather than merely alter how we're bandaging it. We must build reliable ways of engaging with these existential realities that do not automatically elicit defensiveness.

Humility can help address the five existential fears of freedom/ groundlessness, isolation, identity, death, and meaninglessness.[37] Starting from a place of security, in which we know that we have inherent worth and dignity, cultivating humility allows us to find our rightful place among the inevitabilities of being human. Freedom or groundlessness refers to the anxiety-provoking feeling of having to make a decision in the absence of a clear direction or in which multiple options can lead to radically different life outcomes. What job should I take? Which partner should I pursue? Where should I live? How should I spend my time? Humbly acknowledging that we're finite, owning our limitations as humans, and realizing that we're not always going to get it right—because there really isn't one right way to do life—can alleviate some of this pressure and reduce anxiety. In the same way, the fear of isolation—in which we realize that we all come into and leave the world alone, and that we're having unique experiences from one another—can cause us to act on our anxiety and respond aggressively or defensively. By admitting that each person's unique perspective is valid, and that we can work to understand and empathize with their experience, we can reduce feelings of isolation. Identity-related concerns emerge when we have to figure out who we are and how to relate to the world. A humble response may be to understand that people grow and change. The realization that death is the only certainty gives rise to considerable dread and can make us particularly defensive. Humbly accepting the fact that we will, indeed, one day perish should help us realize that our time is precious, that we are no more entitled to escape the inevitability of mortality and should spend what time we do have making the world more loving, just, and whole. And finally, the fear of meaninglessness, that life lacks any objective and easily recognizable meaning, can be mollified by humility. Humbly acknowledging that there are things well beyond our understanding and outside of our intellectual capacity to comprehend will help us live with a reality that we cannot neatly explain. The common thread through all these existential concerns is coming to terms with objective reality and beginning to see them as "facts and not fears."[38]

Seeking Cultural Humility

Now that you know how cultural humility can transform your relationships with people who hold different identities or perspectives, here are some tips to make the hard work a bit easier.

- **You will make mistakes.** Change is hard and often slow. It takes continual effort to retrain yourself to escape your predominant perspective and gain a broader appreciation for how you approach the world. Your prevailing worldview has been ingrained in your mind, body, and actions since birth—its grooves are deep. This means that you *will* make mistakes. You're more likely to rely on your default narrative when you're stressed, overwhelmed, distracted, or under threat. So, when mistakes happen and you don't act humbly, take a step back and realize that this is part of the process and commit to doing better. Don't abandon your quest to become more culturally humble because you mess up. And in the same way, understand that others make mistakes as well. Grant them the space to try again— and hold them to that commitment as they move forward—and it will go a long way in developing a more culturally humble society.

- **Progress over perfection.** If I had a mantra for developing cultural humility, it would be "Be better than yesterday." As just discussed, you're going to make mistakes, but that's no excuse for a lack of effort. Each day, stive to be humbler than the day before. Don't get lost in the unattainable quest for perfection, but do demonstrate continual progress. Each day, do better. Set your daily intention to improve how you interact with those who hold different cultural worldviews. Over time, this intention coupled with deliberate work will become more natural and can re-train your cognitive, emotional, and behavioral patterns to reset your default.

- **Don't stop learning.** You can't ever "master" cultural humility (or any feature of humility, for that matter). It's a moving target because culture is evolving. So, to continue making progress, you need to continually learn. One way to ensure that you're broadening your perspective is to listen to a diverse set of voices, drawn from people who represent a wide range of identities and who are telling myriad stories about their lived experiences. Some might find it more comfortable to start by seeking new sources of information from additional news or media channels. Others may want to read books or articles by authors or thinkers of different identities or who embrace different perspectives. Still, perhaps most valuable, is finding people who are already in your life, such as at work or in your community, who are different from you and initiate a genuine relationship; ask them to coffee or invite them on a walk. Reaching out to them will be a good first step. Moving out of your echo chamber and beyond conversation partners who hold your same cultural perspective will change how you see the world.

- **Language is important.** Finally, pay attention to your language. Language is the tool that shapes how you think about and experience the world. It conveys meaning and points toward larger assumptions you hold about yourself, others, and the nature of the world. It's the door you open to the inner workings of the mind and the depths of your emotions. It's how you express your deepest desires and longings, share your vulnerabilities or sadness, and lash out in anger or fear. Language matters. And it matters for those who hear you speak. It can affirm others and convey belonging and inclusion. It can shape shared narratives. It's powerful and worth paying attention to. Be intentional about the language you use and how it can help others feel visible, included, and loved.

Building Bridges

Our deep divides are wounds that we carry in our bodies and that are expressed in our instinctual responses. There's no simple fix to mend the damage caused by so much contempt, hatred, and acrimony. Humility is not a simple life hack that can quickly get society back on track. These problems are complex, and some people fear that they can't be solved. But I believe that humility can slowly transform *us* and, over time, contribute to a healthier society that begins to prioritize the health of its community over being right or seeking power.

Humility works by changing how we engage this broken and beautiful world, altering how we see disagreement or difference as an invitation to learn rather than as a threat we need to defend against. It beckons us to see diversity as a gift, and the panoply of ideas as part of the rich fabric of our community. Life is best lived *together*, which is messy and hard, but also necessary. Seeking cultural humility can help us build the bridges across our existential wounds as a way of ensuring that each member of the community, including the marginalized and most forgotten, are cared for, valued, listened to, respected, and viewed as equals. Without that, we can't start the work of building a more loving and just society.

9

—

Making Progress

M Y DAD TAUGHT ME how to drive when I was sixteen. I had bought the old family heirloom, a 1964 Chevrolet Nova station wagon that sported multiple colors of paint and a rust-colored roof, because it had survived several accidents at the hands of multiple drivers. This car was once the family car, then sold to my brother for the cost of repairs after it broke down somewhere in the New Mexico desert during our move from California to Colorado, and eventually bequeathed to me from my brother for the hefty sum of $1. Of course, my dad later added a $499 "household tax" to that sale price to "teach me a lesson in responsibility," but this thing was a fortress on wheels and worth every penny. With no air conditioning, no power brakes, crank windows, and a radiator that needed more hydration than an endurance athlete, this mobile brick was where I learned to drive.

After being reminded to wear my seat belt and that I couldn't transport more than one friend at time for fear my car would turn into a portable party palace, my dad told me a simple rule for driving: Place your hands at ten and two o'clock. This position on the steering wheel was thought to provide maximal control over the car and ensure safety.

The problem is that old advice is now just plain wrong.

It was fine advice at the time, or perhaps just for my car, which was nearly thirty-five years old. It barely had functioning heat, let alone any safety features. I can't remember if there was a defroster, but it obviously didn't have an airbag. And that's why the advice for ten and two was fine then but terribly unsafe now. Given that all cars now come with airbags, if drivers leave their hands at ten and two and get into an accident, the airbag will launch their hands into their forehead, possibly breaking their thumbs and definitely knocking themselves silly. Instead, driving instructors now tell their students to keep their hands at nine and three o'clock, which allows plenty of room for the airbag to deploy without injuring their hands or face.

It's good advice. Several cars later, in graduate school, still in a cloud of grief after the tragic death of my brother just days prior, I totaled my (newish) car coming home from the university. Distracted with grief, I rear-ended the car in front of me, and the airbag deployed and spared me from serious injury. And my hands were at nine and three and pushed safely to the side. Everyone was fine, and I was grateful that I walked out relatively unscathed.

Life has plenty of "airbag" lessons to teach us if we're willing to learn. But it takes a certain kind of humility—*intellectual humility*—to ensure that we continue to learn as individuals and that societies continue to make progress. When we rely too much on tradition or "the ways things used to be," we fail to grow or adapt to new ways of being in the world. We can stagnate, and sometimes our lack of new information can be dangerous. It's both incredibly fun and terribly frustrating that knowledge is ever evolving and we're constantly learning new and better ways. It means that we'll always be mentally engaged as we tackle new challenges, but it also means that we must be open and willing to learn, rather than bringing dated expertise that's no longer tenable.

The central premise of this chapter is that any progress—personally, organizationally, societally, culturally, globally—requires intellectual humility. If we're so convinced that we're right that it keeps us from learning or growing, we're going to become intellectually dormant and personally stale. Our work will stop being innovative, and our societies will flounder, failing to meet the needs of its citizens. Our organizations will shrink as people leave for communities that can better adapt to the changing landscape of business and technology.

Change doesn't have to be scary. It can be exhilarating and meaningful—and it can save our lives.

Progress Requires Humility

The march toward progress requires humility. You don't have to go very far into history to realize how strongly some people have held beliefs—and even killed others who didn't share their beliefs—that ended up being wrong. Galileo's writings that the earth rotates around the sun, based on Copernicus's theories, were roundly criticized as heretical by the Catholic Church, which sentenced him to house arrest. Certain that such scientific theories were wrong because they contradicted long-standing beliefs about the earth's centrality in the universe based on biblical accounts, the Church persecuted scholars who advanced this view, subjecting them to ridicule and religious punishment. However, as we all learned in grade school, Galileo was right: The earth rotates around the sun. But the prevailing cultural and religious norms were steadfastly committed to the tradition of their beliefs and were unwilling to consider alternative views, even when accompanied by evidence. There was a gross lack of humility.

That's precisely why humility is so important to progress. We need to be able to admit the weaknesses of our views and the limitations of our own perspectives; to consider data and change our mind when strong evidence is provided; to admit when we're wrong and be eager to grow. If we didn't, just think of all the scientific and cultural progress we would have missed, due to sheer arrogance and unrelenting commitment to the status quo.

Research has demonstrated how intellectual humility is related to the acquisition of knowledge.[1] Five different studies paint a picture of how powerful intellectual humility can be: Those who rank high in this humility are more likely to have an accurate perception of how much they know, and those with low intellectual humility are more likely to claim to know what they don't. In addition, this type of humility is associated with greater curiosity, open-mindedness, collaboration, and an intrinsic desire to learn. Intellectual humility may be a pathway to gaining more knowledge.

There are some drawbacks of intellectual humility. Intellectually humble people are more likely to underestimate their cognitive abilities. That is, they might sell themselves short in how smart they are. Certainly, confidence and ambition are often the fuel necessary to drive innovation and accomplishment, but without the grounding of intellectual humility, they can be ruinous. Instead, researchers have recommended a good strategy: balancing confidence and timidity.[2] Intellectual humility—where we rest in the knowledge of what we do know—might be that golden mean.

Recall that humility is an *accurate* assessment of our abilities. It's not shrinking when we're the expert or conflating confidence with expertise. It's knowing what we know, as well as what we don't. And intellectual humility is not being an intellectual pushover or lacking conviction; rather, it's engaging ideas and beliefs with openness and a desire for evidence. This approach has considerable advantages. For example, previous research has found a positive relationship between intellectual humility and cognitive flexibility.[3] The more intellectually humble report greater

willingness to revise beliefs in light of evidence, which is a skill
that can catalyze personal growth as well as social change and
innovation.

As we'll soon see, we can cultivate intellectual humility, but it
starts with an acknowledgement that certain features of how we
think can change. For example, one study found that having people read that intelligence was not fixed and can be changed—
indicating a growth mindset—resulted in increased intellectual
humility, which, in turn, led them to be more respectful of a person they disagreed with and have greater openness to learning
from opposing views.[4] By being reminded that we *can* change, it
helps us become more open to *actually changing* when confronted
with views that differ from or oppose our own. Another study
found that people experiencing relationship security, marked by
a secure attachment style, were more intellectually humble.[5] This
supports the notion that humility springs from security. We must
start from a place of knowing our inherent worth and value—
and being sure that it is not contingent on being right all the
time—in order to become open to different ways of experiencing
and understanding the world.

What Is Intellectual Humility?

Researchers have provided different perspectives about what
constitutes intellectual humility, but current research presents an
interlocking set of characteristics.

- **Intellectually open.** Prior research has found that
  people high in intellectual humility are open to new
  ideas and values.[6] This can look like holding religious
  or spiritual beliefs more tentatively and being more
  tolerant of ambiguity and uncertainty. Conversely,
  they reject dogmatism and refuse to hold beliefs
  rigidly. Others have suggested that intellectual
  openness means encouraging others' viewpoints, being

open to ideas, enjoying diverse perspectives, and exhibiting a lack of defensiveness when in disagreement.[7] Those high in intellectual humility are also more willing to consider opinions that go against their own views.[8] Rather than holding their beliefs with defensiveness and walking through life with a closed mind, they are open to different views and comfortable with the anxiety that comes with not knowing.

- **Curious.** Intellectually humble people are also curious. They desire to know and have a strong need for cognition—that is, they like to think. They enjoy wrestling with topics and want to get to the bottom of ideas.[9] They seek out views that differ from their own and enjoy weighing competing ideas.[10] And their curiosity is rooted in a belief that they could change their mind if the evidence warranted it.[11] They consider ignorance a challenge and are constantly looking for new ways to expand their perspective and beliefs. And they realize the surest way to do this is to look for solid evidence.

- **Realistic.** Intellectual humility requires the security to be aware of and admit our intellectual shortcomings. A key marker of intellectual humility is admitting that our view has weakness and owning those limitations.[12] Intellectually humble people admit that they could be wrong and their beliefs might change.[13] They can acknowledge that they don't know it all, or even know everything about a particular topic. They embrace their inherent restrictions of being human, realize their own biases, and can use that awareness to alter how they approach new ideas and people who hold divergent beliefs.

- **Teachable.** When people are intellectually open, curious, and can acknowledge and own their limitations, they often are quite teachable. They're willing to accept feedback because they seek the truth and can do so nondefensively. They are curious and open-minded and see changing their mind as good. They look forward to the promise of knowing more— and being more accurate—tomorrow than they do and are today. They learn and then alter their behavior accordingly.

Intellectually humble people are less likely to view those who change their minds as "wishy-washy" or "flip-flopping."[14] Because they see the value of aligning their beliefs with data, they don't punish others who change their attitudes when they've encountered sufficient proof. And they're good at determining what makes for a strong argument relative to a weak one. They know quality persuasion when they come across it. They also don't need to get the last word in an argument or act like a know-it-all, and following an offense, they're more likely to offer forgiveness.[15]

In relationships, intellectual humility is on display when admitting we're wrong, revising our beliefs in response to a good argument, avoiding arrogance or superiority when presenting our views, welcoming feedback, being curious about new ideas and alternative viewpoints, and interacting with others who hold different opinions with respect and empathy.

In our current culture, that seems like a tall order. We're often rewarded for doubling down on our views and ignoring (or disparaging) those who disagree. But it's critical to the success of our—or any—society's long-term health. Without intellectual humility, communities and organizations stagnate, miss opportunities for advancement, lag behind on discoveries and technologies, and become entrenched in anachronistic approaches to solving problems that no longer exist while failing to address new ones that surface. Intellectual arrogance is a death knell for progress. Conversely, individuals and organizations that prioritize intellectual humility understand that learning and adapting to new information are key in ever-evolving industries.[16]

When communities can cultivate intellectual humility, they're more likely to experience growth and stimulate the components necessary for discovery and innovation. Sadly, people today are often unwilling to entertain differing opinions. Many of us have become intellectually closed and only to listen to voices that sound like ours, proclaiming messages we believe and arriving at conclusions with which we already agree. But many scholars have suggested that intellectual humility is needed for healthy public discourse,[17] including in colleges and universities.[18] With narcissism on the rise,[19] especially among college-aged adults,[20] the need for intellectual humility has never been greater.

It's important to clarify some important nuances. Intellectual humility is not a lack of conviction or commitment. We can be committed to our beliefs and still be open to rethinking in light of new evidence. We can pursue truth without being arrogant and can speak with others with care and concern. Our desire for growth and curiosity to learn can operate in parallel with our best version of beliefs—knowing that we'll likely revise. Seeing our worldview as a "draft" rather than a final version may help us go a long way.

My colleague David Myers, a true humility exemplar, holds the following two axioms to be true: "There is a God," and "It's not you and it's not me." This conveys intellectual humility because he's committed to two core beliefs, the latter of which affirms that he is neither all-knowing nor all-powerful, that he has plenty to learn. A consummate learner and educator (as well as productive textbook author), David's beliefs are, in his words, "ever reforming" as he continues to learn. He doesn't believe *nothing*; he believes *something* until there's sufficient evidence to believe *something else* new.

Intellectual Humility in Action

Societies need intellectual humility to experience any significant
and lasting advancement: They need the ability to continually
revise their ideas, to avoid becoming stagnated in their beliefs.
However, beliefs are hard to change. Some of my own previous
research has found that people who left their religion still think,
feel, and act in ways that resemble religious individuals—a phenomenon we called *religious residue*.[21] Across four different countries (the United States, the Netherlands, Hong Kong, and New
Zealand), the effect of people's religion persisted even after they
stopped identifying as religious. A similar obstacle has been
found for atheists: Early socialization for nonbelief was negatively
associated with intellectual humility.[22] When people attach
themselves to an idea or belief system that becomes deeply
encoded into their cognitive framework, it is hard to modify. We
get stuck in our patterns of thinking. But these deep grooves run
counter to the need for expansion, curiosity, and innovation.

There is a great need for intellectual humility when it comes to
traditions, many of which have developed as overgeneralized
communal agreements on how to solve a pressing problem and
often carry the wisdom of a foregone time. Before tossing a tradition out the window, we should put it to a two-step test: Is the
problem still pertinent, and for whom was the practice developed? Sometimes, the problem has been solved and no longer
exists, and so the tradition can be modified or discarded. Other
times, the practice was only designed for a select (privileged) few
in society, excluding marginalized members of the community.
For example, we have traditionally said "God bless you" after
someone sneezes, for fear that a sneeze would expel their spirit
and they needed a blessing after losing their divine spark. Of
course, we know this is not the case, rendering the problem obso-
lete. We also realize that not everyone is religious, making this
tradition a bit exclusive (if not offensive to some). To be sure,

broader and more far-reaching traditions might need to be reconsidered beyond a substitution for "Gesundheit."

Revisions to long-held practices must be made with nuance. For example, research has found a negative link between intellectual humility and several religious and spiritual beliefs.[23] However, on closer analysis, *how* these beliefs were held explained the relationship: intellectual humility is inversely related to holding religious beliefs with dogmatic certainty and moral superiority. When beliefs are deeply intertwined with protecting the status quo, they can impede intellectual humility. On the other hand, when people are intellectually humble, they are more willing to change their traditions.[24]

Putting intellectual humility into action also means relying on evidence to make decisions. One study of intellectual humility within politics revealed that humility is associated with greater interest in politics and less motivation to avoid political discussions; that is, intellectually humble people are more likely to want to be engaged in potentially contentious areas of disagreement.[25] Critically, although all participants in the study preferred their own political party to others, intellectually humble folks demonstrated this bias to a lesser degree; they also were less likely to engage in reasoning that supported their own claims when presented with politicized evidence. They sought accuracy over the defense of their own beliefs. Why is this important? Given that future advancements of any significance will likely require buy-in from constituents across the political aisle and stakeholders representing myriad beliefs, intellectual humility enables us to work with others with whom we disagree. It will help us engage in tough discussions and effect positive change for everyone, no matter their political beliefs.

Finally, intellectually humble people seek out new information. Research has found that intellectually humble people pay greater attention to novel information, such as spending more time reading arguments that run counter to one's own views.[26] They are also better at recognizing what they know and what they can learn. Taken together, these studies suggest that intellectual humility can help change society.

How Humility Brings About Change

How might intellectual humility bring about lasting change? After all, don't the loudest voices win and the strongest personalities overpower? How might an even-handed approach that relies on deep curiosity and demands stringent evidence—and might be considerably slower at reaching decisions—be a better decision-making, change-producing strategy? One mini-intervention study looked at an attempt to enhance intellectual humility among a sample of diverse college students by providing a lesson on intellectual humility at the beginning of the five-week course (versus courses that did not).[27] The results were mixed: Participants didn't report being any more intellectually humble at the end of the class, suggesting that increasing intellectual humility is not as simple as just educating people on what it is. However, two things did change over those five weeks: People who participated in the lesson saw their classmates as more intellectually humble. Perhaps learning what intellectual humility is helped people identify it in others; or perhaps there was *some* change that was undetectable to themselves but more apparent to others. In addition, an analysis of students' written arguments revealed that they were more likely to seek compromise when considering situations of cultural conflict.

It might be tempting to think that humility runs counter to ensuring equity and the liberation of oppressed groups. After all, compromise isn't necessarily the stuff needed to fight systemic oppression systems and the persecution of marginalized groups, right? To be sure, dominant groups have often told minority groups to be humble as a way of maintaining their own position of power and controlling resources. However, humility can be seen as a *liberatory virtue*, or a character strength that can lead to liberation. Philosopher Heather Battaly argues this position cogently.[28] She contends that virtues such as humility must be employed with sound judgment and wisdom, which can help people bring about efforts for equality and justice. Those in power can realize and own the limitations of their liberation work (namely, the areas where they are not doing the good work of fighting for justice and falling into traps of assigning blame) and be motivated to liberate others. Those who are oppressed can likewise use humility to anchor necessary courageous acts to disrupt and rebalance the power dynamics, realizing that long-term strategies of arrogance will inevitably lead to a new system of oppression. She also suggests that on its own, humility won't do the trick—only in concert with other virtues, such as courage or justice, can it bring about liberation. Here, we see the critical importance of humility among those in positions of power, as well as among those who are experiencing oppression to balance the necessary resistance required to enact lasting change. Those with privilege cannot leave the work of liberation to those who are oppressed. Humility helps bring about this critical realization so that they can engage in the necessary work of making the world more equitable.

We need to consider our positions of power and privilege. Where do we hold ideological positions of superiority—where our view is prioritized and our voice given more weight? In what domains is our word taken as evidence, without requiring data? Let me be clear: We have liberatory work to do. Until everyone's view is considered as valuable as ours, the system is tilted toward inequity and imbalance. Perennially dominant groups need to listen to historically oppressed or marginalized groups. Intellectual humility can help bring about this necessary correction and usher in lasting change.

The effort required to overturn inequity is great. Inevitably, there will be mistakes and perhaps even egregious offenses. Intellectual humility can also help in this challenging process by eliciting interpersonal forgiveness. One study I collaborated on examined the role of intellectual humility in promoting forgiveness of religious leaders.[29] In two different samples totaling more than four hundred people, we asked participants to recall a time when their religious leader committed an actual offense. They rated how intellectually humble their leader was about their religious beliefs and how much they forgave the leader for the offense. Even when accounting for the hurtfulness of the offense and general humility, an intellectually humble leader elicited greater forgiveness. This effect was more pronounced when the offense was related to an area of strong conviction. When we're intellectually humble, and in visible positions of leadership with a considerable amount at stake, others are more willing to forgive us. They see that we're open to receiving feedback rather than arrogantly holding on to our beliefs. As we seek to improve ourselves in any domain of civic life, we will make mistakes, but being intellectually humble takes some of the sting of out of our missteps.

Intellectual Humility in the Wild

Not only is intellectual humility key in creating lasting change, but it is also critical in education, relationships, and mental health. In education, it helps foster curiosity, teachability, the demand for evidence, and open-mindedness. Without these strengths, it would be hard for students to succeed academically and contribute to society, much less navigate life. According to one philosophical account, humility is designed precisely to help people manage their confidence,[30] a dose of which is necessary in education: Students need to know that they are mastering the material sufficiently enough to put it into practice. However, overconfidence can be detrimental. Recall that humility is about being the *right size*—and intellectual humility can temper over-confidence that skews our view of ourselves.

We can also see intellectual humility in relationships, especially in intellectually vibrant relationships in which both partners share ideas, are willing to explore complex topics, and offer mutual excursions into the landscape of their rich inner lives. For many, this type of disclosure conveys a special type of intimacy. After all, sharing some of our deeply held convictions or even tentative ideas leaves us feeling rather vulnerable. It can be scary to share what we truly think or believe, especially if we desire our partner to see us in a favorable light; at the very least, we might seek validation for our experiences with the world from those we love and with whom we are the closest. Having a partner invalidate our beliefs can be painful and might cause deep ruptures in the relationship. However, when a partner is attentive and responsive, we might be less defensive and more open—in short, more intellectually humble.[31] Sharing our thoughts is less scary when we inhabit a safe space with our partner in which to explore and wrestle with our ideas, including ones that are unformed or tentative. And given that disclosure brings people in relationships closer together, building intellectual humility might lead partners to share more with each other. The loop between intellectual humility and disclosure can strengthen relationships.

There is strength in "unknowing." Some research even suggests the mental health benefits of "unknowing"—a humble detachment from struggles that people cannot explain.[32] When it comes to religion, people hold convictions with a particular kind of zeal. However, some adopt stances that embrace a lack of certainty. For example, people often get stuck in patterns of rumination or repetitive thinking when they cannot solve certain religious paradoxes (such as God's role in suffering, or the existence of evil). Those who can humbly assert that they simply "don't know" reap the benefits of reduced anxiety and more cognitive expansiveness by getting off the carousel of negative thoughts. Admitting our intellectual limitations can be incredibly freeing and psychologically rewarding: We no longer make decisions simply to avoid uncertainty but can explore potentially unknown futures that may be exciting and new.

This played out in my own life when my wife and I moved to a new town, and I was trying to impress a couple with whom we had become friends. Both partners had graduate degrees from prestigious institutions and led intellectually and culturally rich lives. They read voraciously, appreciated art and music, traveled to interesting and exotic locations with regularity, and had a taste for fine food and wine. Around them I felt insecure and intimidated. Early on, in an attempt to appear more erudite and cultured than I am, I would often claim to have heard of a musician or read an author I knew nothing about. In the moment, I thought it saved my embarrassment. But then, I was often confused for the next few minutes while they shared a story or anecdote about that famous person. After doing this a few times, I made a resolution to stop entirely. If they brought up something I didn't know or someone I hadn't heard of, I would just be honest. The first time I tried this new approach, I was terrified. I imagined they would laugh at me, with my admission revealing me to be the uneducated imposter I regularly feared I was. And so, I was blown away with delight when they simply replied, "Oh, you haven't heard of them? You'd love them! Let me get their book for you to borrow." They didn't shame me. They shared with me. I learned from them, and my world expanded. Since then, I've encountered countless authors, musicians, poets, restaurants, trips, games, TV shows, movies, and experiences I would have missed out on had I protected my ego and listened to my shame. Instead, I now have a richer set of experiences because of my honesty. But I had to admit that I didn't know something first.

Building Intellectual Humility

Here are some practical strategies that will help you cultivate intellectual humility.

- **Identify areas where you don't have expertise.** We all have cognitive limitations. An important part of intellectual humility is owning those limitations. A well-worn joke in academia is that when you graduate from college, you're pretty sure of all the things you know. Then, when you go to graduate school, despite your exponential learning on a narrow subject, you begin to realize how much you don't know. In fact, education often helps us see how little we actually know—and not just within academia. I'll be the first to admit that I don't know most things. Take a moment to make a list of things you *do not* know. It can range from particle physics to the intricacies of human anatomy to the nature of the universe or the mating habits of ancient crustaceous sea life. Unless you're a surgeon, you likely don't know how to (successfully) remove someone's spleen. And few people can know much about several different topics. We might develop expertise in one area, but not in *all* areas. The longer the list, the better. Let this serve as a visual reminder of your intellectual limitations.

- **Recall the last time you were wrong.** I know we don't like to dwell on past mistakes. Besides being unpleasant, we don't like to think of ourselves as limited or wrong. But none of us is right all the time. Revisit a time when you were wrong. Think about how you might have been sure that you were right beforehand, and how detrimental it might have been to hold on to the persistent belief that you were right. Keeping that moment fresh in your mind can remind you to pause, challenge your default assumptions, and seek evidence and alternative viewpoints.

- **Think of a time when you changed your mind and life got better.** When you get stuck in an ideological rut, you can forget how valuable changing your mind can be. Sometimes, it's revising your views on sushi (delicious, not scary), but other times, it's something much more substantive, like revising your religious traditions or political beliefs. But this change doesn't mean that your life is now somehow worse. In fact, many people report life being better after making an ideological adjustment. Perhaps they've jettisoned some of their positive illusions, but at least they're more aligned with the empirical evidence offered by a more objective evaluation of the world around them.

- **Read and write (and argue) against yourself.** Think of the last few books you read or consider where you normally get your news. Do most of your sources of information conform to what you already believe? If you're politically conservative and only watching Fox News or liberal and only getting your information from MSNBC, chances are you're not diversifying your information streams. You're exposed to ideologically confirming information. It's easy, it feels good, and it makes intellectual humility incredibly hard. If you really want a more balanced and even-handed ideological approach, you need to intentionally seek out sources that go against what you believe. Read articles from authors who argue against your views, or a critical book review of a book you loved, and do so openly rather than defensively. Seek to engage your empathy and understand the opposite perspective. Another

option is to write against yourself. Consider a position
you hold strongly. Write down how you might be wrong
and the opposing position might be right. In fact, argue
for that opposing view as convincingly as possible. These
practices will help build habits that broaden your
perspective.

Avoiding Pitfalls

Why is intellectual humility so difficult to practice? In addition to
the usual suspects of cognitive biases and the limitations of
self-insight, this form of humility is up against additional forms of
pressure to bolster preexisting beliefs. Last chapter, we discussed
the problem of *group polarization*, in which our original attitude
strengthens through conversations with like-minded others.[33]
This means that the mere act of discussing topics we care about,
when done with people who share our convictions, can leave us
more entrenched in our ways of thinking. We don't become more
open-minded through such conversations, but less. The upshot is
that we should be thoughtful about seeking out people in our life
with whom we disagree, striving for diversity in our social and
professional networks. Although on some level, it might feel easier
or more comfortable to gravitate toward people with whom we
are ideologically similar, it makes it harder to cultivate an openness toward new ideas and diverse perspectives. Crafting ideological echo chambers is an act of arrogance. It signals that we're so
convinced we're right, we only need other people around who
will affirm the superiority of our beliefs.

A second stumbling block is *groupthink*, which pops up when we
are part of a group tasked with making a challenging decision.
Momentum to affirm the group's decision suppresses individual
or dissenting voices,[34] for example, when experiencing time pressure, working under a strong and directive leader, or in our social
media echo chamber. Although members may separately

maintain concerns or may have creative ways of tackling a problem at hand, they hold back their opinions and yield to the group's will. As a result, the group often engages in a cursory and narrow-minded analysis of the situation, which can result in suboptimal decision-making. Groupthink stifles intellectual humility by rewarding compliance with the dominant idea. Those in power often punish dissenters rather than appreciating a diverse perspective that challenges the momentum of the group. To combat this pressure, groups should encourage divergent thoughts, allow people to provide feedback anonymously, allow for "second-chance" voting (that happens anonymously), and welcome outside experts or consultants who are not as entrenched in the group's or organization's "culture" and can see things a bit differently.

A troubling trend that bogs down our quest toward intellectual humility is the desire to uphold the status quo. Cultures tend to develop patterns of behavior that are reinforced and defended over time—even, and perhaps most strongly, by those who do not benefit from its policies.[35] For example, research has shown that people work hard to validate and protect the existing social order. This process of *system justification* is often implicit, and people can begin to internalize the norms of a particular setting into their own identity, even when it makes them worse off. For many of us, we simply like things to be as they've always been. We crave the stability of an unchanging world, even if it is unfair or bad for us. However, if we hear the excuse, "We've never done it that way before," an alarm bell should ring in our head, signaling that new ideas are not welcome and will be met with resistance. We might have even held some of these implicit beliefs or uttered those same words. The problem is that it closes us off to new and perhaps fairer ways of thinking and acting. Our natural tendency is to stagnate and defend larger systems, taking up the mantle for a set of beliefs that doesn't work for everyone and may not even work for us. If we hear that excuse, it should not be a deterrent but rather an acknowledgement that we have our work cut out for us.

So how do we address these three threats of group polarization, groupthink, and system justification? Conquering them all would be a tall order. Rather, I think it's first important to acknowledge that they operate so we can start to identify these patterns in our life. We should consider our social group: Is it exclusively composed of people who think, act, talk, and look like us? Where do we get our news: Do we rely on only one source? How can we add diversity to our social and informational networks? In what ways can we intentionally look to broaden our intellectual world by inviting a range of voices and perspectives? Similarly, when in a group setting, how can we structure it to avoid groupthink and encourage dissent or individual opinions? How can we welcome outside contributions? And how can we encourage new and different ways of doing things that might never have been done before? Can we conceptualize "new" and "different" as potentially positive and transformational rather than threatening and undermining? Perhaps the reason we (or our group) need to solve a particular problem is precisely because we've always done it the same way. We might be relying on a solution to a problem in the past; newer problems require newer solutions. Intellectual humility will help us seek out, and be responsive to, such new approaches.

Balancing Commitment and Curiosity

How do we balance our core commitments while remaining open-minded and curious? In research I conducted on religious beliefs, my colleagues and I proposed a model of the trade-offs of security and growth.[36] On the one hand, people are committed to their beliefs and want certainty. This certainty, which can show in places like religious fundamentalism or political extremism, has significant psychological benefits: It provides clarity and reduces anxiety, and people feel calmer when they have an organized, if not rigid, way of making sense of the world. The downsides are interpersonal: Holding certainty-focused beliefs means that people are generally less tolerant and more prejudiced toward those who differ from them. On the other hand, people who operate from a place of growth can be more focused on open-mindedness. They're willing to change their beliefs and revise their attitudes based on new evidence or conversations with other people. They tend to be more tolerant and willing to learn and grow. But intrapersonally, there are costs: They are more anxious and don't have the clarity or certainty that other more security-focused beliefs give them. So, it seems that security and growth might reside at opposite poles.

However, I believe the relationship is more nuanced. We need security before we can grow. When we're under threat, we experience a sympathetic nervous system response often referred to as "fight, flee, or freeze." We can't grow if we feel like we're under attack. So, we need a measure of security first before we can start exploring new ideas and testing alternative perspectives. Others have similarly argued that self-expansion can only take place once there is sufficient security.[37] Humility—which is rooted in a deep inherent sense of self-worth and value—can offer some of that security, as can identifying core commitments that are relatively nonnegotiable while leaving the rest of our belief structure flexible.[38] Those core axioms (like David Myers's two beliefs) can provide a rough framework for holding security while allowing for a great deal of evolution, growth, and change.

This balancing act is not easy. Chances are, we'll get it wrong at some point, oscillating between too rigid and too flexible. But if we check in with ourselves and are willing to revise our process, we'll keep getting closer to an equilibrium that works: a set of beliefs that provides us security without the toll of closed-mindedness, and that allows us to engage the world with a sense of wonder and eagerness to learn.

Forever Students

I admit that I'm biased in my appreciation for intellectual humility, not because I'm flush with it, but because I'm fortunate enough to work in a collegiate setting, where I am constantly introduced to new ideas, take part in intellectual discussions, and am engaged in the scientific process by testing my ideas empirically. Dozens of peer reviewers who thought my ideas were terrible have rejected my papers, and many more have offered incisive feedback on how to improve the work—all in the name of science. Every professional contribution I've made has been improved by the feedback and suggestions of others who have helped me see the limitations of my work and allowed me to improve my research. Science, like other parts of life, is a team sport, and we have to be able to work together to improve our collective knowledge. But we need to be humble enough to learn, and relearn, based on the best available information. Just like having to retrain ourselves to not hold the steering wheel at ten and two, we can revise our other beliefs and opinions when there's evidence. Otherwise, misinformation can be downright dangerous.

10

—

A Flourishing Community

THE GREEK WORD FOR the good life is *eudaimonia*. Well, technically *eu* means "good" and *daimon* means "spirit"; together they convey well-being, wholeness, or welfare. It represents flourishing. It's not necessarily happiness, which is *hedonia*, but something richer or deeper. It's a quality of life marked by goodness, which contributes to a sense of meaning and purpose. But I tend to think that in the quest between being happy and living a fulfilling life, the latter wins out each time. Happiness is fleeting, and evolution has predisposed us to be increasingly dissatisfied, stuck on what researchers call the hedonic treadmill, when we continually adapt to our new levels of happiness and compare ourselves to others who always seem to have more of what we want. Our happiness erodes, but we can build a meaningful life that lasts—and humility can help us cultivate it. In fact, humility can help us develop flourishing communities.

We've seen the power of humility in facilitating authenticity and wholeness in our lives. We've explored how it may very well help bridge social divides that show up in our various relationships and in civic life. But over time, humility can transform the places we live and those closest to us by helping communities flourish. We can think of the power of humility starting within our own mind, next affecting our close relationships, spreading to the circles of influence we have at work and in our neighborhood, and finally saturating a larger community. Of course, humility is not magic. Simply taking feedback isn't going to solve poverty and hunger or cure disease—per se. But humility is a necessary component of our communal work toward flourishing. How can we see poverty and hunger as a problem without the empathic humility needed to think beyond ourselves and consider how we may play a role in sustaining these injustices? How can we change what we think and adapt to the evidence that is required to make significant breakthroughs in medicine? Perhaps just as powerfully, how can we live a virtuous and good life if the center of our attention resides squarely on ourselves?

The central thrust of this last chapter is this: Humility can make us better people, both inside and out. It helps us become more virtuous and prosocial. It helps us appreciate the good things in our life with a deep sense of gratitude. It allows us to be overwhelmed with awe and the enjoyment of something larger than ourselves. Humility can motivate a set of virtuous responses that transforms us and those around us. And humility can help us craft lives of meaning and significance. So, if we move collectively toward humility, we can see the larger effects of this shift toward experiencing the value and purpose that is found in doing good, seeking justice, and loving others. But don't take my word for it; the science backs me up.

Relational Humility

The type of humility in which going beyond ourselves really shines is *relational humility*—the expression of humility within our close relationships. Often, it is assessed by asking others to rate how humbly we act in three key domains: self-awareness, lack of superiority, and prioritizing the needs of others.[1] By getting feedback from a range of relationships, we can have a textured and more complete view of how humble we are in our interactions with others. After all, what good is it to say that we're humble with others if they don't agree or they see us as arrogant? Moreover, humility helps us check our selfish motives, when we tend to give priority to our own views at the cost of others' and seek praise while shirking blame. It opens us up to a wider set of perspectives from those around us and beckons us to share the praise and accept responsibility. And when we do, we're more likely to think of the needs of others, consider their emotional experience and perspective, and prioritize their well-being. It breaks us out of our singular self-view and allows us to change the lives of those around us.

Transcending the Self

Humility helps us transcend ourselves. Research has found that people high in humility are likely to act in positive, helpful, and generous ways across situations, including when there is no reward.[2] In one study, humble participants gave away more of their monetary endowment in a dictator game. In another behavioral assessment, people were given money and told they could keep all of it for themselves or split it evenly with their study partner. Humble partners gave more. Why might this happen? A different study of more than four hundred participants in China suggests that humble people are more likely to take the perspectives of other people and may be prone to feeling more guilt when they act selfishly or inconsiderately.[3] Humble people are more attuned to others and understand how failing to consider their needs makes them feel; they're more in touch with themselves and others.

Quite a bit of psychological research has linked humility with prosociality (meaning positive interactions with other people that enhance their belonging and acceptance—any behavior that benefits others).[4] Some have argued that humility is a virtue that can explain a variety of positive psychological states.[5] The research is clear: Humility promotes prosocial actions and virtues. The benefits are significant: Humility can unleash a host of prosocial virtues that will improve our life and that of those around us, eventually transforming our communities. Let's examine a few virtues where we might see this power of humility emerge.

Humility improves *forgiveness*. Prior research has found links between humility, empathy, and forgiveness. For example, it takes both empathy to consider an offender's perspective and humility to admit that we're just as fallible as the offender in order to engage in deep and lasting forgiveness.[6] This is particularly important in families, where people regularly (even if inadvertently) offend each other, but they love one another and are committed to maintaining a lasting relationship. Forgiveness helps those ongoing relationships thrive, but humility is needed to facilitate such forgiveness. Other research has shown that not only does humility make us more likely to *forgive others*, but it can also make us easier to be forgiven *by others*. Some of my own research found that people were more likely to forgive humbler partners than less humble partners when under relationship stress.[7] That makes sense: It requires humility to admit when we're wrong and own up to our mistakes. Arrogance and stubborn pride often obstruct true confessions or genuine apologies, but a humble person can admit when they've hurt someone they care about and love.

When this relational humility extends to *sacred relationships*, we also see the benefits. People who were rated as being humble toward the sacred (such as God, spirits, whatever they consider divine) are more likely to be granted forgiveness by those they harmed.[8] When we see our offender as having some form of spiritual or religious humility, we're more likely to grant them forgiveness. Humility is also associated with dimensions of spiritual transcendence: Humble people are more likely to report perceiving a common bond with all of humanity or feeling wholeness in times of prayer or meditation.[9] More specifically, the combination of high humility and high spiritual transcendence often produces relatively high levels of forgiveness. We might imagine that this view of common humanity and a connection to something greater helps people see those who hurt them with compassion, understanding that we're all in this common plight of humanity together.

Humility can also help us become more *grateful*. Gratitude is described as the positive feelings and thoughts we experience when someone bestows a gift or benefit upon us that we didn't seek out.[10] Rather, we received this benefit purely because of the positive intention and motivation of some other person or external factor. Being grateful reflects how we've benefited from the actions of someone or something else. For example, we might feel grateful for a thoughtful card or phone call from a friend, or when someone gives us a compliment. We might experience gratitude for having a job when we know many others are looking for meaningful work. We might feel grateful for our ability to taste our morning coffee, read a book, or simply be alive. Gratitude is related to better well-being.[11] It feels good to reflect on our privileges rather than dwell solely on our burdens.

Research has found that humility and gratitude build on each other. A set of studies found that writing a letter of gratitude increases how humble you feel. And over time in our daily lives, experiencing gratitude predicts humility and vice versa; the authors concluded that the two are mutually reinforcing.[12] Other research has confirmed the relationship between humility and gratitude toward God.[13] Given that humility helps us "right-size" in relation to others and the transcendent, it makes sense that we would experience a deep sense of gratitude for others (and perhaps God, if we're religious) for the positive things we've experienced because of their actions. When we move ourselves out of the center of our own universe, we can see how other people have played such an important role in our successes and triumphs. Humility grants us the perspective—and checks our egoistic tendency toward entitlement—that allows us to see and appreciate these gifts from others. If we mistakenly hold the arrogant belief that we're owed the positive things we have, we'll miss out on the gratitude that comes from acknowledging the roles that others had in making our lives better.

Research is clear that humility is also related to *generosity*. Arrogant people don't often give, not unless they're praised for doing so—they're more concerned with making sure they get what they believe they are rightfully entitled to (which happens to be a larger share than other people). When we believe that we're superior and that, at the end of the day, because there's only so much to go around, we need to take care of ourselves first, we're operating out of a scarcity model. This is a fear-based approach, in which we see everything, from relationships to resources, as depletable: If someone else has something we want, there is less for us. And it conveys a deep sense of insecurity and lack of trust: We simply don't believe our needs will be taken care of unless we act selfishly.

Humble people, on the contrary, have the security to act generously and are often thinking of others. Previous research has shown that humble people donate more money, including to people they haven't met.[14] In one study, humble participants were willing to give money to future research participants they did not know. And this generosity wasn't due to personality, religious observance, or simply acting in socially desirable ways; humility motivated these generous actions. When we are secure in who are, and we believe that we have enough, we can empathically attend to the needs of others and are motivated to give.

We also see this generosity in the form of helpfulness. A set of studies found that humility, assessed both through self-report as well as via implicit measures, predicts greater helpfulness toward others.[15] Here, too, we see the benefit of prioritizing the needs of others and exercising empathy to make their lives better. Humility helps us go beyond ourselves with both our money and time. In addition, humble people are better able to receive kindness from others.[16] Whereas prideful people might feel shame, obligation, or view receiving help as a weakness, humble people feel positive rather than negative emotions after receiving kindness. Humility helps motivate prosocial behavior and allows us to cheerfully be the recipient of such actions.

Finally, humility is associated with *wisdom*. A large-scale study of more than 1,500 adults (middle- and older-aged) revealed a positive relationship between the two virtues.[17] Moreover, there's an interactive effect between the two on life satisfaction. Humble people are more satisfied with their lives, but this relationship is stronger among those who are also wise. The author of the study argued that, given the delicate balance of humility, it may require wisdom to know how to use humility effectively in one's life. Those who have cultivated wisdom can do so in ways that improve their life satisfaction. Other research suggests that there might be a broader set of virtues that is associated with both greater humility and wisdom.[18] That is, people who are more virtuous are both humble and wise. In any case, the two are intimately related.

This resonates with some of the earlier findings we've discussed. When a humble person has an arrogant romantic partner or spouse, it can be ruinous for the relationship, as well as the humble person's mental health. Some people may try to exploit us for being humble. We've also examined the importance of balancing a healthy (though not over-inflated) ego. These nuances are important to ensure that we can embrace humility in ways that improve our life and that of others. Knowing how to navigate these different demands, including when our expression of humility may also require other valuable virtues (such as courage and justice), requires wisdom. Some have suggested that wisdom helps us decide which virtuous response is most appropriate in any given situation; humility is no exception.

The Meaningful Life

Living virtuously can transform communities. Imagine a network of people committed to being more forgiving, grateful, generous, and wise. These people prioritize working through their interpersonal hurts in ways that are healthy and honest, appreciate the gifts they've received from others, give away their time and resources to those who need them, and can balance the demands of deciding how to act virtuously. A community committed to these values, and composed of people who live out these virtues, would flourish, which can mean many different things. I tend to think of flourishing as having moments when life feels meaningful and full; when we're connected with those we love and able to share who we truly are; when we're free to pursue our passions; when each other person in the community is valued, cared for, and listened to; when there's a sense of communal thriving—when we're all healthy, growing, and enjoying the richness of life. A flourishing community is vibrant, interactive, trusting, open, and oriented toward growth. It's a place where people feel safe to be themselves and care deeply about those around them.

Humility not only helps communities flourish—it helps us flourish as well. By unleashing many virtues, humility can make our lives more meaningful. We tend to feel as though life is meaningful when we feel significant and have a purpose.[19] One of the most reliable sources of meaning is our relationships.[20]

Relationships check several boxes: They can help us make sense of this world through another person and give us a sense of significance, and for many, meaning comes through improving life for others (such as by being a teacher or doctor). In the quest for a meaningful life, relationships are perhaps the most critical component.

Virtues improve our relationships. Scholars have highlighted that our moral processes, or how we think about right and wrong, are geared for social interactions and so are inherently social.[21] When we're more forgiving, generous, and helpful, it improves our relationships. Because of this, when we act virtuously, our life feels more meaningful. Some of the research I started in graduate school examined how prosocial behaviors (behaviors intended to benefit or improve the lives of others) can make life more meaningful. In a series of studies I led, we examined the link between people's self-reported altruism (how much they helped people) and their reported meaning in life. Even after accounting for personality and self-esteem, helping was associated with greater meaning in life.[22] Our follow-up experiments dug deeper. In one study, we had some participants write four letters of gratitude, some about their most valuable trait (self-affirmation), and some about four things they planned to do the next week. We measured meaning in life before and after this task and found that participants assigned to write gratitude letters reported the highest levels of meaning after the mini-intervention; higher than the control and slightly higher than the self-affirmation task. Expressing gratitude increases people's perception of meaning in life. In a final study of more than four hundred participants, we found that the link between altruism and meaning in life is mediated by relationship satisfaction. That is, people who are more helpful report being more satisfied with their relationships, which, in turn, is associated with feeling that life is more meaningful.

Other research has supported the link between prosociality and meaning in life. One study found that engaging in prosocial behaviors increases meaning.[23] Other research has highlighted the positive associations of humility, gratitude, and forgiveness with well-being.[24] My dissertation explored how forgiveness might offer the same existential benefits over time: Examining more than one hundred romantic couples over six months, I found that consistently forgiving your partner increases meaning in life.[25] Various strains of research converge on the idea that when we act morally or virtuously—considering and caring for the needs of others—life becomes more meaningful. And a meaningful life is a flourishing life.

The Connected Life

There's another way that humility helps us flourish: It improves our relationships, which give our lives meaning, and in turn combats loneliness, anxiety, and depression. Indeed, the virtuous and flourishing life is a connected life. Research has found that our desire for meaning motivates us to invest in our communities, through such actions as volunteering and donating.[26] In this way, our desire for a flourishing life leads us directly to others. Other research has found that people who have a secure attachment style—marked by the ability to trust others, the willingness to disclose their needs and desires, and a pattern of relying on those around them—are more likely to report greater levels of forgiveness, gratitude, and—critically—humility.[27] People who have others they can trust and rely on often have the security required to act virtuously toward others; they can recover from adversity knowing that they have support. We must start from a place of trust and security in order to fully live a humble and virtuous life.

Humility can radically transform our behavioral motivations. It allows us to shift away from the strong cultural pressure for success and ego enhancement toward a more holistic and loving pursuit of whole and healthy relationships, marked by love, justice, and equality. We can prioritize the well-being of those around us when we have the security of knowing that we're enough and have the courage to stop pursuing hollow praise. We can free ourselves from the fetters of others' approval, which emboldens us to stand up for our convictions and respect others while not sacrificing our message, precisely because our cause is *motivated by the well-being of others*. And that's precisely how humility is incredibly liberating: When our mission is to improve life for others, we can engage in that mission boldly, secure in the reality that what matters more is not the acclaim we get for acting virtuously but rather the change that we're laboring to usher in. We do the hard work precisely because it's good and right to do—even when no one is looking.

Humility is a communal effort. If we want our societies to feel the positive effects of humility, we need to be working together toward this change. Of course, it *begins with us*—to change our relationships and surroundings, we have to put in the work. We can't tell other people to work on their own humility; doing so simply betrays our own arrogance. However, we can desire to work collectively together—in our close relationships, and then in smaller groups, at school and work, and eventually in our neighborhoods—we might see momentum building to create positive spirals of change. We won't always get it right, but we can't do it alone. We need each other to share a similar vision, to encourage one another along the way, and to help each other along when we mess up.

Working collectively toward humility has practical effects. My own research on couples has revealed that couples thrive when both partners are humble, whereas an imbalance can lead to dissatisfaction and stress for the humble partner.[28] And many people are hesitant to act humbly for fear of exploitation. We might be reserved because we think that if we're humble, other arrogant or narcissistic people will take advantage of us—and this fear has some merit. Many parts of the industrialized world have become increasingly individualistic. Larger economic systems, such as capitalism, often reward individual greed and selfish ambition. Shifts away from communal interdependence have given way to people prioritizing their own desires and motivations. In turn, we've also become more isolated and insular, despite its cost to our mental health and well-being. But when we collaboratively work toward humility, we start to upend these currents: We signal to others that authenticity and mutual regard are valued in our relationships; demonstrate that the perspectives and well-being of others matter to us; actively seek feedback, admit when we're wrong, and can change together. The strength of the few can become the power of the many, and we can begin to chart a different course for what we value in our societies and how we treat others. We can affect the world around us.

The Quiet Power of an Ancient Virtue

Despite the negative perceptions some people hold about humility, it's remarkably powerful. Humility has been on the intellectual and moral scene for a while. Philosophers loved talking about it. For example, first-century philosopher Epictetus is attributed to having said, "If anyone tells you that a certain person speaks ill of you, do not make excuses about what is said of you but answer, 'He was ignorant of my other faults, else he would not have mentioned these alone.'" Of course, clergy love humility as well. Seventeenth-century French priest Vincent de Paul contended that "humility is nothing but truth, and pride is nothing but lying." Writers and poets have also lauded the virtue. Maya Angelou is known for having said,

You don't want modesty, you want humility. Humility
comes from inside out. It says, someone was here before me
and I'm here because I've been paid for. I have something
to do and I will do that because I'm paying for someone else
who has yet to come.

Despite all these positive sentiments toward the virtue, humility is
largely underappreciated. Critics suggest that humility is for the
weak—a claim we've seen doesn't hold up to empirical scrutiny.
We've reviewed the evidence that humility improves our personal
well-being, relationships, jobs, and larger societies. It takes considerable strength and security to accept feedback, reduce defensiveness, cultivate empathy, and continue to invest in the long,
hard work of personal change to become humbler. Let's take a
look at what the research has to say about the strength of humility
in child and adolescent development, schools, and religious
settings.

  Humility plays a role in child and adolescent development. One
study found that humility is related to lower aggression among
children: A large longitudinal study of more than 1,200 children in
elementary and middle school revealed that humility was associated with less aggression a year later.[29] Interestingly, aggression
predicted less future humility as well, suggesting a mutual relationship between the two: People who struggle with being humble are
also aggressive, and aggressive folks are more likely to be arrogant.
Other research has examined how humility can explain the link
between negative early life experiences and social behavior. One
study examining nearly 3,000 middle school students from China
found that negative early experiences, such as unpredictability or
negative interactions with a parent, can lower trust and humility,
which, in turn, are associated with less positive behavior toward
others.[30] Experiences that erode trust and security can make it
harder to be humble, which gives way to selfishness.

Humility also strengthens schools. One study surveying more than 300 German students (grades eight to ten) found that humility was positively associated with positive social intentions, such as helping a fellow classmate, and negatively associated with antisocial intentions, such as joining in on bullying, within the school setting.[31] Of note, humility more strongly reduced negative responses than enhancing positive ones within this context; it was especially important to be humble in order to avoid negative antisocial intentions. Given that there is a reactionary asymmetry in which acting aggressively is often punished more severely than acting positively is rewarded—a phenomenon in psychology known as "bad is stronger than good"—it seems relevant that the strength of humility revealed in this one study is keeping students out of trouble. Taken together, these studies on development, both in the school setting and at home, suggest that cultivating humility among children and adolescents is incredibly valuable; it can predict positive outcomes immediately, as well as later in life. It's never too early to start prioritizing humility.

Finally, we see the importance of humility in religious settings. Often a place where humility is taught but where many have experienced a lack of humility, houses of worship stand to gain a lot from developing this ancient virtue. Scholars have noted that although pastors often laud humility, there is a notable degree of narcissism among many church leaders.[32] However, a lack of humility from religious leaders may cause pain or trauma among congregants. Churchgoers might feel deceived or experience abuse at the hands of arrogant leadership, and their complaints or concerns may largely go unnoticed or unaddressed. Given that humility is so important for religious leaders, how might they cultivate it? Recent research suggests five potential pathways for religious leaders to enhance their humility: strengthening relationships with

others (being vulnerable, seeking feedback, asking for accountability), private worship practices (prayer, meditation, reading
scripture), self-reflection (introspection, time in nature),
self-care (rest, exercise), or service (helping others at home or
at church).[33]

It turns out, it's hard to change a congregation's humility.
Some colleagues and I conducted a study in which we tested
an intervention from positive psychology on different church
groups. In order for the churches to agree to participate, we
had to adopt a design that wasn't ideal for social science: We
let churches self-select into the humility treatment group or
the neutral control group. The intervention group had participants work through a sixteen-exercise workbook over the
course of four weeks. We obtained both self- and other-ratings
of the participants' humility before and after the intervention.
Unfortunately, that wasn't sufficient to affect humility, though
it did increase the agreement between self- and other-ratings
of the target's humility. That is, participants did become more
accurate in assessing their own humility thanks to the intervention. But sadly, the intervention didn't make them any
humbler, in their own eyes or in the eyes of other people. This
means that more work needs to be done on humility interventions, both in general and in religious settings.

There have been some positive efforts to formalize a humility intervention. A colleague of mine, Psychologist Caroline
Lavelock, led a project to test the efficacy of a humility intervention workbook.[34] The workbook, which took participants
roughly seven and a half hours to complete over the span of
two weeks, randomly assigned people to the humility workbook or a control condition (where they just filled out the sur-
veys without the intervention). Participants in the intervention
group were instructed to focus on five steps to build humility,
based on the acronym PROVE:

P ick a time when you weren't humble.

R emember the place of your abilities and achievements within the big picture.

O pen yourself and be adaptable.

V alue all things to lower self-focus.

E xamine your limitations and commit to a humble lifestyle.

These five activities helped people know themselves, check themselves, and go beyond themselves. After all, by reflecting on a time when we were humble and acknowledging our limitations, we increase our self-awareness and begin to take responsibility for some of our shortcomings. By opening ourselves up to other perspectives and valuing others, we reduce our preoccupation with ourselves and begin to prioritize the needs of others. And committing to living humbly moving forward, while admitting that we have some limitations that might make this difficult, can help us in the long, hard work of cultivating a humble life.

Two weeks after returning the workbook, participants were surveyed again. We found that over time, the humility intervention increased not only their dispositional humility but also their levels of forgivingness and patience. This valuable intervention study revealed two critical insights: First, humility can be changed with intention over time. Committing oneself to do the work over two weeks began to produce reliable changes. Second, focusing on humility had positive spillover into other virtues, suggesting that humility can be so radically transformative that it contributes to other aspects of developing a flourishing life. When we work to become humbler, a side effect is becoming more virtuous in other areas along the way.

Building Relational Humility

Of course, there are other ways to relational humility beyond my colleague's (freely accessible) workbook.[35] Let's look at other ways to enhance relational humility in your own life:

- **Experience awe.** Previous research has shown that people who regularly experience awe are rated as humbler by others, and experimentally inducing awe led people to behave more humbly.[36] Awe is the feeling of amazement, wonder, or being overwhelmed that you get when you experience or observe something beyond your comprehension. In some cases, you might be in awe of other people, such as when seeing an athlete or musician perform at a high level or an artist create a moving piece of art. Or you may feel awe when you see a profound act of virtue or selflessness, such as witnessing the heroism of someone risking their life to save another's. You might also experience awe when in nature. For example, people often feel a sense of awe and wonder at the Grand Canyon, when peering into a telescope, when surrounded by the ocean, or immersed in an old forest.

- **Nurture gratitude.** You've seen how gratitude and humility are mutually reinforcing. When you're grateful, you're more likely to be humble, and humble people are more grateful. Make a practice out of expressing your gratitude to others and look for ways to share your appreciation. Communicate your thanks to people who have invested in your life. Take time, each day, to consider how life itself is a gift. It may motivate you to use that gift wisely and intentionally. As I mentioned before, in one study, we had participants write short letters of gratitude to three to four people in

their lives who had made a positive difference and for
whom they were thankful. Participants didn't even have
to send the letters to achieve an effect—it was simply the
act of expressing gratitude that was positive. Similarly,
writing the ways that you are grateful, such as in a
journal or through actual letters to those who have
cared for you, can be powerful.

- **Work on relational security.** The research we reviewed
  showed the importance of security in humility.
  Authentic humility comes from a place of feeling secure.
  Part of that security comes from the belief that your
  worth is inherent, and external standards do not dictate
  your value or esteem. But another part of that security
  comes from healthy relationships with other people. You
  need to have people in your life who are honest with you
  and with whom you can be honest; you need equality
  and mutuality in your relationships, and you need
  people around who will support you. Humility is hard
  work, and knowing you have people to rely on during
  adversity or when you struggle is key. Investing in
  creating healthy relationships, and instituting clear
  boundaries, can help create space for humility to grow.

- **Find a humility role model.** Social psychologists know
  how powerful role models can be for motivating
  behavior. You may hold certain people in high esteem
  for characteristics you'd like to emulate, and you can
  begin to shape your behavior in ways that line up with
  theirs. Think of someone in your life who demonstrates
  the rich and authentic humility you'd like to emulate. It
  might be that this person is a relative stranger, someone
  whose humility is inspiring but whom you don't know
  well. In such cases, you might take note of how they
  carry themselves and respond in stressful situations in

which an egoistic response would be typical. Keeping
them in mind as someone to imitate could help you
begin to shape your life and relationships with a clear
picture of humility. Or you might know this person well
and gain greater insight into and appreciation of their
humble behavior. You can develop a closer relationship
with this person and be honest about your desire to
pursue humility. Ask them if they would be willing to
mentor you about cultivating humility in your own life.
They may defer or react with surprise when you
mention how humbly you perceive them. And even if
they decline to provide mentorship, spending time with
those who are humbler will begin to shape how you
respond in similar situations. After all, a good start to
the journey of humility is to admit that you'll need a bit
of help along the way.

Flourishing Together

Our cultures often prioritize selling cheap and quick happiness.
If we simply buy the right product, look a certain way, or have
enough success in one area of our lives, we're told that we'll be
happy. But an authentically meaningful life looks different. We
see the power of cultural humility in helping us build bridges
across our social divides to appreciate and value those who are
different from us. We understand the value of intellectual humility in admitting what we don't know and remaining curious and
teachable as a path to growth and progress. And we know the
importance of relational humility in improving our communities
and enhancing our relationships. Genuine flourishing is a state of
enduring well-being in which we and those around us are
engaged in the good work of improving our collective wholeness,
where we build a community in which each of us belong and are
valued. It's a life in which we commit to doing well by doing

good—engaging in virtuous behaviors and connecting with others beyond ourselves. Humility helps us transcend our selfish quest toward momentary happiness for the nobler pursuit of communal flourishing, where the needs of every member in society is valued. Humility will help us break free from the trappings of a narcissistic world and find freedom in the pursuit of what really matters.

Conclusion

If I'm honest, at times I struggle to move humility from an academic focus of research to a virtue I embody in each area of life. I'm human, and my drive for selfishness, like everyone's, is strong and evolutionarily rewarded. But my desire to live more humbly is not merely based on scientific proof; rather, I have had experiences that made it clear to me that humility is the only *reasonable* response to being alive. As humans, we are social animals with the capacity to wrestle with big existential questions—and sometimes this wrestling leads us to a greater sense of humility.

I experienced the importance of humility in a deep and profound way on a trip to Iceland. Sara and I booked a three-day trip to see the northern lights, which she had always wanted to see. Having done extensive research prior to our trip, Sara found several online resources for tracking the best locations and times to view the lights based on the current conditions. During dinner on our first day, she shared that her predictions revealed that that very night was our best and likely only chance to view the aurora borealis. The peak visibility was around 2:00 AM, about an hour outside of Reykjavik, where we were staying.

At first, I balked. I was jet-lagged and exhausted after not sleeping more than thirty minutes on our overnight flight, which had arrived pre-dawn that morning. We'd been up for nearly thirty-six hours already, save the half-hour nap on the plane and another twenty minutes of rest parked safely on the side of the road after I almost fell asleep driving to a glacier. Plus, I was training for another marathon and was planning a long run in the morning to see the city before our day of adventure. I wanted to rest up.

After plenty of complaining, I finally listened and changed my mind. Sara convinced me that this might be our only shot at ever seeing this natural marvel. After dinner, we headed to bed, setting the alarm for shortly after midnight. A few minutes after our alarm woke us, we were in the car heading away from the glow of the city. A little before 2:00 AM, we pulled into an unmarked parking lot off the highway that aligned with the GPS coordinates Sara had found. There was one other car nearby, also holding two bleary-eyed and exhausted travelers. We stood around scanning the sky for almost an hour, nearly ready to give up.

Suddenly, the northern lights opened and swirled around us. It felt as though we were going to be swallowed by the changing, swirling sky as we were engulfed by green, blue, purple, and yellow bands of changing light. At one point, it seemed as though the heavens would engulf us entirely. It was almost too beautiful and majestic to comprehend, and I had never felt smaller, more afraid, and simultaneously at peace. Neither of us could speak; we were both brought to tears. It was the closest I had ever felt to something transcendent and larger than myself.

I felt small—appropriately small—in the scope of the universe. This experience carried on for nearly forty-five minutes as we stood in silence in the cold night. We didn't talk much on the drive back to our room either, but it left me feeling profoundly changed, deeply humbled, and extremely grateful.

I started this book talking about how humility is, in part, about being the *right size*. Sometimes, and in some scales, that size is rather small. I'm not suggesting that we shrink in relation to other people or cower at stronger or louder voices. But when our reference is grander in scope, we can't help but resonate with feeling small. Sometimes, being little is a great relief. It offers us *existential* humility.

A Final Reminder

We humans share an uncomfortable reality: Evolution has gifted us sophisticated brains that grant superior intelligence relative to other animals, including the capability for self-awareness and the ability to think symbolically. This means that we're smart enough to solve complex evolutionary problems, but we're also burdened with knowing that one day we're going to die.[1] Our finitude is the only certainty in an otherwise uncertain world, and we're constantly reminded of our mortality through grief and loss, whether from large-scale atrocities or saying goodbye to a family pet. We're reminded that we're destined to perish, and this reminder can be rather humbling.

We've discussed how each of us is offered competing cultural narratives for how to live the most meaningful life—all of which are couched within a broader context of narcissism. In our consumerist culture, we are oriented toward making the most money possible so that we can buy the most stuff possible, with the hopes that one such purchase might imbue our life with the worth and significance we so desperately crave. We are sold the myth that with a large-enough house, enough material possessions, or a certain number in our bank account or stock portfolio, we will finally matter. We mindlessly agree to becoming a cog in a grand capitalistic wheel in the larger service of creating "more," regardless of the human cost or environmental degradation. In doing so, we risk forfeiting our lives for the relentless pursuit of more, only to find that this endeavor is a fool's errand: In the competitive game of materialism, there are no winners.

Similarly, narcissistic success begs our time be spent climbing—whether toward the top, up a corporate ladder, or over other people—all in the name of notoriety and pride. We seek significance through admiration, status, and respect. We console ourselves that our peers might not like us, but at least they'll respect us. We often embody an inexhaustible drive for greater accomplishment, regardless the cost. We resign ourselves to never settling, which looks more like never being settled, and embracing discontent in the service of constant striving. Here it is often too late before we realize that all of this climbing has been in vain, because, as Franciscan priest Richard Rohr argues: All along, our ladder was leaning against the wrong house. We missed the point of our strivings and have invested our time and energy in the fleeting, vapid pursuits of shallow accolades and meaningless praise. After all, who has ever, on their deathbed, looked back and said, "I wish I had spent more time working"?

Perhaps a more pernicious trap is the allure of piety, a misplaced conviction in your own righteousness that looks like religion but lacks the compassion or courage of an embodied relationship with the divine, or the humility or empathy of true community with others. It's a feigned imposter of a true well-spring of meaning. And piety need not be relegated to religion: Each of us serves a god of our choosing—work, politics, nationalism, money, fame, safety, security, comfort. And when ideology becomes our god, we offer our time and allegiance as dutiful sacrifices. We convince ourselves that our motives are noble and our intentions pure; we surround ourselves with people who share the same beliefs and scoff at those who differ from us. We draw increasingly narrow circles and are unwilling to engage with those with whom we disagree. Our worlds shrink. We forget how to listen. And we convince ourselves that we're right and others are wrong. Let us beware of self-assurance. We must realize that whenever we feel as though we know something completely, it is a warning sign; we must be vigilant to resist closed-mindedness, work to remain open, listen to others, and continue learning.

All these cultural myths that promise meaning but never deliver are couched in the biggest lie of them all: There will always be more time. Like a procrastinator's trusty assurance, we soothe ourselves with the illusion that our life will span endlessly, and one day we can get around to doing good, giving back, fighting for justice, standing up for the oppressed, taking that trip, telling that person we love them, enjoying that sunset, or soaking up a golden-splashed afternoon by the water. We assume we'll have time to course-correct, begin living intentionally in five, ten, twenty years. We'll get around to it—eventually. But these are bets on an unguaranteed future, and as life progresses, the days get long but the years get short. Time accelerates.

With our limited time, we get to decide how we live—where we spend our time, in whose lives we invest, and in what ways we have labored to make this beautiful and terrible world more loving, more just, more compassionate, more free, more authentic, and more whole. We need to ask ourselves: What part have we played in bringing healing into this world?

Let us expose these cultural myths of meaning for what they are: inauthentic imposters attempting to offer us what only a genuine engagement with the world can provide. No amount of money will grant us any more value than we already inherently possess. *You are already enough.* No position, title, degree, or achievement will affirm our dignity or lend us approval we already have. *You are already worthy.* No misplaced righteous conviction that alienates others and refuses to change or grow can offer the deep meaning that we crave. *You are already loved.*

Humility can help us make the most of the time we have in life. We've seen how it can help transform our relationships—weaving meaning into our lives, as other people are often the source of our most significant moments. But too often, we fail to love others authentically. When we operate out of insecurity, we fear being rejected—or perhaps truly known and rejected—so we hide the true parts of ourselves. We fail to be authentic with others, staying on the surface, where it is safe. But it is precisely in the moments when we can truly be ourselves that another person can see us for who we are and love us deeply. Of course, authenticity is risky and can hurt, but it also opens the door for true and deep love. And we ought not take that deep love for granted; we must cultivate it, prioritize it, and work at it—constantly.

Humility gives life meaning, in which each moment matters, where we choose love over fear and authenticity over perfection, where we are curious to learn and open to grow, and where we are unafraid of the hard work required to bring about a just future. And when we don't know when our last day will come, humility ensures that we're making the most of each moment, living more authentically and lovingly, and making the lives of others better and richer each day.

Toward a Humility Revolution

The existential reality of our own finitude can embolden us to live authentically and with radical humility. When we understand that our time is limited, it compels us to make the most of the moments we have and reveal the cultural myths of narcissistic trappings as the hollow and unfulfilling distractions that they are. We realize how foolish it would be to spend a life crafted around seeking praise and jockeying for domination over others, just to stroke our overinflated egos. And this realization grants us the *freedom to truly live.*

Humility liberates us from a wholly narcissistic self. There is relief in knowing that we're all imprisoned in this same selfish penitentiary. We all share the same struggle. We are all limited, biased, and saddeningly subjective. But there's beauty in our brokenness, our common humanity. None of us is immune from the gravitational pull of narcissistic self-interest, and because of that, we share a common dilemma. Realizing that we're all flawed should spark just a bit more empathy for one another.

If we truly want a humility revolution—not only in our own lives but in our families, among our friends, at our workplaces, in our communities, and for our world at large—we'll need a dose of existential humility. We need to be comfortable with the realization that the world is not about us and that we occupy but a miniscule place in it. The dreadful awe of realizing that the world existed just fine before we got here and will continue long after we're gone helps us know that our right size—in both time and space—is excruciatingly fleeting and maddeningly small. But no matter how miniscule our time or small our space, we are still meaningful and can make a difference. In fact, because our life is so short, how we spend our time is incredibly significant. We need to build intentionality in our life—and that takes humility.

Our societies are designed to reward self-aggrandizing behavior. It takes intentionality to live differently. To truly live a life that is not all about us requires a humility that goes beyond ourselves. We all need an *existential humility*, in which we can revel in our smallness in the scope of the universe, feel grateful to simply be alive, realize that there are deep and enduring questions about life that we will never solve, and still find peace in the unknowing—to rest in the comfort of knowing that we all share a similar, human fate, and our core fears are shared by all. We're not alone in our angst, our questioning, our uncertainty, or our suffering. And in our smallness, we can begin to develop a gratitude for our life, however short it might be or small it may feel.

An authentic humility provides us with deep and lasting security. Knowing our sense of worth helps us face the big questions with equanimity and resolve—by realizing that we can hold our beliefs tentatively and embrace uncertainty.

Together, we can build humbler communities, but the work starts with us. We can't expect others to be humble if we don't do the hard work first. Once we do, we'll become a role model, inviting others to be humbler. And when we succeed, we will feel the power of humility in our relationships, workplace, and communities. We won't get it right every time, but we can continue to put in the work, expecting to be a little better today than we were yesterday. Let's prioritize humility, together. Let's persevere when it feels daunting and hold on to the hope that humility can help build a world that is more just and loving. Let's commit to being humbler—it's precisely what this world needs right now.

Notes

Introduction

1. N. G. Cuellar, "Humility: A Concept in Cultural Sensitivity," *Journal of Transcultural Nursing* 29, no. 4 (2018): 317.

2. D. R. Van Tongeren et al., "Religious Differences in Reporting and Expressing Humility," *Psychology of Religion and Spirituality* 10 (2018): 174–84.

3. "'Pride': The Word That Went from Vice to Strength," merriam-webster.com.

4. J. Balakrishnan and M. J. Griffiths, "An Exploratory Study of 'Selfitis' and the Development of the Selfitis Behavior Scale," *International Journal of Mental Health Addiction* 16, no. 3 (2018): 722–36.

5. J. S. Mills et al., "'Selfie' Harm: Effects on Mood and Body Image in Young Women," *Body Image* 27 (2018): 86–92.

6. J. M. Twenge and J. D. Foster, "Birth Cohort Increases in Narcissistic Personality Traits Among American College Students, 1982–2009," *Social Psychological and Personality Science* 1, no. 1 (2010): 99–106.

7. J. M. Twenge and W. K. Campbell, *The Narcissism Epidemic: Living in the Age of Entitlement* (New York: Atria, 2010).

8. J. M. Twenge, "The Evidence for Generation Me and Against Generation We," *Emerging Adulthood* 1, no. 1 (2013): 11–16.

9. D. R. Van Tongeren et al., "The Complementarity of Humility Hypothesis: Individual, Relational, and Physiological Effects of Mutually Humble Partners," *Journal of Positive Psychology* 14 (2019): 178–87.

10. M. Haggard et al., "Finding Middle Ground Between Intellectual Arrogance and Intellectual Servility: Development and Assessment of the Limitations-Owning Intellectual Humility Scale," *Personality and Individual Differences* 124 (2018): 184–93.

11. T. Pyszczynski et al., "Why Do People Need Self-Esteem? A Theoretical and Empirical Review," *Psychological Bulletin* 130, no. 3 (2004): 435–68.

12. C. C. Banker and M. R. Leary, "Hypo-Egoic Nonentitlement as a Feature of Humility," *Personality and Social Psychology Bulletin* 46, no. 5 (2020), 738–53.

13. R. D. Goodwin et al., "Trends in Anxiety Among Adults in the United States, 2008–2018: Rapid Increases Among Young Adults," *Journal of Psychiatric Research* 130 (2020): 441–46.

14. Anxiety and Depression Association of America, "Facts and Statistics," adaa.org.

15. J. M. Twenge, *iGen: Why Today's Super-Connected Kids Are Growing Up Less Rebellious, More Tolerant, Less Happy—and Completely Unprepared for Adulthood—and What That Means for the Rest of Us* (New York: Atria, 2017).

16. Mental Health America, "The State of Mental Health in America," mhanational.org.

17. United Nations Department of Economic and Social Affairs, "Mental Health and Development," un.org/development/desa/disabilities.

1 | Awareness and Acceptance

1. K. W. Brown, R. M. Ryan, and J. D. Creswell, "Mindfulness: Theoretical Foundations and Evidence for Its Salutary Effects," *Psychological Inquiry* 18, no. 4 (2007), 211–37.

2. L. Cardaciotto et al., "The Assessment of Present-Moment Awareness and Acceptance: The Philadelphia Mindfulness Scale," *Assessment* 15, no. 2 (2008): 204–23.

3. N. Krause, "Religious Involvement, Humility, and Self-Rated Health," *Social Indicators Research* 98, no. 1 (2010): 23–39.

4. D. R. Van Tongeren et al., "The Complementarity of Humility Hypothesis: Individual, Relational, and Physiological Effects of Mutually Humble Partners," *Journal of Positive Psychology* 14 (2019): 178–87.

5. L. L. Toussaint and J. R. Webb, "The Humble Mind and Body: A Theoretical Model and Review of Evidence Linking Humility to Health and Well-Being," in *Handbook for Humility*, ed. E. L. Worthington Jr., D. E. Davis, and J. N. Hook (New York: Routledge, 2017), 178–91.

6. J. P. Tangney et al., "Are Shame, Guilt, and Embarrassment Distinct Emotions?," *Journal of Personality and Social Psychology* 70, no. 6 (1996): 1256–69.

7. C. Sedikides, L. Gaertner, and Y. Toguchi, "Pancultural Self-Enhancement," *Journal of Personality and Social Psychology* 84 (2003): 60–79.

8. S. J. Heine et al., "Is There a Universal Need for Positive Self-Regard?" *Psychological Review* 106 (1999): 766–94.

9. S. J. Heine, T. Proulx, and K. D. Vohs, "The Meaning Maintenance Model: On the Coherence of Social Motivations," *Personality and Social Psychology Review* 10, no. 2 (2006): 88–110.

10. T. Pyszczynski et al., "Why Do People Need Self-Esteem? A Theoretical and Empirical Review," *Psychological Bulletin* 130, no. 3 (2004), 435–68.

11. S. E. Taylor, "Adjustment to Threatening Events: A Theory of Cognitive Adaptation," *American Psychologist* 38, no. 11 (1983), 1161–73.

12. C. Lee, "Awareness as a First Step Toward Overcoming Implicit Bias," in *Enhancing Justice: Reducing Bias*, ed. S. Redfield (Chicago: American Bar Association, 2017), 289–302.

13. E. Pronin, D. Y. Lin, and L. Ross, "The Bias Blind Spot: Perceptions of Bias in Self Versus Others," *Personality and Social Psychology Bulletin* 28, no. 3 (2002): 369–81.

14. D. R. Van Tongeren and S. A. Showalter Van Tongeren, *The Courage to Suffer: A New Clinical Framework for Life's Greatest Crises* (West Conshohocken, PA: Templeton Foundation Press, 2020).

15. S. A. Deffler, M. R. Leary, and R. H. Hoyle, "Knowing What You Know: Intellectual Humility and Judgments of Recognition Memory," *Personality and Individual Differences* 96 (2016): 255–59.

16. Ibid.

17. D. R. Van Tongeren and J. L. Burnette, "Do You Believe Happiness Can Change? An Investigation of the Relationship Between Happiness Mindsets, Well-Being, and Satisfaction," *Journal of Positive Psychology* 13, no. 2 (2018): 101–9.

18. J. L. Burnette et al., "Mind-Sets Matter: A Meta-Analytic Review of Implicit Theories and Self-Regulation," *Psychological Bulletin* 139, no. 3 (2013): 655–701.

19. J. T. Thurackal, J. Corveleyn, and J. Dezutter, "Personality and Self-Compassion: Exploring Their Relationship in an Indian Context," *European Journal of Mental Health* 11, no. 1–2 (2016): 18.

20. N. Krause et al., "Humility, Stressful Life Events, and Psychological Well-Being: Findings from the Landmark Spirituality and Health Survey," *Journal of Positive Psychology* 11, no. 5 (2016): 499–510.

21. N. Krause and R. D. Hayward, "Humility, Lifetime Trauma, and Change in Religious Doubt Among Older Adults," *Journal of Religion and Health* 51, no. 4 (2012): 1002–16.

2 | Authentic Relationships

1. C. E. Rusbult and P. A. M. Van Lange, "Interdependence Processes," in *Social Psychology: Handbook of Basic Principles*, ed. E. T. Higgins and A. W. Kruglanski (New York: Guilford Press, 1996), 564–96.

2. N. A. Yovetich and C. E. Rusbult, "Accommodative Behaviors in Close Relationships: Exploring Transformation of Motivation," *Journal of Experimental Social Psychology* 30 (1994): 138–64.

3. W. K. Campbell, C. A. Foster, and E. J. Finkel, "Does Self-Love Lead to Love for Others? A Story of Narcissistic Game Playing," *Journal of Personality and Social Psychology* 83, no 2 (2002): 340.

4. G. W. Lewandowski, N. Nardone, and A. J. Raines, "The Role of Self-Concept Clarity in Relationship Quality," *Self and Identity* 9 (2010): 416–33.

5. J. K. Mogilski et al., "The Primacy of Trust Within Romantic Relationships: Evidence from Conjoint Analysis of HEXACO-Derived Personality Profiles," *Evolution and Human Behavior* 40 (2019): 365–74.

6. D. E. Davis et al., "Humility and the Development and Repair of Social Bonds: Two Longitudinal Studies," *Self and Identity* 12 (2013): 58–77.

7. D. R. Van Tongeren, D. E. Davis, and J. N. Hook, "Social Benefits of Humility: Initiating and Maintaining Romantic Relationships," *Journal of Positive Psychology* 9, no. 4 (2014): 313–21.

8. J. E. Farrell et al., "Humility and Relationship Outcomes in Couples: The Mediating Role of Commitment," *Couple and Family Psychology: Research and Practice* 4, no. 1 (2015): 14–26.

9. A. S. Peters, W. C. Rowatt, and M. K. Johnson, "Associations Between Dispositional Humility and Social Relationship Quality," *Psychology* 2, no. 3 (2011): 155–61.

10. Farrell et al., "Humility and Relationship Outcomes in Couples."

11. C. Dwiwardani et al., "Spelling HUMBLE with U and ME: The Role of Perceived Humility in Intimate Partner Relationships," *Journal of Positive Psychology* 13, no. 5 (2018): 449–59.

12. Van Tongeren, Davis, and Hook, "Social Benefits of Humility."

13. C. J. Holden et al., "Personality Features and Mate Retention Strategies: Honesty–Humility and the Willingness to Manipulate, Deceive, and Exploit Romantic Partners," *Personality and Individual Differences* 57 (2014): 31–36.

14. R. F. Baumeister and M. R. Leary, "The Need to Belong: Desire for Interpersonal Attachments as a Fundamental Human Motivation," *Psychological Bulletin* 117, no. 3 (1995): 497–529.

15. I. D. Yalom, *Existential Psychotherapy* (New York: Basic Books, 1980).

16. J. Maltby et al., "The Position of Authenticity Within Extant Models of Personality," *Personality and Individual Differences* 52, no. 3 (2012): 269–73.

17. Davis et al., "Humility and the Development and Repair of Social Bonds."

18. S. E. McElroy-Heltzel et al., "Cultural Humility: Pilot Study Testing the Social Bonds Hypothesis in Interethnic Couples," *Journal of Counseling Psychology* 65, no. 4 (2018), 531–37.

19. Van Tongeren, Davis, and Hook, "Social Benefits of Humility."

20. Davis et al., "Humility and the Development and Repair of Social Bonds."

21. C. A. Bell and F. D. Fincham, "Humility, Forgiveness, and Emerging Adult Female Romantic Relationships," *Journal of Marital and Family Therapy* 45, no. 1 (2019): 149–60.

22. M. N. Pham et al., "Dishonest Individuals Request More Frequent Mate Retention from Friends," *Personal Relationships* 24, no. 1 (2017): 102–13.

23. F. Wang, K. J. Edwards, and P. C. Hill, "Humility as a Relational Virtue: Establishing Trust, Empowering Repair, and Building Marital Well-Being," *Journal of Psychology and Christianity* 36, no. 2 (2017): 168–79.

24. D. R. Van Tongeren et al., "The Complementarity of Humility Hypothesis: Individual, Relational, and Physiological Effects of Mutually Humble Partners," *Journal of Positive Psychology* 14, no. 2 (2019): 178–87.

25. J. S. Ripley et al., "Perceived Partner Humility Predicts Subjective Stress During Transition to Parenthood," *Couple and Family Psychology: Research and Practice* 5 (2016): 157–67.

26. C. A. Reid et al., "Actor-Partner Interdependence of Humility and Relationship Quality Among Couples," *Journal of Positive Psychology* 13 (2018): 122–32.

27. J. L. Burnette et al., "Forgiveness Results from Integrating Information About Relationship Value and Exploitation Risk," *Personality and Social Psychology Bulletin* 38 (2012): 345–56.

3 | Ambition and Achievement

1. C. Caldwell, R. Ichiho, and V. Anderson, "Understanding Level 5 Leaders: The Ethical Perspectives of Leadership Humility," *Journal of Management Development* 36 (2017): 724–32.

2. M. Frostenson, "Humility in Business: A Contextual Approach," *Journal of Business Ethics* 138, no. 1 (2016): 91–102.

3. A. Argandona, "Humility in Management," *Journal of Business Ethics* 132, no. 1 (2015): 63–71.

4. D. Vera, and A. Rodriguez-Lopez, "Strategic Virtues: Humility as a Source of Competitive Advantage," *Organizational Dynamics* 33, no. 4 (2004): 393–408.

5. M. Sousa and D. van Dierendonck, "Servant Leadership and the Effect of the Interaction Between Humility, Action, and Hierarchical Power on Follower Engagement," *Journal of Business Ethics* 141, no. 1 (2017): 13–25.

6. K. Breevaart and R. E. de Vries, "Supervisor's HEXACO Personality Traits and Subordinate Perceptions of Abusive Supervision," *Leadership Quarterly* 28, no. 5 (2017): 691–700.

7. C.-W. Jeung and H. J. Yoon, "Leader Humility and Psychological Empowerment: Investigating Contingencies," *Journal of Managerial Psychology* 31, no. 7 (2016): 1122–36.

8. A. J. Barends, R. E. de Vries, and M. van Vugt, "Power Influences the Expression of Honesty-Humility: The Power-Exploitation Affordances Hypothesis," *Journal of Research in Personality* 82 (2019): 1–14.

9. R. Nielsen, J. A. Marrone, and H. S. Slay, "A New Look at Humility: Exploring the Humility Concept and Its Role in Socialized Charismatic Leadership," *Journal of Leadership and Organizational Studies* 17, no. 1 (2010): 33–43.

10. P. Liborius, "What Does Leaders' Character Add to Transformational Leadership?," *Journal of Psychology* 151, no. 3 (2017): 299–320.

11. X. Li et al., "Leader Humility and Employee Voice: The Role of Employees' Regulatory Focus and Voice-Role Conception," *Social Behavior and Personality: An International Journal* 47, no. 6 (2019): 1–12.

12. X. Lin et al., "Why and When Employees Like to Speak Up More Under Humble Leaders? The Roles of Personal Sense of Power and Power Distance," *Journal of Business Ethics* 158. No. 4 (2019): 937–50.

13. Y. Chen et al., "Can Leader 'Humility' Spark Employee 'Proactivity'? The Mediating Role of Psychological Empowerment," *Leadership and Organization Development Journal* 39 (2018): 326–39.

14. L. R. Shannonhouse et al., "The Behaviors, Benefits, and Barriers of Humanitarian Aid Leader Humility," *Journal of Psychology and Theology* 47, no. 3 (2019): 143–59.

15. A. Rego and A. V. Simpson, "The Perceived Impact of Leaders' Humility on Team Effectiveness: An Empirical Study," *Journal of Business Ethics* 148, no. 1 (2018): 205–18.

16. M. P. Trinh, "Overcoming the Shadow of Expertise: How Humility and Learning Goal Orientation Help Knowledge Leaders Become More Flexible," *Frontiers in Psychology* 10 (2019): 2505.

17. L. Wang et al., "Exploring the Affective Impact, Boundary Conditions, and Antecedents of Leader Humility," *Journal of Applied Psychology* 103, no. 9 (2018): 1019–38.

18. B. P. Owens, M. D. Johnson, and T. R. Mitchell, "Expressed Humility in Organizations: Implications for Performance, Teams, and Leadership," *Organization Science* 24, no. 5 (2013): 1517–38.

19. A. Y. Ou, D. A. Waldman, and S. J. Peterson, "Do Humble CEOs Matter? An Examination of CEO Humility and Firm Outcomes," *Journal of Management* 44, no. 3 (2018): 1147–73.

20. C.-Y. Chiu, B. P. Owens, and P. E. Tesluk, "Initiating and Utilizing Shared Leadership in Teams: The Role of Leader Humility, Team Proactive Personality, and Team Performance Capability," *Journal of Applied Psychology* 101, no. 12 (2016): 1705–20.

21. B. Oc et al., "Humility Breeds Authenticity: How Authentic Leader Humility Shapes Follower Vulnerability and Felt Authenticity," *Organizational Behavior and Human Decision Processes* 158 (2020): 112–25.

22. J. S. Bourdage, J. Wiltshire, and K. Lee, "Personality and Workplace Impression Management: Correlates and Implications," *Journal of Applied Psychology* 100, no. 2 (2015): 537–46.

23. J. Yang, W. Zhang, and X. Chen, "Why Do Leaders Express Humility and How Does This Matter: A Rational Choice Perspective," *Frontiers in Psychology* 10 (2019): 1925.

24. D. R. Van Tongeren et al., "The Financial Appeal of Humility: How Humble Leaders Elicit Greater Monetary Contributions" (unpublished manuscript).

25. F. Zhou, and Y. J. Wu, "How Humble Leadership Fosters Employee Innovation Behavior," *Leadership and Organization Development Journal* 39 (2018): 375–87.

26. Y. Wang, J. Liu, and Y. Zhu, "How Does Humble Leadership Promote Follower Creativity? The Roles of Psychological Capital and Growth Need Strength," *Leadership and Organization Development Journal* 39 (2018): 507–21.

27. J. Hu et al., "Leader Humility and Team Creativity: The Role of Team Information Sharing, Psychological Safety, and Power Distance," *Journal of Applied Psychology* 103, no. 3 (2018): 313–23.

28. S. Liu, L. Chen, and S. Wang, "Modesty Brings Gains: The Effect of Humble Leader Behavior on Team Creativity from a Team Communication Perspective," *Acta Psychologica Sinica* 50, no. 10 (2018): 1159–68.

29. Y. Zhu, S. Zhang, and Y. Shen, "Humble Leadership and Employee Resilience: Exploring the Mediating Mechanism of Work-Related Promotion Focus and Perceived Insider Identity," *Frontiers in Psychology* 10 (2019): 673.

30. J. Wiltshire, J. S. Bourdage, and K. Lee, "Honesty-Humility and Perceptions of Organizational Politics in Predicting Workplace Outcomes," *Journal of Business and Psychology* 29, no. 2 (2014): 235–51.

31. J. Mao et al., "Growing Followers: Exploring the Effects of Leader Humility on Follower Self-Expansion, Self-Efficacy, and Performance," *Journal of Management Studies* 56, no. 2 (2019): 343–71.

32. T. T. Luu, "Can Sales Leaders with Humility Create Adaptive Retail Salespersons?," *Psychology and Marketing* 37, no. 9 (2020): 1292–315.

33. Y. Lee, C. M. Berry, and E. Gonzalez-Mulé, "The Importance of Being Humble: A Meta-Analysis and Incremental Validity Analysis of the Relationship Between Honesty-Humility and Job Performance," *Journal of Applied Psychology* 104, no. 12 (2019): 1535–46.

34. K. N. Walters and D. L. Diab, "Humble Leadership: Implications for Psychological Safety and Follower Engagement," *Journal of Leadership Studies* 10, no. 2 (2016): 7–18.

35. J. Zhong et al., "Can Leader Humility Enhance Employee Wellbeing? The Mediating Role of Employee Humility," *Leadership and Organization Development Journal* 41 (2019): 19–36.

36. A. Rego et al., "How Leader Humility Helps Teams to Be Humbler, Psychologically Stronger, and More Effective: A Moderated Mediation Model," *Leadership Quarterly* 28, no. 5 (2017): 639–58.

37. X. Qin et al., "Humility Harmonized? Exploring Whether and How Leader and Employee Humility (In)congruence Influences Employee Citizenship and Deviance Behaviors," *Journal of Business Ethics* 170, no. 1 (2021): 1–19.

38. H. Zhang et al., "CEO Humility, Narcissism and Firm Innovation: A Paradox Perspective on CEO Traits," *Leadership Quarterly* 28, no. 5 (2017): 585–604.

39. B. P. Owens, A. S. Wallace, and D. A. Waldman, "Leader Narcissism and Follower Outcomes: The Counterbalancing Effect of Leader Humility," *Journal of Applied Psychology* 100, no. 4 (2015): 1203–13.

40. L. Yuan, L. Zhang, and Y. Tu, "When a Leader Is Seen as Too Humble," *Leadership and Organization Development Journal* 39 (2018): 468–81.

41. D. K. Bharanitharan et al., "Seeing Is Not Believing: Leader Humility, Hypocrisy, and Their Impact on Followers' Behaviors," *Leadership Quarterly* 32, no. 2 (2021): 101440.

42. K. Yang et al., "The Dark Side of Expressed Humility for Non-Humble Leaders: A Conservation of Resources Perspective," *Frontiers in Psychology* 10 (2019): 1858.

43. I. Cojuharenco and N. Karelaia, "When Leaders Ask Questions: Can Humility Premiums Buffer the Effects of Competence Penalties?," *Organizational Behavior and Human Decision Processes* 156 (2020): 113–34.

4 | Seeking Feedback

1. J. Crocker and L. E. Park, "The Costly Pursuit of Self-Esteem," *Psychological Bulletin* 130, no. 3 (2004): 392–414.

2. R. S. Nickerson, "Confirmation Bias: A Ubiquitous Phenomenon in Many Guises," *Review of General Psychology* 2, no. 2 (1998): 175–220.

3. K. P. Sentis and E. Burnstein, "Remembering Schema-Consistent Information: Effects of a Balance Schema on Recognition Memory," *Journal of Personality and Social Psychology* 37, no. 12 (1979): 2200–11.

4. A. H. Hastorf and H. Cantril, "They Saw a Game; A Case Study," *Journal of Abnormal and Social Psychology* 49, no. 1 (1954): 129–34.

5. C. Sedikides and M. J. Strube, "Self-Evaluation: To Thine Own Self Be Good, to Thine Own Self Be Sure, to Thine Own Self Be True, and to Thine Own Self Be Better," *Advances in Experimental Social Psychology* 29 (1997): 209–69.

6. C. Sedikides and J. D. Green, "Memory as a Self-Protective Mechanism," *Social and Personality Psychology Compass* 3, no. 6 (2009): 1055–68.

7. C. Sedikides et al., "Mnemic Neglect: Selective Amnesia of One's Faults," *European Review of Social Psychology* 27, no. 1 (2016): 1–62.

8. J. D. Green and C. Sedikides, "Retrieval Selectivity in the Processing of Self-Referent Information: Testing the Boundaries of Self-Protection," *Self and Identity* 3, no. 1 (2004): 69–80.

9. B. Pinter et al., "Self-Protective Memory: Separation/Integration as a Mechanism for Mnemic Neglect," *Social Cognition* 29, no. 5 (2011): 612–24.

10. J. D. Green et al., "Two Sides to Self-Protection: Self-Improvement Strivings and Feedback from Close Relationships Eliminate Mnemic Neglect," *Self and Identity* 8, no. 2–3 (2009): 233–50.

11. C. S. Dweck and E. L. Leggett, "A Social-Cognitive Approach to Motivation and Personality," *Psychological Review* 95, no. 2 (1998): 256–73.

12. J. L. Burnette et al., "Mind-Sets Matter: A Meta-Analytic Review of Implicit Theories and Self-Regulation," *Psychological Bulletin* 139, no. 3 (2013): 655–701.

13. D. R. Van Tongeren and J. L. Burnette, "Do You Believe Happiness Can Change? An Investigation of the Relationship Between Happiness Mindsets, Well-Being, and Satisfaction," *Journal of Positive Psychology* 13, no. 2 (2018): 101–9.

14. J. L. Burnette et al., "Growth Mindsets and Psychological Distress: A Meta-Analysis," *Clinical Psychology Review* 77 (2020): 101816.

15. J. D. Green, B. Pinter, and C. Sedikides, "Mnemic Neglect and Self-Threat: Trait Modifiability Moderates Self-Protection," *European Journal of Social Psychology* 35, no. 2 (2005): 225–35.

16. Green et al., "Two Sides to Self-Protection."

17. J. Crocker and C. T. Wolfe, "Contingencies of Self-Worth," *Psychological Review* 108, no. 3 (2001): 593–623.

18. R. F. Baumeister, L. Smart, and J. M. Boden, "Relation of Threatened Egotism to Violence and Aggression: The Dark Side of High Self-Esteem," *Psychological Review* 103, no. 1 (1996): 5–33.

19. B. J. Bushman and R. F. Baumeister, "Threatened Egotism, Narcissism, Self-Esteem, and Direct and Displaced Aggression: Does Self-Love or Self-Hate Lead to Violence?," *Journal of Personality and Social Psychology* 75, no. 1 (1998): 219–29.

20. B. R. Meagher, "Ecologizing Social Psychology: The Physical Environment as a Necessary Constituent of Social Processes," *Personality and Social Psychology Review* 24, no. 1 (2020): 3–23.

5 | Reducing Defensiveness

1. S. L. Koole, J. Greenberg, and T. Pyszczynski, "Introducing Science to the Psychology of the Soul: Experimental Existential Psychology," *Current Directions in Psychological Science* 15, no. 5 (2006): 212–16.

2. I. D. Yalom, *Existential Psychotherapy* (New York: Basic Books, 1980).

3. T. Pyszczynski, S. Solomon, and J. Greenberg, "Thirty Years of Terror Management Theory: From Genesis to Revelation," in *Advances in Experimental Social Psychology*, vol. 52, ed. J. M. Olsen and M. P. Zanna (New York: Academic Press, 2015), 1–70.

4. T. Pyszczynski et al., "Mortality Salience, Martyrdom, and Military Might: The Great Satan Versus the Axis of Evil," *Personality and Social Psychology Bulletin* 32, no. 4 (2006): 525–37.

5. T. Pyszczynski et al., "Why Do People Need Self-Esteem? A Theoretical and Empirical Review," *Psychological Bulletin* 130, no. 3 (2004): 435–68.

6. S. J. Heine, T. Proulx, and K. D. Vohs, "The Meaning Maintenance Model: On the Coherence of Social Motivations," *Personality and Social Psychology Review* 10, no. 2 (2006): 88–110.

7. F. Martela and M. F. Steger, "The Three Meanings of Meaning in Life: Distinguishing Coherence, Purpose, and Significance," *Journal of Positive Psychology* 11, no. 5 (2016): 531–45.

8. L. S. George and C. L. Park, "Meaning in Life as Comprehension, Purpose, and Mattering: Toward Integration and New Research Questions," *Review of General Psychology* 20, no. 3 (2016): 205–20.

9. C. G. Lord, L. Ross, and M. R. Lepper, "Biased Assimilation and Attitude Polarization: The Effects of Prior Theories on Subsequently Considered Evidence," *Journal of Personality and Social Psychology* 37, no. 11 (1979): 2098–109.

10. L. Festinger, H. W. Riecken, and S. Schachter, *When Prophecy Fails* (Minneapolis: University of Minnesota Press, 1956).

11. D. R. Van Tongeren and J. D. Green, "Combating Meaninglessness: On the Automatic Defense of Meaning," *Personality and Social Psychology Bulletin* 36 (2010): 1372–84.

12. F. Heider, *The Psychology of Interpersonal Relations* (New York: John Wiley & Sons, 1958).

13. A. Waytz, H. E. Hershfield, and D. I. Tamir, "Mental Simulation and Meaning in Life," *Journal of Personality and Social Psychology* 108, no. 2 (2015): 336–55.

14. Yalom, *Existential Psychotherapy*.

15. Heine, Proulx, and Vohs, "The Meaning Maintenance Model."

16. C. M. Steele, "The Psychology of Self-Affirmation: Sustaining the Integrity of the Self," in *Advances in Experimental Social Psychology*, vol. 21, ed. L. Berkowitz (New York: Acadmic Press, 1988), 261–302.

17. B. J. Schmeichel and A. Martens, "Self-Affirmation and Mortality Salience: Affirming Values Reduces Worldview Defense and Death-Thought Accessibility," *Personality and Social Psychology Bulletin* 31, no. 5 (2005): 658–67.

18. D. R. Van Tongeren et al., "A Meaning-Based Approach to Humility: Relationship Affirmation Reduces Cultural Worldview Defense," *Journal of Psychology and Theology* 42 (2014): 62–69.

19. D. Whitcomb et al., "Intellectual Humility: Owning Our Limitations," *Philosophy and Phenomenological Research* 94, no. 3 (2017): 509–39.

20. D. Kahneman, *Thinking, Fast and Slow* (New York: Macmillan, 2011).

21. Heider, *The Psychology of Interpersonal Relations*.

22. J. L. Davis and C. E. Rusbult, "Attitude Alignment in Close Relationships," *Journal of Personality and Social Psychology* 81, no. 1 (2001): 65–84.

23. G. W. Allport, *The Nature of Prejudice* (Reading, MA: Addison-Wesley, 1954).

6 | Building Empathy

1. R. Elliott et al., "Empathy," in *Psychotherapy Relationships That Work*, ed. J. Norcross, 2nd ed. (New York: Oxford University Press, 2011), 132–52.

2. C. N, DeWall and B. J. Bushman, "Social Acceptance and Rejection: The Sweet and the Bitter," *Current Directions in Psychological Science* 20, no. 4 (2011): 256–60.

3. M. H. Davis, "Measuring Individual Differences in Empathy: Evidence for a Multidimensional Approach," *Journal of Personality and Social Psychology* 44, no. 1 (1983): 113–26.

4. M. Iacoboni, " Imitation, Empathy, and Mirror Neurons," *Annual Review of Psychology* 60 (2009): 653–70.

5. C. D. Batson et al., "Empathic Joy and the Empathy-Altruism Hypothesis," *Journal of Personality and Social Psychology* 61, no. 3 (1991): 413–26.

6. C. D. Batson et al., "Five Studies Testing Two New Egoistic Alternatives to the Empathy-Altruism Hypothesis," *Journal of Personality and Social Psychology* 55, no. 1 (1988): 52–77.

7. C. D. Batson et al., "Moral Hypocrisy: Addressing Some Alternatives," *Journal of Personality and Social Psychology* 83, no. 2 (2002): 330.

8. C. D. Batson et al., "Moral Hypocrisy: Appearing Moral to Oneself Without Being So," *Journal of Personality and Social Psychology* 77, no. 3 (1999): 525.

9. J. L. Burnette et al., "Forgiveness Results from Integrating Information About Relationship Value and Exploitation Risk," *Personality and Social Psychology Bulletin* 38 (2012): 345–56.

10. M. E. McCullough et al., "Interpersonal Forgiving in Close Relationships: II. Theoretical Elaboration and Measurement," *Journal of Personality and Social Psychology* 75, no. 6 (1998): 1586.

11. L. B. Luchies et al., "The Doormat Effect: When Forgiving Erodes Self-Respect and Self-Concept Clarity," *Journal of Personality and Social Psychology* 98, no. 5 (2010): 734–49.

12. D. E. Davis et al., "Relational Humility: Conceptualizing and Measuring Humility as a Personality Judgment," *Journal of Personality Assessment* 93, no. 3 (2011): 225–34.

13. M. H. Davis and H. A. Oathout, "Maintenance of Satisfaction in Romantic Relationships: Empathy and Relational Competence," *Journal of Personality and Social Psychology* 53, no. 2 (1987): 397–410.

14. D. Cramer and S. Jowett, "Perceived Empathy, Accurate Empathy and Relationship Satisfaction in Heterosexual Couples," *Journal of Social and Personal Relationships* 27, no. 3 (2010): 327–49.

15. E. C. Long et al., "Understanding the One You Love: A Longitudinal Assessment of an Empathy Training Program for Couples in Romantic Relationships," *Family Relations* (1999): 235–42.

16. R. A. Emmons, "Narcissism: Theory and Measurement," *Journal of Personality and Social Psychology* 52, no. 1 (1987): 11–17.

17. P. J. Watson et al., "Narcissism and Empathy: Validity Evidence for the Narcissistic Personality Inventory," *Journal of Personality Assessment* 48, no. 3 (1984): 301–5.

18. K. Ritter et al., "Lack of Empathy in Patients with Narcissistic Personality Disorder," *Psychiatry Research* 187, no. 1–2 (2011): 241–47.

19. W. K. Campbell and C. A. Foster, "Narcissism and Commitment in Romantic Relationships: An Investment Model Analysis," *Personality and Social Psychology Bulletin* 28, no. 4 (2002): 484–95.

20. S. N. Wurst et al., "Narcissism and Romantic Relationships: The Differential Impact of Narcissistic Admiration and Rivalry," *Journal of Personality and Social Psychology* 112, no. 2 (2017): 280.

21. B. M. Farrant et al., "Empathy, Perspective Taking and Prosocial Behaviour: The Importance of Parenting Practices," *Infant and Child Development* 21, no. 2 (2012): 175–88.

22. M. E. McCullough, E. L. Worthington Jr., and K. C. Rachal, "Interpersonal Forgiving in Close Relationships," *Journal of Personality and Social Psychology* 73, no. 2 (1997): 321–36.

23. Luchies et al., "The Doormat Effect."

24. B. J. Zinnbauer and K. I. Pargament, "Spiritual Conversion: A Study of Religious Change Among College Students," *Journal for the Scientific Study of Religion* (1998): 161–80.

25. B. L. Fredrickson, "The Role of Positive Emotions in Positive Psychology: The Broaden-and-Build Theory of Positive Emotions," *American Psychologist* 56, no. 3 (2001): 218–26.

26. B. L. Fredrickson, "Positive Emotions Broaden and Build," in *Advances in Experimental Social Psychology*, vol. 47, ed. P. Devine and A. Plant (New York: Academic Press, 2013), 1–53.

7 | The Importance of Self-Regulation

1. P. Hampson, "'By Knowledge and by Love': The Integrative Role of Habitus in Christian Psychology," *Edification* 6 (2012): 5–18.

2. J. D. Green and D. R. Van Tongeren, "Self-Regulation and a Meaning-Based Approach to Virtues: Comments on Hampson's Habitus," *Edification* 6 (2012): 19–23.

3. K. D. Vohs and R. F. Baumeister, "Understanding Self-Regulation," in *Handbook of Self-Regulation: Research, Theory, and Applications* (New York: Guilford Press, 2004), 1–12.

4. T. E. Moffitt et al., "A Gradient of Childhood Self-Control Predicts Health, Wealth, and Public Safety," *Proceedings of the National Academy of Sciences* 108, no. 7 (2011): 2693–98.

5. A. L. Duckworth, "The Significance of Self-Control," *Proceedings of the National Academy of Sciences* 108, no. 7 (2011): 2639–40.

6. J. B. Schweitzer and B. Sulzer-Azaroff, "Self-Control: Teaching Tolerance for Delay in Impulsive Children," *Journal of the Experimental Analysis of Behavior* 50, no. 2 (1998): 173–86.

7. M. Muraven, R. F. Baumeister, and D. M. Tice, "Longitudinal Improvement of Self-Regulation Through Practice: Building Self-Control Strength Through Repeated Exercise," *Journal of Social Psychology* 139 (1999): 446–57.

8. M. Muraven, "Building Self-Control Strength: Practicing Self-Control Leads to Improved Self-Control Performance," *Journal of Experimental Social Psychology* 46, no. 2 (2010): 465–68.

9. T. F. Denson et al., "Self-Control Training Decreases Aggression in Response to Provocation in Aggressive Individuals," *Journal of Research in Personality* 45, no. 2 (2011): 252–56.

10. M. Milyavskaya et al., "Saying 'No' to Temptation: Want-To Motivation Improves Self-Regulation by Reducing Temptation Rather than by Increasing Self-Control," *Journal of Personality and Social Psychology* 109, no. 4 (2015): 677.

11. M. R. Leary, C. E. Adams, and E. B. Tate, "Hypo-Egoic Self-Regulation: Exercising Self-Control by Diminishing the Influence of the Self," *Journal of Personality* 74, no. 6 (2006): 1803–32.

12. E. M. Tong et al., "Humility Facilitates Higher Self-Control," *Journal of Experimental Social Psychology* 62 (2016): 30–39.

13. Z. Yu et al., "Humility Predicts Resistance to Substance Use: A Self-Control Perspective," *Journal of Positive Psychology* 16, no. 1 (2021): 105–15.

14. J. J. Sosik et al., "Self-Control Puts Character into Action: Examining How Leader Character Strengths and Ethical Leadership Relate to Leader Outcomes," *Journal of Business Ethics* 160, no. 3 (2019): 765–81.

8 | Bridging Divides

1. J. N. Hook et al., "Cultural Humility: Measuring Openness to Culturally Diverse Clients," *Journal of Counseling Psychology* 60, no. 3 (2013): 353–66.

2. D. G. Myers and H. Lamm, "The Group Polarization Phenomenon, *Psychological Bulletin* 83, no. 4 (1976): 602–27.

3. S. Iyengar and S. J. Westwood, "Fear and Loathing Across Party Lines: New Evidence on Group Polarization," *American Journal of Political Science* 59, no. 3 (2015): 690–707.

4. J. Goplen and E. A. Plant, "A Religious Worldview: Protecting One's Meaning System Through Religious Prejudice," *Personality and Social Psychology Bulletin* 41, no. 11 (2015): 1474–87.

5. H. A. McGregor et al., "Terror Management and Aggression: Evidence That Mortality Salience Motivates Aggression Against Worldview-Threatening Others," *Journal of Personality and Social Psychology* 74, no. 3 (1998): 590–605.

6. C. Foronda et al., "Cultural Humility: A Concept Analysis," *Journal of Transcultural Nursing* 27, no. 3 (2016): 210–17.

7. I. Martín-Baró, *Writings for a Liberation Psychology*, ed. A. Aron and S. Corne (Cambridge, MA: Harvard University Press, 1994).

8. P. Freire, *Pedagogy of the Oppressed*, rev. ed., trans. M. B. Ramos (New York: Penguin, 1996).

9. E. Duran, J,. Firehammer, and J. Gonzalez, "Liberation Psychology as the Path Toward Healing Cultural Soul Wounds" *Journal of Counseling and Development* 86, no. 3 (2008): 288–95.

10. M. Lehmann, A. N. Kluger, and D. R. Van Tongeren, "Am I Arrogant? Listen to Me and We Will Both Become More Humble" (forthcoming).

11. N. Haslam, "Dehumanization: An Integrative Review," *Personality and Social Psychology Review* 10, no. 3 (2006): 252–64.

12. K. Kristofferson, K. White, and J. Peloza, "The Nature of Slacktivism: How the Social Observability of an Initial Act of Token Support Affects Subsequent Prosocial Action," *Journal of Consumer Research* 40, no. 6 (2014): 1149–66.

13. R. Menakem, *My Grandmonther's Hands: Racialized Trauma and the Pathway to Mending Our Hearts and Bodies* (Las Vegas: Central Recovery Press, 2017).

14. M. Clair and J. S. Denis, "Sociology of Racism," *International Encyclopedia of the Social and Behavioral Sciences* 19 (2015): 857–63.

15. J. F. Dovidio and S. L. Gaertner, "Aversive Racism," in *Advances in Experimental Social Psychology*, vol. 36, ed. M. P. Zanna (London: Elsevier Academic Press, 2004), 1–52.

16. G. Hodson, J. F. Dovidio, and S. L. Gaertner, "Processes in Racial Discrimination: Differential Weighting of Conflicting Information," *Personality and Social Psychology Bulletin* 28, no. 4 (2002): 460–71.

17. D. E. Davis et al., "Microaggressions and Perceptions of Cultural Humility in Counseling," *Journal of Counseling and Development* 94, no. 4 (2016): 483–93.

18. K. M. King, L. D. Borders, and C. T. Jones, "Multicultural Orientation in Clinical Supervision: Examining Impact Through Dyadic Data," *Clinical Supervisor* 39, no. 2 (2020): 248–71.

19. M. J. Brandt, J. T. Crawford, J and D. R. Van Tongeren, "Worldview Conflict in Daily Life," *Social Psychological and Personality Science* 10 (2019): 35–43.

20. A. S. Hodge et al., "Political Humility: Engaging Others with Different Political Perspectives," *Journal of Positive Psychology* 16, no. 4 (2021): 526–35.

21. A. S. Hodge et al., "Political Humility and Forgiveness of a Political Hurt or Offense," *Journal of Psychology and Theology* 48, no. 2 (2020): 142–53.

22. J. E. Farrell et al., "Religious Attitudes and Behaviors Toward Individuals Who Hold Different Religious Beliefs and Perspectives: An Exploratory Qualitative Study," *Psychology of Religion and Spirituality* 10, no. 1 (2018): 63–71.

23. D. E. Davis et al., "Humility, Religion, and Spirituality: A Review of the Literature," *Psychology of Religion and Spirituality* 9, no. 3 (2017): 242.

24. D. R. Van Tongeren et al., "Religious Differences in Reporting and Expressing Humility," *Psychology of Religion and Spirituality* 10, no. 2 (2018): 174–84.

25. E. Woodruff et al., "Humility and Religion: Benefits, Difficulties, and a Model of Religious Tolerance," in *Religion and Spirituality Across Cultures*, ed. C. Kim-Prieto (New York: Springer, 2014), 271–85.

26. S. A. Hodge et al., "Attitudes of Religious Leaders Toward Integrating Psychology and Church Ministry," *Spirituality in Clinical Practice* 7, no. 1 (2020): 18–33.

27. H. Zhang et al., "The Effect of Religious Diversity on Religious Belonging and Meaning: The Role of Intellectual Humility," *Psychology of Religion and Spirituality* 10, no. 1 (2018): 72.

28. D. K. Mosher et al., "Cultural Humility of Religious Communities and Well-Being in Sexual Minority Persons," *Journal of Psychology and Theology* 47 (2019): 160–74.

29. A. A. Singh, "Moving from Affirmation to Liberation in Psychological Practice with Transgender and Gender Nonconforming Clients," *American Psychologist* 71, no. 8 (2016): 755–62.

30. C. D. Olle, "Breaking Institutional Habits: A Critical Paradigm for Social Change Agents in Psychology," *Counseling Psychologist* 46 (2018): 190–212.

31. J. A. Terrizzi Jr., N. J. Shook, and W. L. Ventis, "Disgust: A Predictor of Social Conservatism and Prejudicial Attitudes Toward Homosexuals," *Personality and Individual Differences* 49, no. 6 (2010): 587–92.

32. G. M. Herek and J. P. Capitanio, "'Some of My Best Friends': Intergroup Contact, Concealable Stigma, and Heterosexuals' Attitudes Toward Gay Men and Lesbians," *Personality and Social Psychology Bulletin* 22, no. 4 (1996): 412–24.

33. M. C. Parent, C. DeBlaere, and B. Moradi, "Approaches to Research on Intersectionality: Perspectives on Gender, LGBT, and Racial/Ethnic Identities," *Sex Roles* 68, no. 11 (2013): 639–45.

34. C. C. Bell, "Racism, Narcissism, and Integrity," *Journal of the National Medical Association* 70, no. 2 (1978): 89–92.

35. L. D. Campos-Moreira et al., "Making a Case for Culturally Humble Leadership Practices Through a Culturally Responsive Leadership Framework," *Human Service Organizations: Management, Leadership and Governance* 44, no. 5 (2020): 407–14.

36. S. A. Crabtree et al., "Humility, Differentiation of Self, and Clinical Training in Spiritual and Religious Competence," *Journal of Spirituality in Mental Health* 23, no. 4 (2021): 342–62.

37. S. L. Koole, J. Greenberg, and T. Pyszczynski, "Introducing Science to the Psychology of the Soul: Experimental Existential Psychology," *Current Directions in Psychological Science* 15, no. 5 (2006): 212–16.

38. D. R. Van Tongeren and S. A. Showalter Van Tongeren, *The Courage to Suffer: A New Clinical Framework for Life's Greatest Crises* (West Conshohocken, PA: Templeton Foundation Press, 2020).

9 | Making Progress

1. E. J. Krumrei-Mancuso et al., "Links Between Intellectual Humility and Acquiring Knowledge," *Journal of Positive Psychology* 15, no. 2 (2020): 155–70.

2. M. Haggard et al., "Finding Middle Ground Between Intellectual Arrogance and Intellectual Servility: Development and Assessment of the Limitations-Owning Intellectual Humility Scale," *Personality and Individual Differences* 124 (2018): 184–93.

3. L. Zmigrod et al., "The Psychological Roots of Intellectual Humility: The Role of Intelligence and Cognitive Flexibility," *Personality and Individual Differences* 141 (2019): 200–208.

4. T. Porter and K. Schumann, "Intellectual Humility and Openness to the Opposing View," *Self and Identity* 17, no. 2 (2018): 139–62.

5. M. J. Jarvinen and T. B. Paulus, "Attachment and Cognitive Openness: Emotional Underpinnings of Intellectual Humility," *Journal of Positive Psychology* 12, no. 1 (2017): 74–86.

6. M. R. Leary et al., "Cognitive and Interpersonal Features of Intellectual Humility," *Personality and Social Psychology Bulletin* 43, no. 6 (2017): 793–813.

7. S. E. McElroy et al., "Intellectual Humility: Scale Development and Theoretical Elaborations in the Context of Religious Leadership," *Journal of Psychology and Theology* 42, no. 1 (2014): 19–30.

8. R. H. Hoyle et al., "Holding Specific Views with Humility: Conceptualization and Measurement of Specific Intellectual Humility," *Personality and Individual Differences* 97 (2016): 165–72.

9. Leary et al., "Cognitive and Interpersonal Features of Intellectual Humility."

10. McElroy et al., "Intellectual Humility: Scale Development and Theoretical Elaborations."

11. Hoyle et al., "Holding Specific Views with Humility."

12. D. Whitcomb et al., "Intellectual Humility: Owning Our Limitations," *Philosophy and Phenomenological Research* 94, no. 3 (2017): 509–39.

13. Hoyle et al., "Holding Specific Views with Humility."

14. Leary et al., "Cognitive and Interpersonal Features of Intellectual Humility."

15. McElroy et al., "Intellectual Humility: Scale Development and Theoretical Elaborations."

16. T. L. Friedman, "How to Get a Job at Google," *The New York Times*, February 22, 2014, nytimes.com.

17. M. P. Lynch et al., "Intellectual Humility in Public Discourse," *IHPD Literature Review*, https://humilityandconviction.uconn.edu/wp-content/uploads/sites/1877/2016/09/IHPD-Literature-Review-revised. pdf.

18. C. N. DeWall, "Fostering Intellectual Humility in Public Discourse and University Education," in *Handbook of Humility: Theory, Research, and Applications*, ed. E. L. Worthington Jr., D. E. Davis, and J. N. Hook (New York: Routledge, 2016), 249–61.

19. J. M. Twenge et al., "Egos Inflating over Time: A Cross-Temporal Meta-Analysis of the Narcissistic Personality Inventory," *Journal of Personality* 76, no. 4 (2008): 875–902.

20. J. M. Twenge and J. D. Foster, "Birth Cohort Increases in Narcissistic Personality Traits Among American College Students, 1982–2009," *Social Psychological and Personality Science* 1, no. 1 (2010): 99–106.

21. D. R. Van Tongeren et al., "Religious Residue: Cross-Cultural Evidence That Religious Psychology and Behavior Persist Following Deidentification," *Journal of Personality and Social Psychology* 120 (2021): 484–503.

22. R. John Marriott, M. E. Lewis Hall, and L. A. Decker, "Psychological Correlates of Reasons for Nonbelief: Tolerance of Ambiguity, Intellectual Humility, and Attachment," *Mental Health, Religion and Culture* 22, no. 5 (2019): 480–99.

23. E. J. Krumrei-Mancuso, "Intellectual Humility's Links to Religion and Spirituality and the Role of Authoritarianism," *Personality and Individual Differences* 130 (2018): 65–75.

24. D. Rodriguez et al., "Religious Intellectual Humility, Attitude Change, and Closeness Following Religious Disagreement," *Journal of Positive Psychology* 14, no. 2 (2019): 133–40.

25. E. J. Krumrei-Mancuso and B. Newman, "Intellectual Humility in the Sociopolitical Domain," *Self and Identity* 19, no. 8 (2020): 989–1016.

26. S. A. Deffler, M. R. Leary, and R. H. Hoyle, "Knowing What You Know: Intellectual Humility and Judgments of Recognition Memory," *Personality and Individual Differences* 96 (2016): 255–59.

27. B. R. Meagher et al., "An Intellectually Humbling Experience: Changes in Interpersonal Perception and Cultural Reasoning Across a Five-Week Course," *Journal of Psychology and Theology* 47, no. 3 (2019): 217–29.

28. H. Battaly, "Can Humility Be a Liberatory Virtue?," in *The Routledge Handbook of Philosophy of Humility*, ed. M. Alfano, M. Lynch, and A. Tanesini (New York: Routledge, 2020).

29. J. N. Hook et al., "Intellectual Humility and Forgiveness of Religious Leaders," *Journal of Positive Psychology* 10, no. 6 (2015): 499–506.

30. I. J. Kidd, "Educating for Intellectual Humility," in *Intellectual Virtues and Education: Essays in Applied Virtue Epistemology*, ed. J. Baehr (New York: Routledge, 2015), 54–70.

31. H. T. Reis et al., "Perceived Partner Responsiveness Promotes Intellectual Humility," *Journal of Experimental Social Psychology* 79 (2018): 21–33.

32. J. J. Knabb et al., "'Unknowing' in the 21st Century: Humble Detachment for Christians with Repetitive Negative Thinking," *Spirituality in Clinical Practice* 5, no. 3 (2018): 170–87.

33. D. G. Myers and H. Lamm, "The Group Polarization Phenomenon," *Psychological Bulletin* 83, no. 4 (1976): 602–27.

34. I. L. Janis, *Group Think: Psychological Studies of Policy Decisions and Fiascoes*, 2nd ed. (Boston: Houghton Mifflin, 1982).

35. J. T. Jost, M. R. Banaji, and B. A. Nosek, "A Decade of System Justification Theory: Accumulated Evidence of Conscious and Unconscious Bolstering of the Status Quo," *Political Psychology* 25, no. 6 (2004): 881–919.

36. D. R. Van Tongeren et al., "Security Versus Growth: Existential Tradeoffs of Various Religious Perspectives," *Psychology of Religion and Spirituality* 8, no. 1 (2016): 77–88.

37. T. Pyszczynski, J. Greenberg, and J. L. Goldenberg, "Freedom Versus Fear: On the Defense, Growth, and Expansion of the Self," in *Handbook of Self and Identity*, ed. M. R. Leary and J. P. Tangney (New York: Guilford Press, 2003), 314–43.

38. D. R. Van Tongeren and S. A. Showalter Van Tongeren, *The Courage to Suffer: A New Clinical Framework for Life's Greatest Crises* (West Conshohocken, PA: Templeton Foundation Press, 2020).

10 | Flourishing Community

1. D. E. Davis et al., "Relational Humility: Conceptualizing and Measuring Humility as a Personality Judgment," *Journal of Personality Assessment* 93, no. 3 (2011): 225–34.

2. L. Nockur and S. Pfattheicher, "The Beautiful Complexity of Human Prosociality: On the Interplay of Honesty-Humility, Intuition, and a Reward System," *Social Psychological and Personality Science* 12 (2021): 877–86.

3. Y. Fang, Y. Dong, and L. Fang, "Honesty-Humility and Prosocial Behavior: The Mediating Roles of Perspective Taking and Guilt-Proneness," *Scandinavian Journal of Psychology* 60, no. 4 (2019): 386–93.

4. E. J. Krumrei-Mancuso, "Intellectual Humility and Prosocial Values: Direct and Mediated Effects," *Journal of Positive Psychology* 12, no. 1 (2017): 13–28.

5. P. C. Hill and S. J. Sandage, "The Promising but Challenging Case of Humility as a Positive Psychology Virtue," *Journal of Moral Education* 45, no. 2 (2016): 132–46.

6. E. L. Worthington Jr., "An Empathy-Humility-Commitment Model of Forgiveness Applied Within Family Dyads," *Journal of Family Therapy* 20 (1998): 59–76.

7. D. R. Van Tongeren, D. E. Davis, and J. N. Hook, "Social Benefits of Humility: Initiating and Maintaining Romantic Relationships," *Journal of Positive Psychology* 9 (2014): 313–21.

8. D. E. Davis et al., "Relational Spirituality and Forgiveness: Development of the Spiritual Humility Scale (SHS)," *Journal of Psychology and Theology* 38, no. 2 (2010): 91–100.

9. C. Powers et al., "Associations Between Humility, Spiritual Transcendence, and Forgiveness," in *Research in the Social Scientific Study of Religion*, vol. 18, ed. R. L. Piedmont (Boston: Brill, 2007), 75–94.

10. M. E. McCullough, R. A. Emmons, and J.-A. Tsang, "The Grateful Disposition: A Conceptual and Empirical Topography," *Journal of Personality and Social Psychology* 82, no. 1 (2002): 112–27.

11. R. A. Emmons and M. E. Mccullough, "Counting Blessings Versus Burdens: An Experimental Investigation of Gratitude and Subjective Well-Being in Daily Life," *Journal of Personality and Social Psychology* 84, no. 2 (2003): 377–89.

12. E. Kruse et al., "An Upward Spiral Between Gratitude and Humility," *Social Psychological and Personality Science* 5, no. 7 (2014): 805–14.

13. N. Krause and R. D. Hayward, "Humility, Compassion, and Gratitude to God: Assessing the Relationships Among Key Religious Virtues," *Psychology of Religion and Spirituality* 7, no. 3 (2015): 192–204.

14. J. J. Exline and P. C. Hill, "Humility: A Consistent and Robust Predictor of Generosity," *Journal of Positive Psychology* 7, no. 3 (2012): 208–18.

15. J. P. LaBouff et al., "Humble Persons Are More Helpful than Less Humble Persons: Evidence from Three Studies," *Journal of Positive Psychology* 7, no. 1 (2012): 16–29.

16. J. J. Exline, "Humility and the Ability to Receive from Others," *Journal of Psychology and Christianity* 31, no. 1 (2012): 40–50.

17. N. Krause, "Assessing the Relationships Among Wisdom, Humility, and Life Satisfaction," *Journal of Adult Development* 23, no. 3 (2016): 140–49.

18. N. Krause and R. D. Hayward, "Virtues, Practical Wisdom and Psychological Well-Being: A Christian Perspective," *Social Indicators Research* 122, no. 3 (2015): 735–55.

19. F. Martela, and M. F. Steger, "The Three Meanings of Meaning in Life: Distinguishing Coherence, Purpose, and Significance," *Journal of Positive Psychology* 11, no. 5 (2016): 531–45.

20. M. B. O'Donnell et al., "You, Me, and Meaning: An Integrative Review of Connections Between Relationships and Meaning in Life," *Journal of Psychology in Africa* 24, no. 1 (2014): 44–50.

21. J. Haidt, "The New Synthesis in Moral Psychology," *Science* 316, no. 5827 (2007): 998–1002.

22. D. R. Van Tongeren et al., "Prosociality Enhances Meaning in Life," *Journal of Positive Psychology* 11, no. 3 (2016): 225–36.

23. N. Klein, "Prosocial Behavior Increases Perceptions of Meaning in Life," *Journal of Positive Psychology* 12, no. 4 (2017): 354–61.

24. F. Sapmaz et al., "Gratitude, Forgiveness and Humility as Predictors of Subjective Well-Being Among University Students," *International Online Journal of Educational Sciences* 8, no. 1 (2016): 38–47.

25. D. R. Van Tongeren et al., "Forgiveness Increases Meaning in Life," *Social Psychological and Personality Science* 6, no. 1 (2015): 47–55.

26. T. A. FioRito, C. Routledge, and J. Jackson, "Meaning-Motivated Community Action: The Need for Meaning and Prosocial Goals and Behavior," *Personality and Individual Differences* 171 (2021): 110462.

27. C. Dwiwardani et al., "Virtues Develop from a Secure Base: Attachment and Resilience as Predictors of Humility, Gratitude, and Forgiveness," *Journal of Psychology and Theology* 42, no. 1 (2014): 83–90.

28. D. R. Van Tongeren et al., "The Complementarity of Humility Hypothesis: Individual, Relational, and Physiological Effects of Mutually Humble Partners," *Journal of Positive Psychology* 14 (2019): 178–87.

29. E. T. MacDonell and T. Willoughby, "Investigating Honesty-Humility and Impulsivity as Predictors of Aggression in Children and Youth," *Aggressive Behavior* 46, no. 1 (2020): 97–106.

30. J. Wu, M. Yuan, and Y. Kou, "Disadvantaged Early-Life Experience Negatively Predicts Prosocial Behavior: The Roles of Honesty-Humility and Dispositional Trust Among Chinese Adolescents," *Personality and Individual Differences* 152 (2020): 109608.

31. K. Allgaier et al., "Honesty–Humility in School: Exploring Main and Interaction Effects on Secondary School Sudents' Antisocial and Prosocial Behavior," *Learning and Individual Differences* 43 (2015): 211–17.

32. E. Ruffing et al., "Humility and Narcissism in Clergy: A Relational Spirituality Framework," *Pastoral Psychology* 67, no. 5 (2018): 525–45.

33. P. J. Jankowski et al., "A Mixed-Method Intervention Study on Relational Spirituality and Humility Among Religious Leaders," *Spirituality in Clinical Practice* (2021), advance online publication.

34. C. R. Lavelock et al., "The Quiet Virtue Speaks: An Intervention to Promote Humility," *Journal of Psychology and Theology* 42, no. 1 (2014): 99–110.

35. Everett Worthington, "DIY Workbooks," evworthington-forgiveness.com/diy-workbooks.

36. J. E. Stellar et al., "Awe and Humility," *Journal of Personality and Social Psychology* 114, no. 2 (2018): 258.

Conclusion

1. J. Greenberg, T. Pyszczynski, and S. Solomon, "The Causes and Consequences of a Need for Self-Esteem: A Terror Management Theory," in *Public Self and Private Self*, ed. R. F. Baumeister (New York: Springer, 1986), 189–212.

Acknowledgments

I felt overwhelmed and outmatched writing a book about humility. As I am sure is clear in the stories I share, I am no expert in practicing humility. I'm fortunate to have been able to spend a considerable amount of my professional time researching it, but its full embodiment in my life is still elusive. My sincere hope is that I'm better at practicing it today than I was yesterday.

Writing well is never done solitarily, and I have plenty of people to thank for their investment in this process. I am grateful to my literary agents, Wendy Levinson and Andrea Somberg, for reaching out to me to initiate this process and providing formative feedback at various stages throughout this process. Similarly, I am grateful to Batya Rosenblum for her editorial acumen to help sharpen the words in these pages and focus my writing. This book is markedly better because of her.

All the research in this book is a collaborative effort. I'm grateful to have worked with an outstanding group of colleagues on humility research. My deep thanks go to Don Davis and Josh Hook for our continued collaboration in this area and sustained friendship over the years. This book wouldn't be possible without their collective contributions, nor the work half as enjoyable.

I'm thankful to have learned so much from an outstanding group of humility collaborators and coauthors, including Jamie Aten, Rich Bollinger, Mark Brandt, David Bromley, Kacy Brubaker, Jeni Burnette, Laura Captari, Elise Choe, Ruth Connelly, Richard Cowden, Jarret Crawford, Jody Davis, Ward Davis, Cirleen DeBlaere, Phil Dieke, Franco Dispenza, Carissa Dwiwardani, Dori Eaves, Megan Edwards, Bob Emmons, Jennifer Farrell, Matt Fennell, Rachel Garthe, Aubrey Gartner, Jeff Green, Brandon Griffin, Hanna Gunn, Liz Hall, Annabella Opare-Henaku, Pete Hill, Adam Hodge, Ann Houtman, Tim Hulsey, Jeff Jennings, Kathryn Johnson, Terrence Jordan II, Yuki Kojima, Judith Ansaa Osae-Larbi, Caroline Lavelock-Bratney, Cristine Legare, John McConnell, Mike McCullough, Stacey McElroy-Heltzel, Ben Meagher, Mary Chase Breedlove Mize, David Mosher, Thobeka S. Nkomo, Camilla Nonterah, Osunde Omoruyi, Anna Ord, Jesse Owen, Amber Perkins, Brad Pinter, Marciana Ramos, Ken Rice, Wade Rowatt, Chelsea Reid, Jennifer Ripley, John Ruiz, Constantine Sedikides, James Sells, Nathan Sheff, Laura Shannonhouse, Joshua Stafford, Kelly Teahan, Dave Wang, Elissa Woodruff, Ev Worthington, and Hansong Zhang.

In addition to those named above, I also extend thanks to those who offered insight in the early stages of the book's development, including Kelley Barr Boumgarden, Peter Boumgarden, Tripper Christie, Preston Drobeck, Julie Exline, Todd Hall, Jordan LaBouff, Liz Krumrei Mancuso, Holly Oxhandler, Steve Sandage, Dan Schulte, Kat Schulte, Lynn Stubbs, and Dave Stubbs.

I also wish to thank Yuki Kojima, for her assistance identifying and assembling relevant research articles.

Finally, I am grateful to my wife, Sara, not only for her myriad contributions through ongoing discussions, sharing new perspectives and readings, and providing critically relevant clinical and practical insight, but also for her patience and grace while living with someone who studies humility but is wildly imperfect at it. I am deeply grateful that she read each page and offered valuable and necessary feedback, even when it was hard for me to hear. I thank her for encouraging me to bring my full self to this book and use my voice to champion justice and healing. I am grateful for all the ways she beckons me to live with a greater sense of vulnerability and authenticity.

Index

Page numbers in *italics* refer to tables.

H

habitual humility, 157–58
happiness (*hedonia*), 223
health, 16–17, 25, 38–41, 93,
    214–15
healthy conflict, *50*, 51,
    57–58
hedonia (happiness), 223
helpfulness, 229
honesty, 23–25, 41–42, 100–
    102
hostile sexism, 189
humanitarian organization
    leader study, 70
humiliation, 1–2
humility
    arrogance as opposite of,
        4–5
    comprehensive, 156
    defined, 11
    false, 76
    features of, 11–13, 160
    habitual, 157–58
    humiliation versus, 1–2
    lasting, 155–58
    misconceptions about,
        18–19
    narcissism as opposite of,
        144
    as oppression, 2
    political, 15, 185–86
    power of, 10–11, 17
    psychological research, lack
        of, 3–4
    religious, 15, 186–88
    resilient, 156–56
    types, *14*, 14–16
    See also cultural humility;

existential humility;
    intellectual humility;
    relational humility;
    specific topics
humility intervention
    workbook, 237–38
humility revolution, 248–50
humility role models, 240–41
hypocrisy, moral, 140–41

I

identities
    cultural, racial, and ethnic,
        181–84
    fears about, 196
    gender and sexual, 188–90
    intersecting, 190–91
    political, 175, 184–86
    relational, 71
    religious, 186–88
ideological isolation, 6
illusions, positive, 30, 40, 217
implicit prejudice, 182–83
implicit theories, 102–3
impression management, 72
incremental theories, 71,
    102–4
individualistic cultures, 3–4, 9,
    16, 29, 234
information consumption, 174–
    75, 184–85, 210–11, 217
inner state, as context, 108
innovation, 72–73
insecurity. *See* security
intellectual humility
    about, 14, *14*
    in action, 209–11

About the Author

DARYL VAN TONGEREN, PhD, is an associate professor of psychology at Hope College. A social psychologist, he has published over two hundred scholarly articles and chapters on topics such as meaning in life, humility, religion, forgiveness, relationships, and well-being. His research has been covered by numerous media outlets, including *The New York Times, Chicago Tribune, Washington Post, Huffington Post,* NPR affiliate radio stations, *Scientific American,* and *Men's Health.* He has also coauthored *The Courage to Suffer* (with Sara A. Showalter Van Tongeren). Van Tongeren has been supported by numerous grants from the John Templeton Foundation, and his research has won national and international awards. Currently, he is an associate editor of the *Journal of Positive Psychology* and a consulting editor for *Psychology of Religion and Spirituality* and the *Journal of Social Psychology.* He enjoys running, biking, and hiking near where he lives with his wife, Sara, in Holland, Michigan.

darylvantongeren.com

○ darylvantongeren | ▮ drvantongeren

ABOUT US

Welbeck Balance is dedicated to changing lives.
Our mission is to deliver life-enhancing books to help improve
your wellbeing so that you can live with greater clarity and
meaning, wherever you are on life's journey.

Welbeck Balance is part of the Welbeck Publishing Group –
a globally recognized, independent publisher.
Welbeck are renowned for our innovative ideas, production
values and developing long-lasting content. Our books have
been translated into over 30 languages in more than
60 countries around the world.

If you love books, then join the club and sign up
to our newsletter for exclusive offers, extracts,
author interviews and more information.

To find out more and sign up, visit:

www.welbeckpublishing.com

welbeckpublish
welbeckpublish
welbeckuk

WELBECK
BALANCE